COMICS & MEMORY IN LATIN AMERICA

ILLUMINATIONS

CULTURAL FORMATIONS OF THE AMERICAS SERIES

John Beverley and Sara Castro-Klarén, *Editors*

Comics & MEMORY IN LATIN AMERICA

Jorge L. Catalá Carrasco,
Paulo Drinot, and **James Scorer,** editors

UNIVERSITY OF PITTSBURGH PRESS

Published by the University of Pittsburgh Press, Pittsburgh, Pa., 15260

Manufactured in the United States of America
Printed on acid-free paper
10 9 8 7 6 5 4 3 2 1

Cataloging-in-Publication data is available from the Library of Congress

ISBN 13: 978-0-8229-6424-7
ISBN 10: 0-8229-6424-4

Cover art: Introductory scene to the comic *Matagalpa: Insurrección de agosto!* Source: Ministerio de Cultura 1980b, p. 1.
Cover design by Joel W. Coggins

CONTENTS

ACKNOWLEDGMENTS

The editors would like to thank the University of Pittsburgh Press, particularly Josh Shanholtzer, for their support of this project. Thanks also to the editors of Illuminations: Cultural Formations of the Americas for accepting this book and to the anonymous readers for their helpful comments and suggestions. This book began at a conference held in London in 2012. The editors gratefully acknowledge the support of the School of Advanced Study of the University of London, which made that conference possible.

COMICS & MEMORY IN LATIN AMERICA

INTRODUCTION

COMICS AND MEMORY IN LATIN AMERICA

Jorge L. Catalá Carrasco, Paulo Drinot, and James Scorer

Remembering's dangerous. I find the past such a worrying, anxious place.
"The past tense," I suppose you'd call it. Ha ha ha.
THE JOKER

Since the publication of Ariel Dorfman and Armand Mattelart's *Para leer al Pato Donald* in 1971, scholars of Latin America have increasingly turned to comics as objects of study. The analytical framework privileged by most of these scholars has moved beyond Dorfman and Mattelart's somewhat restrictive cultural imperialism hypothesis influenced by dependency theory. Comics, and more recently graphic novels, are increasingly understood as cultural artifacts that open unique and compelling windows not only onto mass or popular culture but also onto social, cultural, and political processes that have helped define the region since comic art began to appear in mass media in the early twentieth century (and in some cases even before) (see, among others, Foster 1989; Rubenstein 1998; Merino 2003 and 2011; Lent 2005; Fernández L'Hoeste and Poblete 2009). This book presents new research from scholars working in different disciplines, including literary theory, cultural studies, and history. The contributions explore the ways in which comics and graphic novels on and from Latin America address and express ongoing processes of memory formation around a number of historical processes. Comics and graphic novels offer a particularly fruitful perspective through which to examine the work of memory in Latin America.

This book builds on the rapidly expanding field of Latin American comics studies. Comics scholarship on and from Latin America has in recent decades resulted in a number of works, including studies on (1) comics as popular culture (Foster 1989); (2) comics as cultural artifacts representing the advent of modernity in the region (Merino 2003); (3) the history of comics throughout the continent (Lent 2005); (4) comics as agents in the configuration of national identities in Latin America (Fernández L'Hoeste and Poblete 2009); and (5) the ideas of canon and margin in the articulation of critical thinking around comics in the Latin American intellectual context (Merino 2011). In Latin America, such initiatives as Alvaro de Moya's first exhibition in Brazil of *quadrinhos* in 1951 or the Primera Bienal de la Historieta y el Humor Gráfico in Argentina in 1968 gave way to early scholarly approaches to comics. These include *C-Línea* in Cuba from 1973 to 1977 and the quarterly Cuban *Revista latinoamericana de estudios sobre la historieta* (RLESH) from 2001 to 2010.[1] Country-focused studies, such as Anne Rubenstein's *Bad Language, Naked Ladies, and Other Threats to the Nation* (1998), about the politics of Mexican comic books, or the collaborative project *Camouflage Comics* (2005), directed by Aarnoud Rommens, about the last Argentine military dictatorship (1976–1983), bear witness to a well-established field. In addition to these, the biannual *International Journal of Comic Art* (IJOCA), established in 1999 and edited by John A. Lent, has consistently included articles dealing with Latin American comics.[2] This edited volume contributes to this body of work by foregrounding the little explored work of memory in Latin American comics.

This introductory chapter examines the history of comics and graphic novels in Latin America, paying particular attention to the production of comics and graphic novels in the countries surveyed in the following chapters. Comics and graphic novels have a long history in the region, although some countries have far more developed comics industries (or comics cultures) than others. While some general trends in the development of the genre are identifiable (for example, the rise of political commentary in comics from the 1960s on), some national comic industries are characterized by idiosyncratic developments that reflect the particular historical processes of each national experience. We also consider the emergence of memory as a field of study and its development in the Latin American context. As a number of scholars have shown, memory has played a key role in the process of transition from dictatorship and armed conflict to democracy throughout the region since the mid-1980s. It has become a privileged, if always contested, perspective from which to engage with the past—particularly the traumatic past. For some, memory is a medium that has the potential to overcome the historical traumas that have plagued the region.

We examine the interplay between memory as one means of engaging with the past (and the present) and comics, the latter taken as both a cultural form and a cultural artifact. Because of their particular formal characteristics, particularly the way they combine text with graphics, comics have allowed, even encouraged, the development of a series of visual techniques that enable the rendering of memory (or memories) in distinct and often sophisticated ways. As a result, and as students of the genre increasingly recognize, comics offer a distinct platform to relate memory (and time and space) graphically. Comics and graphic novels as material (and, when in cyber form, immaterial) objects operate as mediums or technologies of memory, similar to but also distinct from other memory devices such as photographs, memorials, or museums, which have received far more attention from scholars of memory. Comics elicit and mobilize memories in those who read and enjoy them and enable a particular engagement with the past distinct from that which may be experienced through the medium of, say, a film or a battle reenactment.

A BRIEF HISTORY OF LATIN AMERICAN COMICS

The development of Latin American comics does not differ significantly in format, structure, development, and periodization from its European or North American counterparts.[3] In both continents, the use of images in periodical magazines increased markedly in the 1800s as a result of significant improvements in printmaking techniques such as lithography (1796), chromolithography (1837), and the rotary press (1843). Periodicals became a mass phenomenon following the introduction of offset printing (1875) and the creation of the mimeograph machine (1890). These technologies proved particularly helpful to Latin Americans who sought to articulate discourses around the nation-state and to map out the new political entity in visual terms. They enabled the visual representation not only of landscapes, heroes, fauna, and flora but also of iconographic traditions (Fernández L'Hoeste and Poblete 2009). In turn, these technologies brought about the creation of illustrated satirical magazines that commented not just on local folklore or *costumbrismo* but also on political and social struggle.[4] In this context, graphic artists were able to develop professional careers by securing commissioned contributions to magazines and newspapers, effectively making use of graphic humor and, later on, comics as a commodity. Audiences, usually with high levels of illiteracy across the region, used visual imagery to participate in social and political life.

The first steps in the medium of comics are largely indebted to pioneers who experimented with the disposition of images in sequence and the combination of text and image. Serialized fictions peaked in the nineteenth century in periodical publications, providing a favorable environment for the development of comics. If the history of comics in Europe owes much to Rodolphe Töpffer, George Cruikshank, and Alfred Crowquill, to mention just a few names, the modern history of comics in Latin America began with the Italian-Brazilian cartoonist Angelo Agostini (1843–1910) and the Spanish-Cuban painter Víctor Patricio de Landaluze (1828–1889).[5] Agostini arrived in Brazil in 1859. In 1862 he was already established in São Paulo as a "pintor-retratista" (Balaban 2005: 62; Augusto 2008: 82). The "romance illustrado," *As aventuras de Nhô Quim ou Impressões de uma viagem à corte*, was published in the magazine *Vida fluminense* in 1869. This is Latin America's first known comics story with a continuing character (Vergueiro 2000; Lent 2005).

In 1905, Agostini launched *O Tico-Tico*, a publication whose main character, "Chiquinho," was a clear adaptation of "Buster Brown" (Vergueiro 2005: 88), a mischievous young boy from a middle-class family who played practical jokes, created by Richard Felton Outcault and first published in 1902 in the *New York Herald* (Gordon 1998: 44).[6] In Cuba, Landaluze introduced the series of local folklore types with *Los cubanos pintados por sí mismos* (1852), and he published caricatures in several satirical magazines of the time, such as *Don junípero*, *El moro muza*, and *La charanga*. The autobiographical "Estudios sobre el mareo," published in *Don junípero* (1864) is a primitive comic, in which Landaluze crafted twelve sequential panels with text at the bottom on a double page, imaging his forthcoming boat trip after leaving Havana (Barrero 2004: 86–87).

These early comics by Agostini and Landaluze, infused by the *costumbrismo* genre that dealt with customs, habits, or traditions, were followed in the 1900s and 1910s by a second stage in the development of comics in Latin America. The widespread use of comics in the U.S. press and the internationalization of U.S. comics through powerful press syndicates in Latin America became highly influential for the emerging national comics industries, as the case of "Chiquinho" demonstrates. By the 1900s, translations of comics from the United States, such as *Cocoliche* (Happy Hooligan) by

Frederick Burr Opper, made it to Argentina, and U.S. comics appeared in newspapers in Mexico in 1902 (Lent 2005: 5). According to scholar Harold Hinds (1985), the first Mexican comic strip was Andrés Audiffred's "Don Lupito" in 1903, and the first Chilean comic strip appeared in 1906, titled "Federico Von Pilsener," in the magazine *Zigzag*. In Peru the earliest examples are found in the modernist magazine *Monos y monadas*, which lasted from 1905 to 1907. Amid European influences (notably the German magazine *Simplicissimus* and Alphonse Mucha's *Art Nouveau*) and the discovery of Japanese impressionism (Barros 2008), Julio Málaga Grenet (1886–1963) experimented with the transformation of a person into an insect or an animal (metamorphoses that had a clear political motive), demonstrating an intimate relationship between illustration and literature. These developments fostered a distinctive style for Peruvian comics in such magazines as *Fray Simplón* and *Fray K-Bezón*, with an anticlerical bent (Sagástegui 2009: 134; see also Lucioni 2001).

The influence and diffusion of U.S. comics explains the structure and design of the first comic in Argentina with continuing characters and the use of balloons to represent characters' speech. In 1912 the magazine *Caras y caretas* published *Aventuras de Viruta y Chicharrón*. This was a copy of the U.S. comic strip *Spare Ribs and Gravy* by George McManus, which began that same year in the *New York American* (Seoane and Santa María 2008: 58). The comic was initially sent to Argentina for publication but, after negotiations failed, local artists Manuel Redondo and Juan Sanuy took over due to the comic's popularity (Gociol and Rosemberg 2003: 65). Three years later, in 1915, the Cuban magazine *Bohemia* published *Aventuras de Pepito y Rocamora* by Pedro Valer (who wrote under the pseudonym of Peter Relav). It continued weekly publication until at least 1922. The adventures of Pepito and Rocamora depicted various slapstick situations of a swindler couple within a local folklore substratum (Catalá Carrasco 2011: 140; 2015: 52–53).

In the first decades of the twentieth century, comics proved successful in securing audiences and helping to sell publications. By the 1930s newspaper comic strips were widespread throughout Latin America. The increasing readership facilitated comics' new format, the comic book: a publication entirely dedicated to comics. Brazil, Mexico, and the United States were the initiators of this process, which led to comics becoming more independent from the newspaper—a reflection of the stability and strength of their respective national comics industries. The first U.S. comic book appeared in 1933. *Suplemento juvenil* was published in Brazil in 1934. The first Mexican comic book, *Adelaido el conquistador*, included Mexican comics and translated

U.S. comic strips and lasted only two years (1932–1933). However, in 1934, *Paquín* became the first Mexican comic book to find a wide audience, soon followed by *Paquito* (1935), *Chamaco* (1936), and *Pepín* (1936). Reflecting *Pepín*'s prominence in the nascent industry, Mexicans began to refer to comic books as *pepines*. By 1940 comic books in Mexico were as ubiquitous as radio programs and more common than cinema (Rubenstein 1998: 13).

The golden age of comics in Latin America peaked in the 1950s through the 1970s, when the output of comics in such countries as Argentina, Brazil, Chile, Cuba, and Mexico expanded dramatically. In those years the Argentine Héctor G. Oesterheld, one of Latin America's finest comic script writers, established Editorial Frontera and created several milestone publications in the history of comics, such as *Mort cinder* (1962, drawn by the Uruguayan Alberto Breccia) and *El eternauta* (1957–1959, in collaboration with fellow Argentine Francisco Solano López). Oesterheld was disappeared by the Argentine Junta Militar in 1977 because of his involvement in the left-wing guerrilla group Montoneros, for which he authored *Latinoamérica y el imperialismo: 450 años de guerra* and a second version of *La guerra de los Antartes* in 1974 for the publication *Noticias*, which was closely linked to the Montoneros. Argentina's most famous comic strip, *Mafalda*, was created during this period by Joaquín Salvador Lavado, better known as Quino. *Mafalda* was published in magazines and newspapers between 1964 and 1973, quickly becoming a phenomenon throughout Europe and Latin America.

In Brazil, although *O Tico-Tico* came to an end in the 1950s, the same decade saw the consolidation of several publishing houses and the field was very fertile for new ventures. Horror comics, for example, became the most popular genre of comics in Brazil during the 1950s, while the 1960s was the most productive for Brazilian superheroes (Vergueiro 2009: 158–62). However, the most significant moment in modern Brazilian comics came in 1970, when artist Mauricio de Sousa convinced Editora Abril, one of the largest publishing houses in the country, to publish a comic book with his character Mônica. In similar fashion to the Disney Corporation, de Sousa created a merchandising universe around Mônica in Brazil.[7]

In 1949 the most iconic Chilean comics character, "Condorito," created by René Ríos Boettiger (1913–2000), better known as Pepo, was published in *Okey*. In light of its success in representing Chilean identity, Pepo compiled the first Condorito anthology in 1955. Thereafter, Condorito's predominance in the Chilean comics market grew steadily. Nine anthologies were published in 1983 alone (Fernández L'Hoeste and Poblete 2009: 36–37). The three years of Salvador Allende's Unidad Popular (1970–1973) brought about an important transformation in Chilean comics with the publication of such political comics as *La firme* (Kunzle 1978 and 2005) and an innovative orientation to children's comics better exemplified in *Cabro chico*. The national publishing house Quimantú tried to counterbalance the pervasive presence of U.S. comics, especially those produced by Disney.

From this effort sprang the most influential text on comics and mass culture in Latin America: Dorfman and Mattelart's *Para leer al Pato Donald* (1971; How to read Donald Duck), first published in Chile in 1971. Hugely influential for subsequent political readings of comics, *Para leer al Pato Donald* deconstructed Disney comics from a Marxist point of view, emphasizing the underlying ideological manipulation in what seemed to be the archetype of innocent comics for children. This critique coincided with the growing politicization of comics, which increasingly reflected the polarization of Chilean society and which constituted political interventions in their own right. During the Pinochet dictatorship (1973–1990) several magazines shut down as a consequence of severe censorship and/or financial hardship, including *El siniestro Doctor Mortis* in 1974, *Mampato* in 1978, and *Barrabases* in 1979. Quimantú was then directed by General Diego Barros Ortiz and in 1977 was sold to a private investor (Pérez Santiago 2003).

In Cuba in the 1930s, Horacio Rodríguez Suriá and Rafael Fornés, along with Pedro Valer, published comics in *Cárteles* and in *Avance*'s supplement "Revista Rosa." Manuel Alonso, Mike Cárdenas, Silvio Fontanillas, and Antonio Prohías (who went into exile soon after the 1959 Cuban Revolution and became a crucial contributor for the U.S. *Mad* magazine with his comic "Spy vs Spy") were other important figures in Cuba's burgeoning comics world. With the Cuban Revolution, new opportunities emerged, ranging from the avant-garde magazine *El Pitirre* (1960–1961) to the satiric communist magazine *Mella* (where Virgilio Martínez and Marcos Behemaras published several comics) until the mid-1960s. The publisher Ediciones en Colores launched four monthlies from 1965 to 1968—*¡Aventuras!*, *Muñequitos*, *Din Don*, and *Fantásticos*—which satisfied the increasing demand for comics. And in 1970, Juan Padrón published in *Pionero,* the first of many Elpidio Valdés's comics, as well as three films in 1979, 1983, and 1996. Cuban painter Roberto Fabelo declared that "Elpidio is one of the landmarks of current Cuban culture" (Padrón 1999: 68). In the 1980s the Pablo de la Torriente publishing house produced the weekly tabloid *El muñe*, the monthly comic book *Cómicos* and the biannual magazine for adults, *Pablo*, thus building on a readership that had already begun to expand after the general boom in adult comics in the 1970s with underground comics. Many of these initiatives came to an end with the "Special Period," following the collapse of the Soviet Union (1989) and the Socialist Bloc (1991), but comics artists in Cuba remain active, and the main humorous magazine, *Palante* (which began in 1961), stands out for its support of comic strips.[8]

By the 1950s, Mexico had an average of four million to five million comics readers in a nation of twenty-five million inhabitants, which made comics the largest mass-produced and -consumed cultural artifact of the time. Films were also popular, but film audiences visited cinemas no more than twice a week. By contrast, Mexicans listened to the radio and read *pepines* relentlessly (Bartra 2005: 263). A new development emerged in the 1950s and 1960s, the comic novel, with a more traditional narrative structure (introduction, climax, and conclusion), making each comic novel an independent story. Indeed, Mexican comics artists began to target adult readers some forty years before their counterparts in Europe (265). During the second half of the 1960s and early 1970s, Mexican comics reached the high point of their popularity, but clear symptoms of decline began to appear. Eduardo del Río (Rius) began his prolific career at that time with what soon became classic Mexican comics: *Los supermachos* and *Los agachados*.[9] Nowadays, with the lack of stable and financially viable publications, amateurism poses difficulties for professional development. The only genre that has survived the long decline of comics in Mexico are the "Sensacionales" or "La revista vaquera," low-quality black-and-white erotic adult comics, whose pocket-size book format is generally comprised of some one hundred pages, adorned with voluptuous women on their front covers.

In other Latin American countries, where there was no comics industry, comics nonetheless proved influential and became a forum for artistic and political expression. In Nicaragua there had been a weak tradition of comics and political caricatures before the Sandinista revolution. According to historian Christiane Berth in chapter 4 of this volume, the first satirical weekly was the anti-*somocista Los Lunes de la Nueva Prensa* in the 1940s, followed by *Semana Cómica* in the 1950s and 1960s. But the ousting of the Somoza dictatorship in 1979 opened up new spaces for artists in collaboration with the revolutionary government. In Peru, although comics can be traced to the late nineteenth century (Lucioni 2001), the 1950s represented the starting point for a graphic representation of *peruanidad* through an array of comics characters, such as "Serrucho" (an indigenous peasant who had recently arrived in Lima), "Boquellanta" (a blackface child in love with a blonde) and "Sampietri" (a depiction of the typically penniless pleasure-seeker) (Lucioni 2002; Sagástegui 2009: 137).

Among many artists, Juan Acevedo stands out for being the first to organize workshops on popular comics in Ayacucho (1974) and Villa El Salvador (1975–1977) and for introducing overtly political commentary into the comic genre. These workshops led to his book *Para hacer historietas* (To make comics, 1978). Acevedo's most famous comic strip, *El Cuy*, an anthropomorphic comic based on a guinea pig, was published originally in the weekly *La Calle* in 1979 and subsequently in *El diario de Marka*, a left-wing daily, in 1980–1981. A recent edition, *El Cuy tira*, was published in 2011. Acevedo helped pioneer the graphic novel in Peru, with texts such as *Tupac Amaru* and *Paco Yunque* (Nuñez Alayo 2010).[10]

In all of these countries there is clear evidence of comics participating in historical and political processes and of comics depicting those same processes. Given the dynamic and radical nature of Latin American politics and history over the course of the twentieth century, not least in the wake of the Cuban Revolution, comics, just as other cultural forms, have been part and parcel of the contentious debates over memory politics and practices.

MEMORY STUDIES

The field of memory studies, largely nonexistent some thirty years ago, is today well established. Indeed, it is codified in particular ways through the creation of a broad scholarly armature that legitimizes it as a bona fide field of scholarship attracting an increasing number of scholars. A number of journals are dedicated to the field, including the recently launched *Memory Studies* and the more established *History and Memory*. Perhaps more important, studies of memory appear regularly in mainstream disciplinary journals, while monographs and edited collections on all aspects of memory are published by prestigious university presses. Countless conferences are organized each year that bring together scholars from all over the world who work on ever more diverse research and who are organized in transnational memory research networks. Such rapid growth in the field of memory studies has led at least one scholar to speak of a metastasis of collective memory (Olick 2008). Often interdisciplinary, memory studies scholarship takes place in dialogue or within specific academic disciplines such as literary and cultural studies or history. As such, there are arguably different types of memory studies, shaped by different methodologies and concerns, and increasingly by different types of memory studies literatures (Sturken 2008).

Genealogies of memory studies usually reference the sociological work of Maurice Halbwachs on collective memory and the monumental study of *lieux de memoire* (memory places) directed by the French historian Pierre Nora in the 1980s as seminal moments in the establishment of the field.[11] Later scholars have refined the conceptual toolbox of memory studies, contributing such concepts as cultural memory (Assmann 1995, 2011), postmemory (Hirsch 1992–1993, 1997), prosthetic memory (Landsberg 2004), or multidirectional memory (Rothberg 2009) to account for the myriad ways in which memory manifests itself and is operationalized. These concepts express in different ways how memory is increasingly seen as "a dynamic process that is the result of the practices of individuals and groups" rather than as being contained in objects (Sturken 2008: 74). Cultural memory, Egyptologist Jan Assmann (1995: 130) has written, "works by reconstructing, that is, it always relates its knowledge to an actual or contemporary situation." Memory, therefore, is as much about the present as it is about the past. It is mediated by technologies of memory, such as photographs or indeed memorials, in which memories are experienced and produced. While some memories are indeed expressions of lived experience, others can be inherited (Hirsch 1997) or acquired through involvement in mass culture (Landsberg 2004).

Yet while these scholarly origins, and conceptual refinements, are key to the development of the field, the locus and moment of the irruption of memory discourses and practices, which formed the basis for the establishment of memory studies, is of equal importance. As scholar Andreas Huyssen (2000) has suggested, memory discourses emerged in the 1960s in the context of global processes of decolonization and the emergence of diverse social movements. They were given further impetus in the 1980s when attention focused again on the Holocaust and a globalized discourse on the Shoah emerged. Holocaust memory discourse, Huyssen argues, shaped understandings of and responses to the genocides in Rwanda and the Balkans in the 1990s. These, in turn, helped to further establish memory as a way to engage the traumatic past.[12] By the 1990s, memory discourses had spread to most parts of the world and generated locally specific, if transnationally informed, memory discourses and practices. Indeed, the growth in memory discourses and practices globally has led some scholars, including those working on Latin America, to question whether memory has generated its own political economy and whether such a development risks trivializing the work that memory does or the projects of transitional justice that often engage it (Bilbija and Payne 2011).[13]

In Latin America, memory discourses and practices emerged in the context of processes of democratization and armed conflict resolution throughout the 1980s and 1990s. These processes were characterized, at least initially, by postdictatorial or postconflict settlements (most of which were imposed unilaterally) that included amnesties for perpetrators of human rights abuses and, more generally, a politics of amnesia that, so some claimed, would enable countries like Argentina and Chile to leave behind the trauma of the past. In this context human rights organizations and civil society groups such as, most famously, the Mothers of the Plaza de Mayo in Buenos Aires, began to challenge the postdictatorial settlements and to mobilize politically and culturally. As memory entrepreneurs, they began to articulate a memory discourse consonant with their political objectives. A politics of memory (or memory struggles or battles for memory) over the experience of military dictatorship developed, pitting so-called memories of salvation, which drew on narratives that focused on the ways in which the armed forces had intervened to save the nation from Communist threats, against human rights memories, which homed in on the abuses perpetrated by the armed forces and on the need to challenge the culture of impunity that they had imposed.[14]

The establishment of Truth Commissions in several Latin American countries played a key role in the evolving politics of memory. Truth Commissions in Argentina, Chile, Guatemala, Peru, and other countries gave added legitimacy to the challenges posed to the memories of salvation promoted by perpetrators of human rights abuses, such as amnestied generals in the Southern Cone or authoritarian rulers like Peru's Alberto Fujimori. In most cases, the Truth Commissions had as an explicit or implicit objective to establish a narrative on the past that could become official (and hegemonic) and overcome the fractious politics of memory. However, as a number of scholars have shown, Truth Commissions rarely succeeded in implanting such a narrative and, as a result, more often than not became caught up in, rather than being able to overcome, the politics of memory.[15] This outcome owed in part to the fact that often the memory of salvation had powerful backers. But this was only part of the story. In the Peruvian case, for example, a memory discourse put forward by the Truth and Reconciliation Commission (Comisión de la Verdad y Reconciliación, or CVR) at the national level proved of little use to, and indeed came into conflict with, the everyday practices of some of those people trying to reform communities that had been fractured by conflict. These people therefore needed to generate their own mnemonic practices that were not always commensurate with the memory practices privileged by the CVR.[16]

In studying memory discourses and practices in Latin America, scholars have paid particular attention to how memory is mobilized in the context of particular memory sites, such as monuments like the Ojo que llora in

Peru or the Parque de la Memoria in Buenos Aires or places associated with human rights abuses in times of dictatorship or conflict, such as the Escuela de Mecánica de la Armada (ESMA) in Buenos Aires or Villa Grimaldi in Santiago de Chile, which have sometimes been referred to as trauma sites.[17] However, scholars have focused their attention more and more on other, initially less obvious and less material, "sites," or perhaps more properly, technologies of memory. Indeed, scholars increasingly recognize the potential of a whole range of media for mobilizing memory and therefore for functioning as technologies of memory (Sturken 2008). Such media include visual and performance art, music, digital artifacts such as YouTube or Facebook, landscapes, and, of course, comic books and graphic novels.[18] In the main these media constitute, as historian Cynthia Milton (2007) has called them, "unofficial modes of truth telling" and as such are best understood as alternatives to the "official" memories that both Truth Commissions and state-sanctioned memorials seek to present. However, as numerous studies show and as several of the chapters in this volume confirm, neither the official nor the alternative modes of truth telling are uncontested.

The field of memory studies in Latin America is intimately linked to the politics of memory that shape, and are shaped by, historical processes of democratic transition and postconflict settlements. However, scholars are starting to examine memory in other historical contexts or, to put it differently, scholars are increasingly acknowledging the role that memory plays in how Latin Americans make sense of the past, and not just the past shaped by local inflections of the "long" Cold War (the periods of military rule in the Southern Cone, the civil wars in Central America, or the Shining Path insurgency in Peru). Historian Paulo Drinot (2011), for example, has examined how memory discourses on the War of the Pacific (1879–1884) inform the way that Peruvians and Chileans perceive each other (and themselves). Cultural historian Ana Lucia Araujo (2010) has also approached the topic of Atlantic slavery from the perspective of memory. Studies such as these point to the still largely untapped potential of memory, whether in its guise as collective memory, cultural memory, postmemory or prosthetic memory, to act as a productive process for thinking about Latin America past and present, beyond the still dominant focus on the second half of the twentieth century. Comics and graphic novels can amply fulfill this potential.

COMICS AND MEMORY

Given that Latin America has played host to the Cold War act of disappearance and acted as the testing ground for global neoliberal policies that are highly suspicious of holding on to the past, it is unsurprising that the region's comics and graphic novels have played a significant role within the huge corpus of cultural productions that address this history of upheaval and absence. In the Southern Cone alone, to take one illustrative corpus, the dictatorships of the 1970s and 1980s have recurred in graphic form, whether mimetically or obliquely. On the one hand, comics magazines such as *Fierro a fierro* in Argentina or *Trauko* in Chile provided a sphere where activities and interests otherwise repressed by military rule—especially sex, drugs, dress, music, and other forms of counterculture—could be celebrated. On the other hand, comics took the dictatorships and the legacy of trauma as their subject matter.

The artist Carlos Reyes (2011) has highlighted how in *Trauko*, for example, the threat of authoritarianism was evident in stories such as "Si una desconocida te ofrece una flor," written by Leo Prieto and drawn by Patricio De la Cruz (in 1989), which related how a police officer takes advantage of a vulnerable street seller. More recently, scholar Aidalí Aponte (2011) has read the volume *Zombies en la Moneda* (2009) as an attempt to engage with the "disappearance" of the Chilean dictatorship itself within the country's collective memory. In Uruguay the graphic novel *Acto de guerra*, drawn by Matías Bergara and written by Rodolfo Santullo (2010), which draws together four fictional stories based on real-life stories of the Uruguayan dictatorship, has had considerable success. In the wake of works addressing the Argentine dictatorship, including *Buscavidas*, *La batalla de Malvinas*, *Perramus*, and *Sudor sudaca*, Carlos Trillo and Lucas Varela's recent *La herencia del coronel* (2010) provides a sinister portrait of a military repressor's son struggling to come to terms with his sexual and violent fetish for dolls in the postdictatorship period.

Works such as these have played a key function as sites of memory, from the physical copies of historic comics productions, which circulate among collectors and fan clubs, to discussion pages and forums that have provided opportunities for readers and consumers to debate the past. Indeed, the nature of the comics market has meant that during the time of political upheaval and in its aftermath, comics have often been able to respond with great speed and actuality to historical events and debates in the public sphere. The relatively low cost of production, the manner in which comics are often shared between enthusiasts, and the blend of the visual and the written that makes up comics means that they have the potential for fast distribution and dissemination among a large, and often diverse, reading public. At the height of the Argentine dictatorship and despite strict censorship, for example, the satirical comics magazine *Humor* was able to sell some 350,000 copies every fortnight (Ostuni et al. n.d.: 5–6).

Argentina offers some good examples of the ways that comics function as sites of memory beyond the page, having an increasing impact in and on the public sphere. The disappearance of Héctor G. Oesterheld in 1978, one of the most famous victims of the dictatorship, provided a cultural figurehead for the brutality of the dictatorship. An early example of the way that comics were used to frame that disappearance can be seen in the well-known poster "¿DONDE ESTA OESTERHELD?" included in the October 27, 1983, edition of the magazine *Feriado nacional*. The image, drawn by Félix Saborido, depicts the Avenida de Mayo in Buenos Aires, filled with a silent crowd carrying a banner that demands the return of the comics writer. In a clever fusion of comics history with human rights marches, the protesting crowd is entirely made up of characters taken from Oesterheld's works, including Sargento Kirk, Ernie Pike, Mort Cinder, and El Eternauta. The latter, a famous time traveler, was used to pay homage to Oesterheld in a stencil campaign that began in the city of Rosario in 2006. The wanderer went viral via graffiti throughout the country, enshrining the figure as a symbol of resistance. More recently, the artist Lucila Quieto has drawn on the legacy of Oesterheld, fusing scenes from his series *Sargento Kirk*, which relates the friendship struck up between a disillusioned U.S. soldier and Plains Indians in the nineteenth century, with photographs of the 1968 uprising in Córdoba, the Cordobazo, in artworks that play with cultural and political history to construct new visions of the past. Comics thus constitute sites of memory that elicit and mobilize memories of the past, a politics of the present, and a project for the future.

Of course, many comics also recount past events on and through the page as well, adding a further dimension to the way they function as sites of memory. Often, and particularly in the field of graphic biography, the intention is simply to use comics to provide a visual history, a graphic retelling of the past, an approach evident in, for example, several graphic depictions of Latin American lives, including *Castro* (Kleist 2010), *Gabo: Memorias de una vida mágica* (Pantojo et al. 2013), or the graphic biographies of Ernesto "Che" Guevara analyzed by James Scorer (2010)—namely the 1968 work *Che: Vida de Ernesto Che Guevara* (Oesterheld, Breccia, and Breccia 2008) and the more recent *Che: A Graphic Biography* (Rodriguez 2008) and *Che: A Graphic Biography* (Jacobson and Colón 2009). Other works draw heavily on the past to provide a historical context within which to locate a fictional narrative. Oesterheld, for example, made extensive use of history in many of his fictional works: in *Ernie Pike* (1957–1971) he used a World War II journalist to highlight the brutality of conflict for victors and losers alike, and in *Sargento Kirk* (1953–1973) he turned to the frontier struggles of nineteenth-century U.S. history to think through concepts of colonialism and heroism. Similarly, Juan Acevedo's two volumes on Tupac Amaru (1987–1988) recount the life of the leader of the late eighteenth-century Andean rebellion that shook the Spanish Empire.[19] In these works, historical events, periods, and characters (whether fictional or not) are presented with little or no framing that affects the nature of the narrative itself. As a result, the process of history telling and memory are often not self-consciously presented as a theme for reflection.

In other works, however, the comic form is expressly used as a means of engaging with the nature of retelling the past and with practices of memory. Certainly other cultural mediums have their own particularities and potencies when it comes to memory, but comics can mobilize the past in particularly challenging and productive ways. The way that comics can "spatialize memory" (Chute 2011: 108), and use the panel structure to allow for a multiplicity of temporal moments and for moving forward and back in time, indicates how they invite a series of "negotiations" between the reader and the text-image over which path to take when engaging with the narration of time on the page. In some cases, the multilinear narrative lines that result (Bredehoft 2006: 885), combined with the empty spaces of the gutter, have been deployed by comics creators to try and capture the unreliability of single-narrative pasts and the inaccessible voids that inevitably emerge in the process of remembering. Art Spiegelman's *Maus*, the seminal work in any analysis of comics and memory, is a case in point, mobilizing the "trauma fragment" not only to connect past and present (Hirsch 1992–1993: 26) but also to highlight memory's unreliability and the tensions between truth and history, symbolized by the author's treatment of Vladek not remembering the orchestra at Auschwitz (Spiegelman 2011: 29–31).[20] Though obviously not a Latin American work, *Maus* (in a similar vein to the work of Joe Sacco) has been pointed to by scholars like Ana Merino (2010) for its testimonial nature. Latin America is innately tied to the history, development, and theorization of testimony as a memory practice.[21]

Such ties to testimony, itself a hotly contested form of memory, means that it is unsurprising, as this book demonstrates, that Latin American comics creators have also turned to the comic form to express and engage with memory. In *Che: Vida de Ernesto Che Guevara*, for example, Oesterheld's narrative is split between two interweaving histories: the story of Che's life on the one hand (drawn by Alberto Breccia) and his final days in Bolivia on the other (drawn by Enrique Breccia). It is not just the patchwork nature of the narrative, moving back and forth from past to present, that engages with memory; it is also the dramatically different drawing style of Breccia father and Breccia son. Alberto's highly detailed, complex frames, with his sometimes experimental use of graphic patterns, relate to the more precise nature of the "agreed" historical narrative. Here too we find facsimile copies of Che's birth certificate (Oesterheld, Breccia, and Breccia 2008: 10) or his handwritten farewell letter to his children (56), images that exaggerate the authenticity of this part of the narrative. Enrique's frames, on the other hand, are drawn with much less detail and with greater use of block areas of black and white. The shapes of his figures are less precise, and some characters have childlike faces, exaggerating the fantastical, mythic nature of these passages. Enrique's stylistic approach relates more directly to the nature of retelling Che's Bolivian experiences, which were reproduced from Che's own campaign diary and thus more subjective and personal. The dual narrative reflects the beginnings of the transformation of Che the historical figure to Che the myth.

Other stylistic means of engaging with the past in comics can be seen in works like *La herencia del coronel* (Trillo and Varela 2010), where a color shift is used to distinguish between the narrative present (full color) and the memories of the protagonist (blue tone, with the occasional use of red for the images of torture), or *Parque Chas* (Barreiro and Risso 2004), a series comprised of stories told to the protagonist by different inhabitants of the eponymous neighborhood in Buenos Aires. On the first page of the episode titled "Batalla de otoño," for example, one frame includes both past and present by having the foreground of the image depict the hands of the storyteller pouring sugar into his coffee cup inside the bar, whereas through the window we can see his former boyhood self walking down the street with his friends. Such simultaneity of times can also be seen in *Beya (Le viste la cara a Dios)* (Cabezón Cámara and Echeverría 2013), an expressive critique of enforced prostitution. On one page the narrator's voice (expressed via text) initially describes the abuse that was happening to the protagonist, before shifting tenses to describe that abuse as if it were taking place in the present (30). At the same time, the images, which are themselves partly superimposed on each other and on the text boxes, a visual representation of the fragmented nature of what is being related and the nature of the exploited body, depict the abuse that is taking place in both the past and present. The speech box included in one of the frames, in which the abuser insults the women, only intensifies the manner in which what has happened is being played out once more in the here and now. Finally, in the recent Colombian work *Los once*, the use of visually dense images, of quotes from historical testimonies blended with fictional narrative, and of animals to represent humans, intensifies the difficulty of unpacking past events, in this case the 1985 raid on the Palace of Justice in Bogotá by the guerrilla group M-19 and the subsequent confrontation with state forces during which, in addition to many being killed, several people were disappeared (Jiménez, Jiménez, and Cruz 2014).

Whether as memory processes that frame the past (whether fictional or not) to delve into the metanarrative processes of history telling and memory or as sites that provide the means to consume, debate, and work through the vagaries of history and memory, in both form and object comics remain privileged sites for memory in Latin America. Although comics have adopted different historical, aesthetic, thematic, or contextual strategies, they nonetheless form a key formal, cultural, and social space for memory practices and debates about approaches to the past.

DESCRIPTION OF CHAPTERS

The contributors to this volume consider this engagement with memories of the past in Latin America via comics. In chapter 1, Jorge L. Catalá Carrasco considers the Spanish-Cuban-American War (1898) revisited by the Cuban comic *La emboscada* (1982). The comic, by Ernesto Padrón and Orestes Suárez, is a metaphorical reconstruction, influenced by post-1959 historiography, which seeks to reclaim Cuban agency in the conflict. It serves as an example of Alison Landsberg's "prosthetic memory" (2004), allowing Cubans to apprehend a historical narrative with a more personal, deeply felt, memory of a past event with peculiar connotations for Cuban national consciousness. The comic provides a case study for Jan Assmann's concept of "cultural memory" (1995)—more precisely, its *concretion of identity* and its *capacity to reconstruct*, shedding light on how the inscription of a 1980s Cuban revolutionary discourse onto the 1898 Spanish-Cuban-American War, demonstrates the enduring nature of certain collective memories.

In chapter 2, Edoardo Balletta looks at two works by Argentina's most famous comics writer, Héctor G. Oesterheld, both written at a time when Oesterheld was working for the armed left-wing guerrilla organization Montoneros. Balletta highlights how *Latinoamérica y el imperialismo: 450 años de guerra* (drawn by Leopoldo Durañona) and *La guerra de los Antartes* (drawn by Gustavo Trigo) reappropriate the past to intervene in the present as a graphic, revolutionary act. Taking cultural memory to be socially constitutive, Balletta sees these two works as contributing to the way the Peronist Left attempted to position itself as the hegemonic voice of Argentine politics. In *Latinoamérica y el imperialismo*, a revisionist history of rebellion and colonialism in Latin America, the authors try to fuse Latin American insurrection with national-popular Peronist discourse and to use temporal circularity to present past events as explaining and justifying the present and vice versa. *La guerra de los Antartes*, a science-fiction account of how aliens invade Latin America after creating a pact with world superpowers, also engages with such mutable temporalities. Balletta suggests that the revolutionary fervor and potential of *Latinoamérica y el imperialismo* has itself become an inaccessible memory.

In chapter 3, Isabella Cosse examines the ways in which Quino's *Mafalda* has been resignified and mobilized at different times since the 1970s, both within Argentina and internationally. In the 1980s, Cosse shows, *Mafalda* resurfaced in the context of Argentina's democratization, when the comic strip was used by Quino and others to make sense of, and denounce, the experience of the military dictatorship and its impact on Argentine society. In this process, *Mafalda*, and the values associated with it, acquired a talismanic character as a symbol of Argentina's new democratic project. As the neoliberal experiments took hold in Latin America and elsewhere, Cosse argues, *Mafalda* was subjected to the forces of globalization, with its popularity growing throughout Latin America and Europe. Cosse suggests that within this process, *Mafalda* served to mobilize memories about the 1960s and the values that became associated with that period. Cosse concludes by looking at how *Mafalda* has more recently come to connect with, and articulate, an emerging nostalgia in Argentina for the disappearance of the very sector of Argentine society that *Mafalda* was perceived to embody—namely the middle class.

Christiane Berth's chapter 4 focuses on comic books, comic strips in the Sandinista newspaper *Barricada*, and other media such as pamphlets published in the 1980s to analyze how comics were used in political and educational campaigns and how they contribute to Sandinista memory politics. In a largely illiterate society like Nicaragua, Berth suggests, comics could play an important role in disseminating the revolutionary government's message as they had done in Cuba and Allende's Chile, countries that influenced Sandinista visual communication strategies and, more broadly, their popular education campaigns. Comic books on the insurrection sought to construct a collective memory on the prerevolutionary period (linking the Frente Sandinista de Liberación Nacional [FSLN] firmly with Augusto César Sandino's own struggle) and on the heroic nature of the 1979 revolution. At the same time, they constructed an invariably negative image of both Somoza and the United States. Comic strips employed in the health campaigns drew on such representations to present the Sandinista public health strategy as a continuation of the struggle against the social and political legacy of Somoza and his regime, with Somoza often represented as a bacterium. Less successful were the graphic strategies developed in the context of the campaigns to explain the FSLN's economic policies. These comics were overly reliant on text, pointing to the limits of the Sandinista's use of comics as part of its broader education campaigns and the memory politics to which they contributed.

Chapter 5, by Paulo Drinot, considers the ways in which an online version of *El Cuy*, Peruvian comic artist Juan Acevedo's most famous and popular creation, elicits and helps construct memories about recent Peruvian history. Acevedo's "El Diario del Cuy," a blog that the artist manages himself, is updated on a regular basis with a number of different items but most often with a daily upload of the comic strip *El Cuy*, originally published in several Peruvian newspapers in the late 1970s and early 1980s. A highly political strip, which reflected a highly politicized period in Peru's history, and in particular in the history of the Peruvian Left, *El Cuy* left a very deep impression on many readers who read the comic strip when it was first published or who read it subsequently in book form. Drinot analyzes the comments that a number of posters leave on the blog. He focuses on the ways in which the comic qua blog mobilizes memories of the Peruvian Left and the emergence of Shining Path, the insurgent movement that initiated the internal armed conflict in 1980 and that produced some seventy thousand victims, according to Peru's Truth and Reconciliation Commission. Drinot suggests that the memories mobilized by the blog result in a largely critical evaluation of the Left, more specifically of its failure to produce a viable political project in the early 1980s as Peru emerged from over a decade of military dictatorship. These memories reflect a critical evaluation of the Left's position with regard to the rise of Shining Path and more generally of the Left's failure to reemerge as a political force.

Peru's Shining Path receives further consideration in Cynthia E. Milton's chapter 6, which discusses the work of a collective of artists and researchers (Luis Rossell, Alfredo Villar, and Jesús Cossío), particularly the graphic novel *Rupay*, published in 2008, which draws on but departs from the *Final Report* of Peru's Truth and Reconciliation Commission (CVR) in presenting a narrative of the internal armed conflict that Peru experienced in the 1980s and 1990s. In her analysis of *Rupay*, Milton considers the comic book form as a means to recount this violent past and its unresolved legacies. She focuses on a particular episode of the internal armed conflict, the massacre of a group of journalists in Uchuraccay in 1983, a case study chosen by the CVR as emblematic of the conflict. Milton notes the subtle and not-so-subtle differences in the way events or protagonists are depicted in *Rupay* and in the CVR's *Final Report*. These differences, she suggests, are expressive of the editorial decisions taken by the authors of *Rupay* (which in turn reflect the range of sources they used in putting together the graphic novel) but also of the comic book format, which allows for forms of truth telling (for example, the simultaneous presentation of several views of a process) not available to the CVR. In some ways the format enables Cossío and his collaborators to tell a much more complex, if partly fictitious, account of the massacre. Such comics as *Rupay*, Milton concludes, must be understood as important elements in the memory debates in Peru that have developed in the wake of the CVR.

James Scorer's chapter 7 analyzes Gonzalo Martínez's *Road Story*, a graphic adaptation of a short story written by one of the leading figures of the loosely affiliated McOndo generation, Alberto Fuguet. Fusing the theories of prosthetic and cultural memory, Scorer argues that *Road Story*, in its comic rendition, offers a constructive form of memory production. Contrary to the way that Fuguet is often understood, as a figure of Chile's transnational, neoliberal, and ahistorical present, Scorer suggests that Martínez's graphic techniques transform the dangers of postmodern division into a positive multiplicity of fragments. Crucial to that graphic rendition of appropriated cultural memories is the road trip, a genre that he suggests has always been closely tied to Latin America. Drawing on a genre inherently tied to movement and identity transformation, and thus to memory and forgetting, *Road Story* demonstrates how the visual exchanges inherent in contemporary cultural production can be deployed as a means of moving on from the stasis of trauma.

In chapter 8, Edward King highlights how comic book artists and writers in Brazil have used the interstices inherent in the graphic form, itself located between literature and image and between discourse and technique, to reformulate the relationship between individual and collective identities. His essay is focused in particular on *Morro da favela*, a work by André Diniz that blends traditional woodcut styles with photographs (the latter taken by Maurício Hora) to explore the dialogues between individual, regional, and global cultural imaginaries and forms. The woodblock form, for example, allows for a link to be established between the urban favela and the *sertão*, the Brazilian hinterland. On the one hand, King argues, that might be read as reproducing the way spaces of urban poverty are reified as alien to the rest of the city; on the other hand, because the artwork is clearly a digitized rendition of the woodblock, it is also a reminder of the way technology and graphic techniques have participated in negotiations over modernity and its popular memories.

Overall, the chapters in this book exemplify the productive dialogue that can be established between the fields of comics and memory studies in the Latin American context. These contributions show that, because of their graphic form and because of the subjects that they address, comics in Latin America offer a unique and compelling perspective on memory that sheds new light on key historical and cultural processes in Latin America. Comics in Latin America have been rarely explored in terms of how Latin Americans remember, forget, and make sense of a wide range of issues—from the constitution of national identity, to narratives of resistance to colonialism and imperialism, to the construction of revolutionary traditions, to authoritarianism, political violence, and its traumatic legacies. In this sense, this volume should be read as a contribution not just to the fields of comics studies and memory studies but also, and more generally, to Latin American studies—a field that has explored both comics and memory but that has never offered a sustained reflection on the interplay between the two. While certainly not the last word on comics and memory in Latin America, this volume provides insights that others can draw on to examine further how comics can inform not just the study of memory but also other key issues at stake in Latin American studies.

NOTES

Epigraph: Moore and Bolland (2008 [1988]).

1. See *Revista Latinoamericana de Estudios Sobre la Historieta* (RLESH), online at https://archive.is/8eN5.
2. Earlier academic publications in the United States, such as the *Journal of Popular Culture* (first published in 1967) or *Studies in Latin American Popular Culture* (first published in 1982), have also included pieces about Latin American comics. In the United Kingdom three academic journals focusing on comics have been established: *European Comic Art* (since 2008), *Journal of Graphic Novels and Comics* (since 2010), and *Studies in Comics* (since 2010).

3. Some critics and artists (Masotta 1982 [1970]; Del Río 1983; McCloud 2004 [1993]; Merino 2003) take the discussion of the origins back to cave painting, the Trajan Column, or the Bayeux Tapestry—all seen as precursors of modern comics for the primitive sequential disposition of images, one of the main characteristics many scholars attribute to comics. In the Latin American context, the Codex Azcatitlan (1500s) and the *Nueva Crónica y Buen Gobierno* (1615) by Guamán Poma de Ayala are often cited as similar antecedents.
4. For the Peruvian case, see Ayala Calderón (2012).
5. Töppfer is considered the father of comic strips (Kunzle 2007). His *Histoire de M. Vieux Bois* was published in 1837. It was subsequently published in the United States in 1842 as *The Adventures of Obadiah Oldbuck*. For a detailed account of these artists' contributions to the development of early comics, see Smolderen 2009.
6. Outcault was the creator of the "The Yellow Kid," the lead comic strip character in *Hogan's Alley* that ran from 1895 to 1898 in Joseph Pulitzer's *New York World* and later William Randolph Hearst's *New York Journal*. U.S. scholarship on comics has tended to assume "The Yellow Kid" as the foundational moment of modern comics.
7. In 2007, Panini became the publisher of the Mônica conglomerate, using new projects, including a TV show, to diversify consumers by targeting adults as well as children (Vergueiro 2011: 144–45).
8. The *Bienal Internacional de Humorismo Gráfico* (which celebrated its eighteenth edition in March 2013), which highlights graphic humor and comics, is held annually at San Antonio de los Baños.
9. Rius's international success came with the 1976 English-language publication of *Marx for Beginners*, a translation of his *Marx para principiantes* (1972), following the first English edition in 1970 of *Cuba para principiantes*. *Marx for Beginners*, a comic strip representation of the life and ideas of Karl Marx, became an international best seller and kicked off the *For Beginners* series of books from Writers & Readers and later Icon Books.
10. On Acevedo's graphic adaptation of César Vallejo's *Paco Yunque*, see Faverón Patriau (2011).
11. Useful introductions to the field include Olick and Robbins (1998); Huyssen (2000); Klein (2000); and Kansteiner (2002).
12. More recently, the Holocaust memory discourse has been mobilized in the context of Argentine memory struggles as part of an attempt by some to frame the Argentine experience as a genocide. See Robben (2012).
13. On this point, see Sturken (2007) for the U.S. case.
14. The literature on this issue is far too large to cite here. See, however, Jelin (1994, 2003) and Stern (2006).

15. See Grandin (2005); the special issue of *Radical History Review* edited by Grandin and Klubock (2007); and Klep (2012). On Truth Commissions more broadly, see also Hayner (2002) and Payne (2008).
16. See Theidon (2012); and Riaño-Alcalá and Baines (2012).
17. See, among others, Meade (2001); Jelin and Langland (2003); Jelin (2007); Hite (2007); Gomez-Barris (2008); Hite and Collins (2009); Drinot (2009); Bell and Paolantonio (2009); Violi (2012); Milton (2011); Andermann (2012); and Hite (2012).
18. See, for example, Taylor (2003); Drinot (2011); Sosa and Serpente (2012); and Milton (2014).
19. Beyond Latin America, there are a vast number of examples of historical comic narratives. Some notable examples include Jason Lutes's saga *Berlin* (2001) or Vittorio Giardino's 1999–2008 account of the Spanish Civil War *¡No pasarán!* (published in 2011). Spain itself has seen a wealth of publications about the Civil War, including Francisco Gallardo Sarmiento and Miguel Gallardo's *Un largo silencio* (2012), Paco Roca's *Los surcos del azar* (2013), and Vicente Llobell Bisbal's *Un médico novato* (2013). The Ley de Memoria Histórica (Law of historical memory), passed by the socialist government in 2007, has created a context within which comics artists have created a diverse body of work that addresses the legacy of trauma in Spain (Merino and Tullis 2012: 224).
20. Joe Sacco's work, notably *Palestine* (2003), has many similarities with Spiegelman's testimonial approach in *Maus*.
21. Visual engagements with the process of storytelling itself are often even more prevalent in autobiographical comics and graphic novels, works sometimes described as "autographies" (Gardner 2008). This particular genre of memory is less prevalent in Latin America than it is in North America and Europe. Some examples from the latter regions include Craig Thompson's *Blankets*, which includes one frame that is erased on a simultaneously internal and metavisual level by a paint roller that is initially enclosed within a frame but then appears outside the frame, sweeping across the page to eventually leave a white emptiness (Thompson 2005: 540–43); Paco Roca's *Arrugas*, which uses half-drawn blurred faces (Roca 2013: 95) and then an entirely blank two-page "splash" (98–99) to represent the absent memories brought about by Alzheimer's disease; and Alison Bechdel's memoir *Fun Home*, which uses multiple narrative times, frames that function as historical documents (Bechdel 2006: 8, 32), and drawn pictures of photographs (71, 100–101), all of which blur visions of the past and intensify uncertainty over the veracity of memory.

REFERENCES

Andermann, Jens. 2012. "Returning to the Site of Horror: On the Reclaiming of Clandestine Concentration Camps in Argentina." *Theory, Culture, and Society* 29: 76–98.

Aponte, Aidalí. 2011. "¿La desaparición de la dictadura? Zombies en la Moneda." *Cruce*, 1. Online at www.revistacruce.com/artes/item/1067-la-desaparicion-de-la-dictadura-zombies-en-la-moneda. Accessed on July 16, 2013.

Araujo, Ana Lucia. 2010. *Public Memory of Slavery: Victims and Perpetrators in the South Atlantic*. Amherst, NY: Cambria Press.

Assmann, Jan. 2011. *Cultural Memory and Early Civilization: Writing, Remembrance, and Early Political Imagination*. Cambridge: Cambridge University Press.

Assmann, Jan. 1995. "Collective Memory and Cultural Identity." *New German Critique* 65: 125–33.

Augusto, José Carlos. 2008. "Um provinciano na corte: As aventuras de 'Nhô-Quim' e a Sociedade do Rio de Janeiro nos anos 1860–1870." MA dissertation. Universidade de São Paulo.

Ayala Calderón, Kristhian O. 2012. "Representaciones del imaginario de nación en la caricatura política del siglo XIX (1892–1896)." MA dissertation. Pontificia Universidad Católica del Perú.

Balaban, Marcelo. 2005. "Poeta do lápis: A trajetória de Angelo Agostini no Brasil Imperial–São Paulo e Rio de Janeiro 1864–1888." PhD dissertation. Universidade Estadual de Campinas.

Barreiro, Ricardo, and Eduardo Risso. 2004. *Parque Chas*. Rosario: Puro Comic.

Barrero, Manuel. 2004. "El origen de la historieta española en Cuba." *Revista Latinoamerica de Estudios Sobre la Historieta* 4, no. 14: 65–97.

Barros, Bernardo. 2008. *Caricatura y crítica de arte*. Edited by Jorge R. Bermúdez. Havana: Ediciones Letras Cubanas.

Bartra, Armando. 2005. "Dawn, Noon, and Dusk of a Tumultuous Narrative: The Evolution of Mexican Comic Art." In *Cartooning in Latin America*. Edited by John Lent, 253–78. Cresskill: Hampton.

Bechdel, Alison. 2006. *Fun Home: A Family Tragicomic*. London: Jonathan Cape.

Bell, Vikki, and M. di Paolantonio. 2009. "The Haunted Nomos: Activist-Artists and the (Im)possible Politics of Memory in Transitional Argentina." *Cultural Politics* 5: 149–78.

Bergara, Matías, and Rodolfo Santullo. 2010. *Acto de guerra*. Montevideo: Belerofonte.

Bilbija, Ksenija, and Leigh Payne. 2011. *Accounting for Violence: Marketing Memory in Latin America*. Durham, NC: Duke University Press.

Bredehoft, Thomas A. 2006. "Comics Architecture, Multidimensionality, and Time:

Chris Ware's *Jimmy Corrigan: The Smartest Kid on Earth.*" *MFS Modern Fiction Studies* 52, no. 4: 869–90.

Cabezón Cámara, Gabriela, and Iñaki Echeverría. 2013. *Beya (Le viste la cara a Dios).* Buenos Aires: Eterna Cadencia.

Catalá Carrasco, Jorge L. 2015. *Vanguardia y humorismo gráfico en crisis: La guerra civil española (1936-1939) y la revolución cubana (1959-1961).* Woodbridge: Tamesis.

Catalá Carrasco, Jorge L. 2011. "From Suspicion to Recognition? 50 Years of Comics in Cuba." *Journal of Latin American Cultural Studies* 20, no. 2: 139–60.

Chute, Hillary. 2011. "Comics Form and Narrating Lives." *Profession* 11: 107–17.

Del Río, Eduardo. 1983. *La vida de cuadritos: Breve guía de la historieta.* Mexico D.F.: Grijalbo.

Dorfman, Ariel, and Armand Mattelart. 1971. Reprint, 1981. *Para leer al Pato Donald.* Mexico D.F.: Siglo XXI.

Drinot, Paulo. 2011. "Web-Site of Memory: The War of the Pacific (1879–1884) in the Global Age of YouTube." *Memory Studies* 4, no. 4: 370–85.

Drinot, Paulo. 2009. "For Whom the Eye Cries: Memory, Monumentality, and the Ontologies of Violence in Peru." *Journal of Latin American Cultural Studies* 18, no. 1: 15–32.

Faverón Patriau, Gustavo. 2011. "El silencioso viaje de la ideología: El Paco Yunque de Vallejo y la adaptación de Juan Acevedo." *Revista Iberoamericana* 67, no. 234: 111–33.

Fernández L'Hoeste, Héctor, and Juan Poblete. 2009. *Redrawing the Nation: National Identity in Latin/o American Comics.* Basingstoke: Palgrave.

Foster, David William. 1989. *From Mafalda to Los Supermachos: Latin American Graphic Humor as Popular Culture.* Boulder, CO: Lynne Rienner.

Gallardo Sarmiento, Francisco, and Miguel Gallardo. 2012 (1997). *Un largo silencio.* Bilbao: Astiberri.

Gardner, Jared. 2008. "Autography's Biography, 1972–2007." *Biography* 31, no. 1: 1–26.

Giardino, Vittorio. 2011. *¡No pasarán!* Barcelona: Norma.

Gociol, Judith, and Diego Rosemberg. 2003. *La historieta argentina: Una historia.* Buenos Aires: Ediciones de la Flor.

Gomez-Barris, Macarena. 2008. *Where Memory Dwells: Culture and State Violence in Chile.* Berkeley: University of California Press.

Gordon, Ian. 1998. *Comic Strips and Consumer Culture. 1890–1945.* London: Smithsonian.

Grandin, Greg. 2005. "The Instruction of Great Catastrophe: Truth Commissions, National History, and State Formation in Argentina, Chile and Guatemala." *American Historical Review* 110, no. 1: 46–67.

Grandin, Greg, and Thomas Miller Klubock. 2007. "Special Issue: Truth Commissions: State Terror, History, and Memory." *Radical History Review* 97: 1–10.

Hayner, Priscilla B. 2002. *Unspeakable Truths: Facing the Challenges of Truth Commissions*. New York: Routledge.

Hinds, Harold E., Jr. 1985. "Comics." In *Handbook of Latin American Popular Culture*. Edited by Harold Hinds and Charles Tatum, 81–110. Westport, CT: Greenwood Press.

Hirsch, Marianne. 1997. *Family Frames: Photography, Narrative, and Postmemory*. Cambridge: Harvard University Press.

Hirsch, Marianne. 1992–1993. "Family Pictures: *Maus*, Mourning, and Post-Memory." *Discourse* 15, no. 2: 3–29.

Hite, Katherine. 2012. *Politics and the Art of Commemoration: Memorials to Struggle in Latin America and Spain*. New York: Routledge.

Hite, Katherine. 2007. "The Politics of Representing Victims in Contemporary Peru." *A Contracorriente* 5, no. 1: 108–34.

Hite, Katherine, and Cath Collins. 2009. "Memorial Fragments, Monumental Silences, and Reawakenings in 21st-Century Chile." *Millennium—Journal of International Studies* 38: 379–400.

Huyssen, Andreas. 2000. "Present Pasts: Media, Politics, Amnesia." *Public Culture* 12, no. 1: 21–38.

Jacobson, Sid, and Ernie Colón. 2009. *Che: A Graphic Biography*. New York: Hill and Wang.

Jelin, Elizabeth. 2007. "Public Memorialization in Perspective: Truth, Justice, and Memory of Past Repression in the Southern Cone of South America." *International Journal of Transitional Justice* 1: 138–56.

Jelin, Elizabeth. 2003. *State Repression and the Labors of Memory*. Minneapolis: University of Minnesota Press.

Jelin, Elizabeth. 1994. "The Politics of Memory: The Human Rights Movement and the Construction of Democracy in Argentina." *Latin American Perspectives* 21, no. 2: 38–58.

Jelin, Elizabeth, and Victoria Langland. 2003. *Monumentos, memoriales y marcas territoriales*. Madrid: Siglo XXI.

Jiménez, Miguel, José Luis Jiménez, and Andrés Cruz. 2014. *Los once*. Bogotá: Laguna Libros.

Kansteiner, Wulf. 2002. "Finding Meaning in Memory: A Methodological Critique of Collective Memory Studies." *History and Theory* 41: 179–97.

Klein, Kerwin Lee. 2000. "On the Emergence of Memory in Historical Discourse." *Representations* 69: 127–50.

Kleist, Reinhard. 2010. *Castro*. Reprint, 2011. London: SelfMadeHero.

Klep, Katrien. 2012. "Tracing Collective Memory: Chilean Truth Commissions and Memorial Sites." *Memory Studies* 5, no. 3: 259–69.

Kunzle, David. 2007. *Father of the Comic Strip: Rodolphe Töpffer.* Jackson: University Press of Mississippi.

Kunzle, David. 2005. "The Comic Book in a 'Revolutionary Process': Chile in 1973." In *Cartooning in Latin America*. Edited by John Lent, 143–53. Cresskill: Hampton.

Kunzle, David. 1978. "Chile's *La Firme* versus I.T.T." *Latin American Perspectives* 5, no. 1: 119–33.

Landsberg, Alison. 2004. *Prosthetic Memory: The Transformation of American Remembrance in the Age of Mass Culture*. New York: Columbia University Press.

Lent, John A. 2005. "Latin American Comic Art: An Overview." In *Cartooning in Latin America*. Edited by John Lent, 1–24. Cresskill: Hampton.

Llobell Bisbal, Vicente. 2013. *Un médico novato*. Madrid: Sin Sentido.

Lucioni, Mario. 2002. "La historieta peruana, parte 1." *Revista Latinoamericana de estudios sobre la historieta* 2, no. 8: 203–18.

Lucioni, Mario. 2001. "La historieta peruana, parte 2." *Revista Latinoamericana de estudios sobre la historieta* 1, no. 4: 257–64.

Lutes, Jason. 2001. *Berlin: City of Stones: Book One*. Montreal: Drawn and Quarterly.

Masotta, Oscar. 1982 [1970]. *La historieta en el mundo moderno*. Barcelona: Paidós.

McCloud, Scott. 2004 [1993]. *Understanding Comics: The Invisible Art*. New York: Kitchen Sink Press and HarperPerrenial.

Meade, Teresa. 2001. "Holding the Junta Accountable: Chile's 'Sitios de Memoria' and the History of Torture, Disappearance, and Death." *Radical History Review* 79: 123–39.

Merino, Ana. 2010. "Memory in Comics: Testimonial, Autobiographical, and Historical Space in *MAUS*." *Transatlantica*, 1. June 22, 2010. Online at http://transatlantica.revues.org/4941. Accessed on March 4, 2015.

Merino, Ana. 2003. *El cómic hispánico*. Madrid: Cátedra.

Merino, Ana, ed. 2011. *Entre el margen y el canon: Pensamientos discursivos alrededor del cómic latinoamericano*. Special Issue. *Revista Iberoamericana* 67, no. 234: 13–18.

Merino, Ana, and Brittany Tullis. 2012. "The Sequential Art of Memory: The Testimonial Struggle of Comics in Spain." *Hispanic Issues Online* 11: 211–25. Online at http://cla.umn.edu/sites/cla.umn.edu/files/hiol_11_11_merino_the_sequential_art_of_memory.pdf. Accessed April 15, 2016.

Milton, Cynthia. 2014. *Art from a Fractured Past: Memory and Truth-Telling in Post–Shining Path Peru*. Durham, NC: Duke University Press.

Milton, Cynthia. 2011. "Defacing Memory: (Un)tying Peru's Memory Knots." *Memory Studies* 4, no. 2: 190–205.

Milton, Cynthia. 2007. "At the Edge of the Peruvian Truth Commission: Alternative Paths to Recounting the Past." *Radical History Review* 98: 1–33.

Moore, Alan, and Brian Bolland. 2008 [1988]. *Batman: The Killing Joke: The Deluxe Edition.* New York: DC Comics.

Nuñez Alayo, Evelyn Mabel. 2010. "Novela gráfica peruana." MA dissertation. Pontificia Universidad Católica del Perú.

Oesterheld, Héctor G., Enrique Breccia, and Alberto Breccia. 2008. *Che: Vida de Ernesto Che Guevara.* Buenos Aires: Doedytores.

Olick, Jeffrey. 2008. "Collective Memory: A Memoir and Prospect." *Memory Studies* 1: 23–29.

Olick, Jeffrey K., and Joyce Robbins. 1998. "Social Memory Studies: From 'Collective Memory' to the Historical Sociology of Mnemonic Practices." *American Review of Sociology* 24: 105–40.

Ostuni, Hernán, et al. N.d. "Politics, Activism, Repression, and Comics in Argentina during the 1970s." Online at www.camouflagecomics.com/pdf/03_bordel_en.pdf. Accessed on December 12, 2009.

Padrón, Ian. 1999. "Descartes de Palmiche." *Cine Cubano* 145: 64–69.

Pantojo, Óscar, Miguel Bustos, Tatiana Córdoba, Felipe Camargo Rojas, and Julián Naranjo. 2013. *Gabo: Memorias de una vida mágica.* Madrid: Ediciones Sins Entido.

Payne, Leigh. 2008. *Unsettling Accounts: Neither Truth nor Reconciliation in Confessions of State Violence.* Durham, NC: Duke University Press.

Pérez Santiago, Omar. 2003. "Treinta años de cómics chilenos: Desde el golpe de Pinochet a hoy." *Tebeosfera.* Online at www.tebeosfera.com/1/Documento/Articulo/Especial/Chile/1970a2000.htm. Accessed on July 15, 2013.

Reyes, Carlos. 2011. "Arranca, arranca que viene el trauko." *Ergocomics.* Online at http://ergocomics.cl/wp/2011/02/%E2%80%9Carranca-arranca-que-viene-el-trauko%E2%80%9D/. Accessed on July 16, 2013.

Riaño-Alcalá, Pilar, and Erin Baines. 2012. "Special Issue: Transitional Justice and the Everyday." *International Journal of Transitional Justice* 6, no. 3, 385–93.

Robben, Antonius CGM. 2012. "From Dirty War to Genocide: Argentina's Resistance to National Reconciliation." *Memory Studies* 5, no. 3: 305–15.

Roca, Paco. 2013 [2007]. *Arrugas.* Bilbao: Astiberri.

Roca, Paco. 2013. *Los surcos del azar.* Bilbao: Astiberri.

Rodriguez, Spain. 2008. *Che: A Graphic Biography.* London: Verso.

Rothberg, Michael. 2009. *Multidirectional Memory: Remembering the Holocaust in the Age of Decolonization.* Redwood City, CA: Stanford University Press.

Rubenstein, Anne. 1998. *Bad Language, Naked Ladies, and Other Threats to the Nation: A Political History of Comic Books in Mexico*. Durham, NC: Duke University Press.

Sacco, Joe. 2003. *Palestine*. London: Jonathan Cape.

Sagástegui, Carla. 2009. "Acevedo and His Predecessors." In *Redrawing the Nation: National Identity in Latin/o American Comics*. Edited by Héctor Fernández L'Hoeste and Juan Poblete, 131–50. Basingstoke: Palgrave.

Scorer, James. 2010. "Man, Myth, and Sacrifice: Graphic Biographies of Ernesto 'Che' Guevara." *Journal of Graphic Novels and Comics* 1, no. 2: 137–50.

Seoane, María, and Víctor Santa María. 2008. *110 años de Caras y Caretas: La tragedia y la comedia de la Argentina*. Buenos Aires: Octubre.

Smolderen, Thierry. 2009. *Naissances de la bande dessinée: De William Hogarth à Winsor McCay*. Brussels: Les Impressions Nouvelles.

Sosa, Cecilia, and Alejandra Serpente. 2012. "Special Issue: Contemporary Landscapes of Latin American Cultural Memory." *Journal of Latin American Cultural Studies* 21, no. 2: 159–63.

Spiegelman, Art. 2011. *MetaMaus*. London: Viking.

Spiegelman, Art. 2003. *The Complete Maus*. London: Penguin.

Stern, Steve J. 2006. *Remembering Pinochet's Chile: On the Eve of London 1998*. Durham, NC: Duke University Press.

Sturken, Marita. 2008. "Memory, Consumerism, and Media: Reflections on the Emergence of the Field." *Memory Studies* 1, no. 1: 73–78.

Sturken, Marita. 2007. *Tourists of History: Memory, Kitsch, and Consumerism from Oklahoma City to Ground Zero*. Durham, NC: Duke University Press.

Taylor, Diana. 2003. *The Archive and the Repertoire: Performing Cultural Memory in the Americas*. Durham, NC: Duke University Press.

Theidon, Kimberly. 2012. *Intimate Enemies: Violence and Reconciliation in Peru*. Philadelphia: University of Pennsylvania Press.

Thompson, Craig. 2005. *Blankets*. Marietta, GA: Top Shelf.

Trillo, Carlos, and Lucas Varela. 2010 [2008]. *La herencia del coronel*. Madrid: DibBuks.

Vergueiro, Waldomiro C. S. 2011. "De discursos não Competentes a Saberes Dominantes: Reflexões Sobre as Historias em Quadrinhos no Cenário Brasileiro." *Revista Iberoamericana* 77, no. 234: 135–48.

Vergueiro, Waldomiro C. S. 2009. "Brazilian Comics: Origin, Development, and Future Trends." In *Redrawing the Nation: National Identity in Latin/o American Comics*. Edited by Héctor Fernández L'Hoeste and Juan Poblete, 151–70. Basingstoke: Palgrave.

Vergueiro, Waldomiro C. S. 2005. "Children's Comics in Brazil: From Chiquinho to Mônica, a Difficult Journey." In *Cartooning in Latin America*. Edited by John Lent, 85–100. Cresskill: Hampton.

Vergueiro, Waldomiro C. S. 2000. "Brazilian Superheroes in Search of Their Own Identities." *International Journal of Comic Art* (Fall): 164–77.

Violi, P. 2012. "Trauma Site Museums and Politics of Memory: Tuol Sleng, Villa Grimaldi, and the Bologna Ustica Museum." *Theory, Culture, and Society* 29: 36–75.

ONE

RAISING THE CUBAN FLAG

COMICS, COLLECTIVE MEMORY, AND THE SPANISH-CUBAN-AMERICAN WAR (1898)

Jorge L. Catalá Carrasco

Memories were difficult to reconcile. Americans expected gratitude; Cubans harbored grievances. Americans remembered 1898 as something done for Cubans; Cubans remembered 1898 as something done to them.

LOUIS A. PÉREZ JR., *THE WAR OF 1898*

On July 17, 1898, after the defeat of the Spanish fleet at the hands of the modern U.S. Navy in Santiago de Cuba's bay, General Shafter's forces triumphantly entered Santiago. At noon, playing the U.S. national anthem, the U.S. flag was raised at the government palace. General Calixto García's *mambises* (Cuban pro-independence army) were not invited to take part in the ceremony, nor were they informed. Thirty years of struggle against the Spanish colonial power were conveniently omitted from public celebrations. Rituals are performed mainly for their symbolic value. At war, raising the flag inside the enemy's quarters, accompanied by the victorious national anthem, not only puts an end to formal hostilities but marks the transfer of power and/or sovereignty. The same ritual was performed on January 1, 1899, when the Spanish flag was lowered at "El Morro" fortress in Havana and the U.S. flag was raised instead. The Cuban war of independence (1895–1898) and the Spanish-Cuban-American war (1898) had ended with the defeat of

Spain. The terms of the victory, however, were not so straightforward. The Cubans did not achieve full independence, as the U.S. intervention became a military dictatorship that lasted four years (1898–1902). Although the Cuban Republic was officially declared on May 20, 1902, the Platt Amendment, first incorporated into U.S. law and then as an annex to the Republican constitution, ensured that even after independence was granted and the American occupation force gone, the United States would be able to exert colonial control over the island.[1] The phrase "caer como un veinte de mayo," meaning a massive and unstoppable blow, has belonged to the cultural memory of Cubans ever since.

The building of the nation-state was thus politically flawed from its early days, charged not only with the traumatic experiences of the war but with the subsequent U.S. military interventions (1898–1902; 1906–1909; 1912; 1917–1923) in Cuban politics. With the nationalist forces divided, and a political life that became endemically corrupt as a result of a patronage system based on sugar wealth, wartime loyalties, and U.S. tolerance (Kapcia 2005: 61), the new republic meant a betrayal to the thousands of people who died fighting for their independence; a betrayal to Calixto García, who died in December 1898, as it was to Antonio Maceo and, above all, José Martí, the Apostle of Cuba. Destined to be the first president of Cuba, had he not been killed in 1895, José Martí had long warned about the dangers of the great neighbor in the north: "I have lived in the monster and I know its entrails; my sling is David's" (Shnookal and Muñiz 1999: 234).

This is the historical context for the comic *La emboscada* (1982), from the series *Historietas de Inés, Aldo y Beto*, by Ernesto Padrón and Orestes Suárez. The comic provides a fictional setting (the "Loma de La Yagua" fort) in which the memories, tensions, and traumas about the American entrance into Santiago are reenacted. The story suggests the difficulties associated with establishing the nation-state in Cuba after the fight for independence. Crucial to this was the symbolic importance of the Cuban flag and the rituals associated with it, such as the Fiesta de la Bandera, established by Emilio Bacardí, mayor of Santiago de Cuba, on New Year's Day 1902. This aspect features prominently in the ending of *La emboscada*, reminding the reader about the ceremony marking the defeat of Spain and the exchange of power between Spain and the United States, exemplified by the lowering of the Spanish flag and the raising of American one in the fortress of El Morro in Havana as well as in Santiago de Cuba. The comic thus aims to provide a didactic story about the Spanish-Cuban-American war, very much in line with the strong drive toward didacticism that has defined Cuba's national comics industry since 1959. It is more precisely a reenactment, influenced by post-1959 historiography, to reclaim Cuban agency in the Spanish-Cuban-American war, because if Cubans understood 1898 as the point of preemption, then 1959 was the moment of redemption (Pérez 1998: 131). The story unveils the post-1959 Cuban revolutionary vision of the relationship between Cubans and Americans against the Spaniards and the credit the Americans were swift to claim in the theater of war.

Most significantly, it serves as an example of scholar Alison Landsberg's *prosthetic memory* (2004), when she argues that technologies of mass culture function as a prosthesis between an individual and a historical narrative about the past. These prostheses create an experience that makes it possible for a person to "not simply apprehend a historical narrative but . . . [to take] on a more personal, deeply felt memory of a past event through which he or she did not live" (Landsberg 2004: 2). In *La emboscada*, the technology that makes possible the experience of connecting the historical past at a personal level is the *fantasidoscopio*, a fantastic device that allows time traveling and the realization of whatever you are thinking. In this chapter I foreground the importance of (historical) consciousness in the Cuban context as developed by Ché Guevara in 1965 and argue that the comic informs Egyptologist Jan Assmann's concept of *cultural memory* (1995), more precisely its *concretion of identity* and its *capacity to reconstruct*.

Historietas de Inés, Aldo y Beto began publication in 1979 for the comic magazine *Pásalo*, an original initiative that encouraged children to pass on the magazine (as the title indicates) once they had finished reading it, thus creating a symbolic *experiential site* formed by a community of readers. In this particular story, the protagonists time travel from the present (1982) back to 1898, taking an active role in the fight for independence. As Landsberg (2004: 9) has argued, from a position of difference and the recognition that these images and narratives concerning the past are not one's heritage, "people who acquire these memories are led to feel a connection with the past, but, all the while, to remember their position in the contemporary moment." The beginning and the end of the comic take place in the "now" of the story, thus reminding the readers of their distanced position, while the historical adventure is accessed through technology (*fantasidoscopio*) and culture (a book about the 1895–1898 war that Inés brought to the campsite). Cultural memory is characterized by its distance from the everyday and its fixed points, "fateful events of the past, whose memory is maintained through cultural formation (texts, rites, monuments) and institutional communication (recitation, practice, observance)" (Assmann 1995: 129).

In this story the connection with the past is accessed through a purposive use of a radical nationalistic agenda, which originated in the nineteenth-century struggle for independence and continued after the 1959 revolution took power—a reinforcement of what historian Antoni Kapcia (2000: 125) has defined as *cubanía revolucionaria* ("revolutionary Cubanness"). One of the first things that arrests our attention, along with the possibility of actively taking part in past events through time traveling, is the collective character of this comic. Cuban ethnic diversity is taken care of, with Inés and Aldo being white and Beto black. The authors did not approach this historical period through an individual heroic figure.[2] Instead, they deliberately opted to be as inclusive as possible; the three main protagonists aim to represent Cuban children as a whole, as the preface suggests: "Viven en el mismo barrio de una ciudad cualquiera de Cuba" [They live in the same neighborhood of any Cuban town] (Padrón and Suárez 2009a). This chapter discusses the notions of cultural memory and identity, along with the concept of prosthetic memory in the context of the Spanish-Cuban-American war as revisited in *La emboscada*, which was the first time the topic had been presented in comic format.[3] This was largely thanks to the previous archival work undertaken by Juan Padrón (Ernesto's brother) in Cuban and Spanish museums and archives about the war, which resulted in the popular *El libro del mambí* (1985). The comic serves as an example of how Cuban comics help to strengthen national consciousness through cultural memory.

MEMORY AND IDENTITY IN CUBA

Memory and identity are mutually dependent concepts. The construction of one's identity involves the participation in a number of social groups (family, friends, language, religion, nationhood, etc.) through which one becomes aware of the similarities shared with the members of those groups and the differences with those who do not. It is an ongoing process in constant change or "coction," to use anthropologist Fernando Ortiz's term when describing Cuban culture as an *ajiaco* (a stew that combines various indigenous staples—such as yucca, corn, and potatoes—with imported vegetables, meats, and spices).[4] We are constantly revising our memories (ingredients) to suit our current identities (Gillis 1994: 3), for cultural memory is pivotal in the construction of individual and collective identity.[5] When we move from "communicative memory," which includes those varieties of collective memory based on everyday communication, to the realm of objectivized culture, the relationship between memory and identity becomes more noticeable:

"For in the context of objectivized culture and of organized ceremonial communication, a close connection to groups and their identity exists that is similar to that found in the case of everyday memory. We can refer to the structure of knowledge in this case as the 'concretion of identity.' With this we mean that a group bases its consciousness of unity and specificity upon this knowledge and derives formative and normative impulses from it, which allows the group to reproduce its identity" (Assmann 1995: 128).

In the context of the newly established Cuban republic, the "concretion of identity" took place through diverse ceremonies and rituals aimed at strengthening national identity as well as collective memory. On New Year's Day 1902, Emilio Bacardí, mayor of Santiago de Cuba, established the Fiesta de la Bandera, displaying a large Cuban flag on the town hall's flagpole, subsidized by popular subscription and donated to the local council. The act was accompanied by the national anthem, the "Himno de Bayamo." After the ritual, the mayor, a local council delegation, and a large group of *santiagueros* headed toward Antonio Maceo's house to greet his widow, María Cabrales. Eight years later, after the second American military intervention, a decree signed by President José Miguel Gómez in 1910 made the act of swearing allegiance to the Cuban flag in every school official. With the restoration of the republic came what seemed to be a new order. More interestingly, the confrontational language used in this ceremony against the United States served to a reaffirm "Cubanness" as opposed to "the other" (Cordoví 2012: 78).

Soon after, José Martí was incorporated into the Jura de la Bandera ritual. A delegation of students from every Havana school went to the Parque Central to leave flowers at the monument to José Martí. As historian Pierre Nora (1989: 7) has argued, temporal and topographical *lieux de mémoire* emerge at those times and in those places where there is a perceived break with the past. A new republic needs symbols, rituals, and monuments to articulate a sense of being. However, the marginalization of Calixto García's forces in the marching into Santiago by the American army; the shameful ritual of raising the American flag in Santiago and in Havana; the deaths of José Martí in 1895, Maceo in 1896, and García in 1898; the subsequent American military interventions—all those events obscured the establishment of the republic and the end of colonial times. It had become all too apparent that the new republic was ill-fated and fragile and that colonial times might not be over after all.

Although the revolution of 1959 was primarily concerned with a break with the past and the establishment of a new order (as with every revolution), there was also, from its early years, a clear preoccupation with the past and with the construction of a collective memory upon which the nation would base its consciousness of unity. Assmann (1995: 133) has reasoned that "through its cultural heritage a society becomes visible to itself and to others." It is for this reason that Cuban official discourse has taken particular care to integrate the Cuban Revolution led by Fidel Castro with the overarching process of national independence dating back to the nineteenth century. The last episode in the struggle for independence against Spain started in 1895, led by the triumvirate Martí-Gómez-Maceo, which involved U.S. forces in the last phase, following the sinking of the U.S.S. *Maine* in February 1898. The consequences of U.S. participation were wide ranging, changing the war for independence into a war between an emerging superpower and a declining country, ratified in the Treaty of Paris signed in December 1898. On that occasion no Cuban representatives were invited to take part.

Thus, when Fidel Castro spoke to the jubilant people of Santiago de Cuba on January 2, 1959, he remembered 1898 and reminded everyone that this time the revolution would not be fooled: "It will not be like 1895 when the Americans came and took over, intervening at the last moment, and afterwards did not even allow Calixto García to assume leadership, although he had fought at Santiago de Cuba for 30 years" (Castro 1959). Similarly, on October 10, 1968, Fidel Castro declared at La Demajagua that 1868 marked "the beginning of 100 years of struggle and the beginning of the revolution in Cuba [he was referring to the Ten Year War 1868–1878] because there has only been one revolution in Cuba—the one which Carlos Manuel de Céspedes began on 10 October 1868" (Castro 1968).[6] The Cuban leader was not only rewriting history, inscribing the 1959 revolution within the long Cuban struggle for independence, but he was doing so through a purposive use of collective memory.

1898: CONTESTED MEMORIES OF AN INTERVENTION

If Cuban official revolutionary discourse has strived to inculcate the need to protect the social conquests (free access to health care and education), even in the most difficult circumstances (such as the Special Period during the 1990s), history and memory represent a second front aimed at helping to build revolutionary consciousness in the population. There are, according to scholar Peter Hulme (2011), 227 Cuban national monuments. This figure needs to be compared to the prolixity of monuments and memorials that remember the liberation of Cuba thanks to the U.S. intervention. According to Cuban-American historian Louis A. Pérez Jr. (1999: 379), Cuba incurred a debt of gratitude, and "the island filled with markers and statues memorializing the liberation of Cuba by the United States." The profusion of national monuments in Cuba (dedicated to Cuban or U.S. participation in the struggle for independence) can be seen as the writing of an official discourse into the landscape; it is an effort to inscribe collective memory in the national agenda. The U.S. representation of its intervention in Cuba was seen as a project of liberation, ratified by the Joint Resolution of Congress in April 1898, which stated the rightful case for Cuba to become a free and independent nation. This was reinforced publicly by different personalities after the conflict ended. Congressman J. Hampton Moore summarized in plain words the public opinion on this issue: "Cuba was given her liberty through the intervention of the United States" (Pérez Jr. 1999: 359).

For decades, U.S. historiography has recalled the 1898 war as an achievement of altruism, the fulfilment of destiny (President McKinley used this explanation in his evaluation of the conflict) or a war as an accident ("the splendid little war"), but in 1953 when foreign policy expert Robert Endicott Osgood highlighted the full impact of 1898 in the realm of consciousness, he struck a chord among scholars in the field. He wrote that those events brought "the American people to the full consciousness of their power in the world . . . by the end of that war the United States had become a world power" (as quoted in Pérez Jr. 1998: 121). The events of 1898 determined, one way or another, the image of Cuba in the U.S. consciousness: "the sinking of the Maine (remember?); the daring rescue of Evangelina Cisneros, the most beautiful girl in Cuba; the annihilation of the Spanish fleet in Santiago de Cuba; the charge up San Juan Hill; the famous 'message to García' delivered by an intrepid American soldier" (Pérez Firmat 2010: 35). It was also the point at which North Americans subsequently defined their relationship to Cuba: always as benefactor, as protector (Pérez Jr. 1998: 123).

In Cuba the 1898 U.S. intervention was received with enthusiasm, but the mood gradually changed, anchoring grievances. The swift victory against the Spanish forces and the reluctance to abandon the island, or indeed hand over the control of Cuba to the revolutionary forces commanded by Máximo Gómez, seemed to indicate what the old general had feared.[7] Gómez in late 1898 described the situation in these terms: "What is going to be done about independence? The Americans, it seems, are not thinking about it. . . . Even if finally they give it to us, it will be as a gift, while we have gained it.

And more than gained it with continuous efforts during more than half a century" (Pérez Jr. 1999: 363). The previous three years of war seemed to have amounted to nothing. Being given the independence as a gift is to incur a huge debt of gratitude. However, for the Cubans this had been a long war in which they had frustrated Spanish forces with their sheer determination, a war in which several thousand people also died of yellow fever and malaria. With such enormous sacrifices, the idea of being granted independence as a gift from the United States seemed almost grotesque. This is one of the underlying motifs in *La emboscada*: the reaffirmation of Cuban agency in the fight for independence with a protagonist role.

Louis Pérez Jr. situates in the late 1930s and early 1940s the period in which the Sociedad Cubana de Estudios Históricos e Internacionales served as a discussion forum about the historiography of 1898. This led to a decree issued by the Cuban national congress in 1945, for which thereafter all references to the conflict of 1895–1898 were to be known officially as the Spanish-Cuban-American war (Pérez Jr. 1998: 126). Although Pérez Jr. mentions the contribution to this debate undertaken by Cuban historian Emilio Roig de Leuchsenring with his book *Cuba no debe su independencia a los Estados Unidos* (1950), he omits Roig de Leuchsenring's previous articles (under the pseudonym of Enrique Alejandro de Hermann) in the most popular magazine at the time, *Carteles*. For example, on October 23, 1932, Roig de Leuchsenring wrote a piece denouncing the politics used by the United States to take control of Cuba: "force against Spain and Cuban gratitude. That is how they took Cuba in 1898 and 1902. Cuba will not be annexed as a new state to the Union, but the United States will forcefully separate it from Spain and independence will be graciously granted . . . making it a colony, without any responsibility and with the eternal gratitude of Cuba; eternal because it will never fully be repaid" (Roig de Leuchsenring 1932, translation mine).

In fact, Roig de Leuchsenring devoted one article every week from 1932 to March 1933 to discuss the relationship between the United States and Cuba during the nineteenth century, with particular focus on the methods used to exert political and economic influence on the island. The times were changing in Cuba, and August 1933 marked the fall of dictator Machado coinciding with the coming of age of a new generation of anti-imperialist intellectuals, such as Roig de Leuchsenring, Antonio Guiteras, Rubén Martínez Villena, Raúl Roa, and Pablo de la Torriente Brau. Roig de Leuchsenring concluded his explicitly titled monograph, *Cuba no debe su independencia a los Estados Unidos* (1950), in clear terms: "Cuba does not owe its Independence to the United States of North America, but to the efforts of its own people, through their firm and indomitable will to end the injustices, abuses, discriminations, and exploitation suffered under the despotic colonial regime" (Roig de Leuchsenring as quoted in Pérez Jr. 1998: 126).

Post-1959 Cuban revolutionary historiography has repeated the traumas of the U.S. participation in 1898, foregrounding in particular the case of Calixto García and Santiago de Cuba (Tabares del Real 1975: 30; Soto 1977: 46; Torres-Cuevas and Loyola Vega 2006: 395). Testimonial writing such as Miguel Barnet's *Biografía de un cimarrón* (1966) or Flora Basulto's *Una niña bajo tres banderas* (1954) highlight the same episode suggesting a traumatic experience that has become part of the collective memory for all Cubans, whether they lived it or not. In *Biografía*, Esteban Montejo declared "the truth is that in Santiago the one who really fought was Calixto García. . . . Then the Americans raised the flag to let it be known they had taken the city. . . . The worst of it was that the American commander gave the order to bar Cubans from entering the city" (Barnet 1995 [1966]: 196). The same idea is reinforced in *Una niña*: "Of course enthusiasm weakened. The Americans had not yet recognized Máximo Gómez. Calixto García developed the landing plan. His help was decisive at Las Guásimas and El Caney. He made the victory at San Juan possible. Cubans dug the trenches, but only the Americans entered Santiago triumphantly" (Basulto 1963 [1954]: 85, translation mine).

LA EMBOSCADA: CUBAN COMICS AND COLLECTIVE CONSCIOUSNESS

A brief outline of the Cuban comics industry will help to situate *La emboscada* within a wider context, in which certain trends, such as didacticism, activism, and struggle, take special prominence. Cuban comics, or *muñequitos* as they are commonly called in Cuba, have been and still are very popular. The presence of comic strips in Cuban periodicals grew steadily from the second decade of the twentieth century. By the 1930s we find continuity in a number of comics published in different newspapers, such as Manuel Alonso's *Napoleón: El faraón de los sinsabores* in *El País gráfico*, the weekly supplement of *El País*.[8] By the 1940s and 1950s, comics populated the pages of such newspapers and magazines as *Bohemia*, *Carteles*, and the weekly humor magazine *Zig-Zag*, the most popular of its kind until 1959.

With the 1959 revolution, profound changes came to the comics industry. From 1960 to 1961 the weekly humor supplement *El Pitirre* modernized comics and graphic humor in Cuba with its avant-garde approach. The closure of *El Pitirre* marked an important reorganization of publications with the creation of *Palante* (for an adult audience) and *Pionero* (for children) in November 1961. Both magazines have consistently published comics ever since. From 1964 to 1965, the weekly supplement *Muñequitos de Revolución* preluded an important step toward the stability of the industry with the establishment of the publishing house Ediciones en Colores, which published several comic books from 1965 to 1968. The communist magazine *Mella* also included comics, most notably the creations of Virgilio Martínez Gainza in a very characteristic *Mad*-style.

Memory entered the realm of graphic humor and comics very early. In 1959 the *Álbum de la Revolución Cubana* was published, and children exchanged their cards trying to complete the album that recounted the deeds of the brothers Castro and their comrades from 1952 to 1959. The landing of the *Granma* or the attack on the presidential palace are recounted with vivid images that do not spare the infant reader of the blood. The didactic component, mentioned at the beginning of this chapter as one of the salient features of *La emboscada*, became increasingly visible in 1970, when Cuba strengthened its links with the USSR after the failure of the ten million *zafra* (sugar cane harvests). Francisco Blanco and Juan Manuel Betancourt (Betan) published *Matilde y sus amigos*, *Trucutuerca y Trescabitos*, *Los 7 samuráis del 70,* and *Pol Brix contra el ladrón invisible.* While keeping remarkable artistic quality, these are examples of the didactic drive in Cuban comics on, respectively, livestock raising, machinery operating, as well as sugar cane harvest and sugar production.

Central to the recognition of comics in Cuba was the appearance of the most popular hero in Cuban comics, Elpidio Valdés. Created by Juan Padrón Blanco, the adventures of Elpidio Valdés were first published in *Pionero* in 1970. Three feature films have appeared to date, the first one in 1979, followed by a second in 1983 and a third in 1996. Elpidio is by far the most recognizable and successful Cuban comic of all, and the reprints still enjoy a decent readership. In the late 1970s, the new magazine *Pásalo*, entirely devoted to comics, targeted children. This magazine, in which the series *Historietas de Inés, Aldo y Beto* were to be published, was initially published by the Pioneros Organisation and from 1980 by the new publishing house Editora Abril. *Pásalo* was a significant step in the stability of comics in Cuba, as neither *Pionero* nor *Zunzún*, created in 1980, devoted all its content to comics. *Pionero* changed its target audience to teenagers, while *Zunzún* concentrated on children up to seven and eight years old and *Pásalo* covered the nine-to-twelve range.

La emboscada brought together two talented artists: the writer Ernesto Padrón (b. 1948), who is also a filmmaker and became director of *Zunzún* for several years, and the artist Orestes Suárez (b. 1950), one of the best comic artists in Cuba over the past forty years. Suárez has authored comics in nearly every genre (fantasy, terror, humor, science fiction, satire, and historical), maintaining a realistic style, with detailed backgrounds and characters who reflect their psychology in their physical and facial expressions. Suárez became one of the few Cuban artists who combined their work in Cuban publications with collaborations in foreign magazines, such as *El gallito inglés/Gallito comics* (Mexico), *Creepy* (Toutain, Spain), *Napartheid* (Spain), and *Skorpio* and *Lanciostory* (Eura Editoriale, Italy). He also worked on the series *Mister No* (from 1995) and *Tex* (from 2010) for the Italian market.[9]

The main plot in *La emboscada* presents the three protagonists (Inés, Aldo, and Beto), along with their history instructor, Hildita, time traveling to 1898 Cuba, where they find out about the maneuvers of a *mambí* traitor, Aura, who is informing the Spanish forces about movements in the Cuban lines. They decide to help the *mambises*, who are about to be ambushed, by bringing some *pionero* friends using the *fantasidoscopio*. The Americans, who have been informed about the ambush by the four protagonists, are depicted carrying on their military movements (the attack on a Spanish fort) regardless of their allies' situation. After helping the *mambises*, the protagonists all go to help the Americans in the attack on the Spanish fort. In terms of style, *La emboscada* is a full-color realistic comic, which develops a fictionalized account (yet historically accurate in garments, accessories, and overall setting) of treachery amid the Spanish-Cuban-American war of 1898. The use of color helps to recognize objects, landscapes, and characters: "we become more aware of the physical form of objects than in black and white" (McCloud 1994: 189). Whether color comics will always seem more "real" at first glance, as comics artist and theorist Scott McCloud suggests, is debatable. There are far too many examples of comics that, precisely because of the tonalities in the use of black and white, seem very "real." This is the case with the successful detective series *Alack Sinner* (1975–1992) by José Muñoz and Carlos Sampayo or the disturbing *Perramus* (1985) by Alberto Breccia and Juan Sasturain.[10] Although the use of color has dominated superhero comics, and these do not necessarily present a realistic setting (or plot), it is true we inhabit a world in color, and the use of color in a realistic comic is an attempt to reproduce that world and hence produces a sense of familiarity with the story. Color thus helps readers to identify better with the story.

The issue of identification is at the core of this comic, which explains the choice of a realistic style. The series *Historietas de Inés, Aldo y Beto* denotes the development of the Pioneros organization in Cuba; Beto is nine years old and stands for children until fourth grade, eleven-year-old Inés is studying sixth grade, and fourteen-year-old Aldo is in ninth grade. The combination of iconic characters with realistic backgrounds allows readers to "'mask' themselves in a character and safely enter a sensually stimulating world" (McCloud 1994: 43). The didactic component of the comic, facilitated by the *fantasidoscopio* and the history book, which allow for experiencing history "firsthand," coupled by the cartoon effect (a "vacuum into which our identity and awareness are pulled" [36]), create the conditions for readers to "travel in another realm" since we do not just observe the cartoon; we become it (36).

The three characters represent Cuban children and therefore not only act as a model to follow but as an example of what sociologist Maurice Halbwachs (1992 [1925]) has referred to as the social frameworks through which human beings construct their memories. According to Halbwachs, all memories are collective and the construction of memory takes place within the social frameworks of a specific epoch and with the predominant thoughts of the society. Hence these children act as representatives of Cuban children in their understanding of and approach to the struggle for independence and U.S. participation in the hostilities. Children's education is permeated by post-1959 revolutionary discourse in Cuba, rendering the past in accordance with the anti-imperialist stance of the 1959 revolution, but also exhibiting a much longer "tradition" that returned to the memories of 1898, specifically to Santiago de Cuba as the breaking point of the struggle for independence and the subsequent frustrated objectives of national independence.

From the very beginning, the authors introduce a series of scenes that aim to ensure that children are aware of what Cuban daily life during those years of struggle was like. For instance, in figure 1.1 the typical Spanish formal dress does not correspond to a war camp; our protagonists have to imagine the soldier again in his battledress to avoid historical errors. The same applies to figure 1.2, this time when describing the garments of a *mambí* fighter. These two examples reflect the accuracy of the comic when depicting *mambises* or Spaniards, as seen in figure 1.3, featuring Spanish infantry taken from *El libro del mambí* by Juan Padrón (2003 [1985]). The notes and sketches in the preparation of *El libro del mambí*, published in 1985, helped both artists to depict more precisely technical elements of the story. In figure 1.2 we have an example of a change in perspective. In the first panel, Hildita and Beto appear on top of a hill looking down to Aura. The next panel depicts the scene in reverse. The perspective is bottom-up, foregrounding Aura as the protagonists imagine the garment of the *mambí*. In the background we see sketches of Hildita and Beto. What is more relevant is brought to the front by

FIGURE 1.1. Spanish formal dress versus battle dress. *La emboscada* 1982 [2005], p. 2. Reproduced with kind permission of Ernesto Padrón and Orestes Suárez.

FIGURE 1.2. *Mambí* fighter. *La emboscada* 1982 [2005], p. 4. Reproduced with kind permission of Ernesto Padrón and Orestes Suárez.

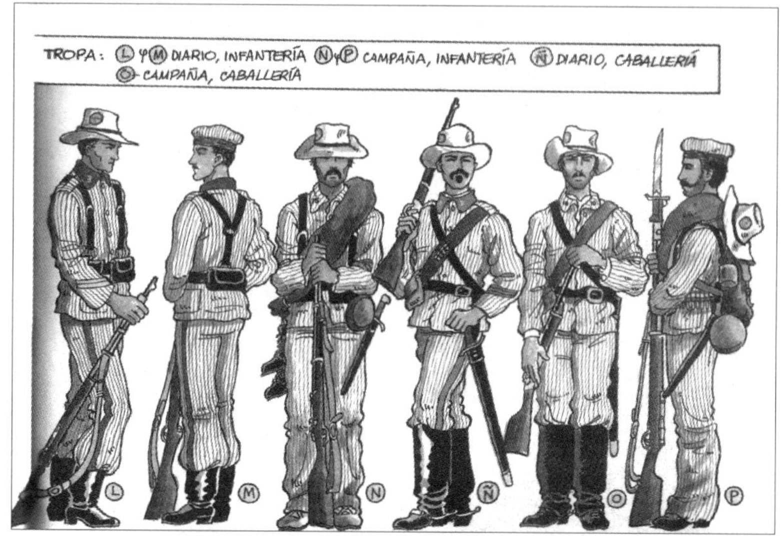

FIGURE 1.3. Spanish infantry. *El libro del mambí* 1985 [2003], p. 117. Reproduced with kind permission of Juan Padrón.

the artist. The third panel represents the correct depiction of Aura in *mambí* attire. But surrounding the rider, we can see little bubbles, the graphic representation symbolizing the rider's disappearance and reappearance thanks to Hildita's imagination.

Other remarkable stylistic features of note are the page composition and the facial expressions to represent the attitudes and psychologies of each character. Suárez combines these with conventional graphic uses in the language of comics, such as the discontinued lines in the speech balloon depicting a whisper or a pronged balloon when someone is shouting. Regarding page composition, the comic gains in dynamism with the ambush against the *mambises* at a gorge. In the lower half of page 8, we see Spaniards and *mambises* shooting at each other from their respective perspectives in different panels, which creates a swift sequence. In his influential *Comics and Sequential Art*, artist Will Eisner (2006: 2) declared that "crucial to the success of a visual narrative is the ability to convey time. It is the dimension of human understanding that enables us to recognize and be empathetic to surprise, humor, terror, and the whole range of human experience."

La emboscada is a realistic comic and consequently conveying "timing" (which is, according to Eisner, the manipulation through the arrangement of panels and page composition of the elements of time to achieve a specific message or emotion) is ever more relevant. Two examples from the comic serve to illustrate the importance of timing in visual narrative. The first example happens in the aforementioned ambush. In the last panel of page 8 (figure 1.4) an embedded close-up is included with the mortal shot against the Spanish captain, who immediately falls off the cliff. The previous panel, arranged as a long and thin frame, depicts the Spanish captain about to shoot one of the *pioneros*. It is a dramatic and quick scene, followed by a much larger panel that acts as a background scene but also moves the story forward, since we see the fall of the Spanish captain. But more interestingly, this panel includes an embedded close-up, which links the action facilitating the sequence. That embedded frame represents a frozen instant in the timeline, a moment of remarkable importance because the Spanish captain has been shot by a *mambí* fighter, who has also saved the *pionero* from a certain death.

The embedded panel resembles a photograph, almost a snapshot taken by a war photojournalist. It is a sudden, dramatic, and emotional scene that compares with the more elongated main panel in which we see who took the mortal shot as well as the fall of the Spanish captain. It is a significant scene in the story because it marks the defeat of the Spanish forces, which retreat instantly. The quickness and/or slowness of narration through panel and page composition is one of the most striking features of narration in comics. Sequences can be distorted and manipulated to highlight a particularly intense moment. In this regard, comics seem especially apt for this material, since time is relative to the position of the observer and readers rely on the memory of experience to measure it and perceive it (Eisner 2006: 25).

The second example is on page 14 (figure 1.5), when the traitor is finally discovered. The artists opted for an "L"-shaped panel without borders that covers half a page. As in the previous example, the artists have opted for embedded frames, guiding the reader toward the top right corner, since the previous two frames decrease in size, creating a diagonal reading. Once we reach the right corner, we are encouraged to slow down our reading and pay attention to the muted grave faces staring at the reader, which are in fact directed toward the traitor. The peculiar arrangement in "L" shape orients our gaze back to the left side of the page, where a small close-up of the traitor sweating gives a clear indication of the time elapsed in the sequence. This elongation of time reinforces the intensity of the scene, one of the story's high points. The traitor is discovered but, more important, past and present are combined here in a collective effort. The *mambises* and *pioneros* have blended in their fight for national sovereignty. In fact, the decisive help from the *pioneros* to take the Spanish fort and uncover the traitor connects past

FIGURE 1.4. Embedded close-up and death of Spanish captain. *La emboscada* 1982 [2005], p. 8. Reproduced with kind permission of Ernesto Padrón and Orestes Suárez.

and present allegorically in a shared collective memory. The new generations need to stand firm in their defense of the nation. This is reflected in the importance given to consciousness in Cuba. As stated by the historian Amos Funkenstein (1989: 12), "historical consciousness is not only the reminder of the past for the purpose of creating collective identity and cohesiveness but it is the attempt to understand the past and give it a meaning." Identity, struggle, and collective memory are therefore reinforced in the comic.

The last part of the comic sees the North Americans running away and losing the battle, but the arrival of the Cuban front changes the situation

FIGURE 1.5. Dramatic slow reading. *La emboscada* 1982 [2005], p. 14. Reproduced with kind permission of Ernesto Padrón and Orestes Suárez.

altogether, especially because of another trick by the *fantasidoscopio*. Beto decides to give the attack a little help by imagining a 1970s mortar. What is most interesting is that they recognize this is anachronistic ("¡Qué anacronismo histórico!" says Inés, on page 11), but nevertheless it is within the ethos of the comic. Let us use our imagination. When the fort falls, the American flag is raised and this prompts anger in our protagonists, although they recognize that is historically accurate: "¡Qué ofensa! ¡Y así fue históricamente! ¡Los yanquis no dejaron entrar en Santiago de Cuba a nuestros mambises!" (on page 12). Beto comes up with another ingenious solution, imagining ropes and the Cuban flag. They raise the flag, to the astonishment of the American commander (figure 1.6), turning the formal ritual into a jubilant celebration for the Cubans. The flag exchange performance is an example of a *lieu de mémoire*, as they "only exist because of their capacity for metamorphosis, an endless recycling of their meaning and an unpredictable proliferation of their ramifications" (Nora 1989: 19).

In this regard, historian Marial Iglesias Utset (2008) reminds us that traditional accounts describing the official transfer of power and sovereignty at the end of 1898 have repeatedly highlighted the popular anger when on January 1, 1899, the Spanish flag was lowered at "El Morro" fortress in Havana and the American flag was raised instead. But collective memory, which is closer to the popular rather than to the official, works with feelings and the manifestation of affect. Hence, what was meant to be an official ceremony of geopolitical power exchange was appropriated by Cuban nationalists and turned into a popular party. Leaflets were distributed in which the modern context was understood as the beginning of a new *époque* for liberties (4).

La emboscada exemplifies the importance of consciousness and historical consciousness in the Cuban revolutionary discourse. Ernesto Guevara in "El socialismo y el hombre en Cuba" (2006 [1965]) developed the idea of *conciencia* (consciousness). Conventional Marxist theory distinguished between a society's "structure" (its economic and class relations) and its "superstructure" (politics and ideology), the former determining the latter. However, Guevara argued that, based on the example of the Cuban Revolution, the

FIGURE 1.6. Raising the Cuban flag. *La emboscada* 1982 [2005], p. 13. Reproduced with kind permission of Ernesto Padrón and Orestes Suárez.

political will of the revolutionaries had led the Revolution to take power in rather adverse conditions. In its simplicity, it was an absolute heresy to traditional Marxism, as the *conciencia* could influence the economic and social conditions. Since then, a plethora of scholars and commentators have stressed the importance of building consciousness in revolutionary Cuba (Fagen 1969; Mesa-Lago 1971; Domínguez 1978; Medin 1990; and Kapcia 2000 and 2009 are among the most relevant studies).

The revolutionary leaders strived to inculcate a certain political culture that emphasized a dissenting ideology throughout Cuban history and highlighted the concept of *struggle* (*lucha*) and *activism*. When analyzing cultural memory, Assmann (1995) has concluded that *the concretion of identity* and its *capacity to reconstruct* are features of cultural memory. The former pinpoints "the store of knowledge from which a group derives an awareness of its unity and peculiarity" (130). In this comic, the values of struggle, activism, national independence, and sacrifice constitute a horizon of identification. The year 1898 is the date, Santiago de Cuba the locus, but the narrative is expanded to the entire history of Cuba since independence, as a constant search and struggle for national sovereignty, which trespasses the "now" of the story (1982) heading toward the future. The reprints of this comic in 2005 and 2009 indicate a continuity of a certain collective memory that goes back to that highly symbolic episode that could have represented the liberation of Santiago de Cuba (of Cuba as a whole) and instead passed into history as a disappointment, an outrage that demanded reparation. In this comic, there is the impossible attempt to right a wrong, mixing history with memories, facts with affect. The outcome is not a material gain. Facts cannot be changed, but they can be manipulated. In fact, the artists do not hide they are using fiction to modify history; the point is rather to remind children and adolescents that the national independence *was not given to them* but achieved with the collective effort of all Cubans. Consequently, despite the uchronia depicted, there is a reinforcement of collective consciousness.

However, through the manipulation of history we get closer to an ideological use of comics to re-create a constructed version of the past suitable for children. According to comics scholar Ana Merino, Cuban comics such as *Elpidio Valdés* "facilitate the new task in revolutionary education, which requires inserting children into a cultural space directed by the organs of power" (Merino 2003: 193, translation mine).[11] It is undeniable that Cuban comics present a very strong didactic component, and cultural policy has been an area of special interest by the Cuban authorities since the onset of the revolution. One could argue that in *La emboscada* there is as much propaganda as re-creation of collective memories and traumas. The depiction of American soldiers is stereotypical, and we should not forget that the United States was formally at war with Spain in 1898. Logically, the victorious side conquers the territory of the defeated and inscribes its power onto it symbolically through the raising of the national flag. But I believe that Merino's point about a cultural space directed by the organs of power represents a top-down approach that overlooks the complexities in power relations as suggested by Michel Foucault (1990: 92): "Power must be understood in the first instance as the multiplicity of force relations immanent in the sphere in which they operate and which constitute their own organization; as the process which, through ceaseless struggles and confrontations, transforms, strengthens, or reverses them." To what extent is the rendition made by Padrón and Suárez in *La emboscada* following what the organs of power (whatever they might be) want to inculcate to children? To what extent is this reconstruction of the past firmly grounded on cultural policy coming from above and not on affective anxieties and traumas arising from a collective memory situated not above or below but, as also happens with power, everywhere?[12]

This leads to a second characteristic of cultural memory. Cultural memory works by reconstruction, as Assmann (1995: 130) has discussed: "It always relates its knowledge to an actual and contemporary situation [and] every contemporary context relates to these differently, sometimes by appropriation, sometimes by criticism, sometimes by preservation or by transformation." The *capacity to reconstruct* in the context of 1982 needs to take into account at least three events that influenced *La emboscada* and determined the *transformation* of the 1898 memories. First, in 1980 the Second Congress of the Communist Party of Cuba took place, which analyzed the previous five-year plan and outlined the strategy for the following years. In the introduction to the official report, there is a clear reference to Cuban history and memory as "our most precious treasure": "The wealth of experience and revolutionary ideas we have inherited from our nation's history and that of humanity is our most precious treasure" (Congresos del PCC, "II Congreso 1980," translation mine). The reference relates to a foundational text for Cuban and Latin American identity: José Martí's "Nuestra América" (1891), because Martí claimed that "knowledge is what counts. To know one's country and govern it with that knowledge is the only way to free it from tyranny" (as quoted in Shnookal and Muñiz 1999: 114). Martí was campaigning against the institutionalized forgetfulness of each Latin American nation about its own history, which privileged European history instead.

By reclaiming the memories ("the wealth of experience") of the Cuban nation, the report implicitly highlights the aforementioned concepts of *struggle* and *activism*. Second, also in 1980, Cuba announced that anyone who wished to leave the country could be picked up at the port of Mariel. The resulting "Mariel Boatlift" took 125,000 new refugees to the United States. Third, in 1981, Ronald Reagan was inaugurated as U.S. president, whereupon he instituted the most hostile policy against Cuba since the invasion of the Bay of Pigs, tightening the existing embargo and, in 1982, reestablishing the travel ban to Cuba that prohibited U.S. citizens from spending money on Cuban soil. Consequently, the *capacity to reconstruct* cultural memory in the example of *La emboscada* and its transformation of 1898 events was, one way or another, influenced by this particularly heated period in Cuban-U.S. relations, by the damage to Cuban morale with the massive exodus of the "Mariel Boatlift," and the recommendation from the Communist Party of Cuba to treasure past Cuban experience in order to move forward.

In *La emboscada* we also need to take into account the target reader for this comic. It is aimed at youngsters, those children and teenagers who are building not only their future but also, more significantly, their memory (Achugar 2004: 130). These readers belong to a generation defined by the expansion of mass cultural forms, which, as a result, has created a form of memory in which individuals from diverse backgrounds experience the past through *prosthetic memories*, creating "a shared archive of experience" (Landsberg 2004: 14). If we add to this that "identities and memories are highly selective, inscriptive, rather than descriptive" (Gillis 1994: 4), comics seem very apt in this regard, as James Scorer suggests in chapter 7 in this volume, "because it is a medium built on the expressive multiplicity of fragments and the synchronicity of possible times."

The inscription of a 1980s Cuban revolutionary discourse onto the 1898 Spanish-Cuban-American war provides a reflection of the endurance of certain collective memories and their symbolic durability. *La emboscada* reaches its climax with the raising of the Cuban flag, first in 1898 among calls of "¡Viva Cuba Libre!" and then on the last page, when our adventurers have returned to their camp in 1982. Most of the page is devoted to a collective rendering of the *pioneros* camp and, at the center, the Cuban flag dominates the scene. Scholars focusing on images as vehicles of memory generally agree on the primacy of the visual (Samuel 1994; Yates 2007 [1996]; Sherman 1999). Comics and memory share the preponderance of the visual element.[13] In *La emboscada*, the representation of the nation embodied in the raising of the Cuban flag, with the revered and solemn salute by the *mambises* and the collective and more joyful stance by the *pioneros*, connects the harmful memories of the American intervention and the march through Santiago de Cuba in 1898. But it also connects the nationalistic 1902 Fiesta de la Bandera in Santiago, the national Jura de la Bandera in 1910, and the singing of the national anthem today (with the Cuban flag in the background) in every Cuban school before classes begin.

NOTES

Epigraph: Pérez (1998).

1 The Platt Amendment was formally abrogated in 1934, but as historian Richard Gott (2004: 110) has pointed out, it continued to echo in the global perception of the United States, notably in the wording of the Helms-Burton Act of 1996.

2. Examples of comics taking individual heroic figures are *El Generalísimo* (2003), about the mayor General Máximo Gómez, script by Rosa Leyva, drawings by Luis Lorenzo and Domingo García; and *Voluntad férrea*, about Antonio Maceo, by Orestes Suárez, originally published in 1985 and reprinted in the collection *Historias Mambisas* (2008).

3. Ernesto Padrón confirmed this in an e-mail, December 9, 2012.

4. Fernando Ortiz first used the *ajiaco* metaphor in a 1939 lecture at the University of Havana. See Ortiz, "Los factores humanos de la cubanidad," *Revista Bimestre Cubana* (La Habana) 14, no. 3 (March–April 1949): 161–86.

5. For this, see Ben-Amos and Weissberg 1999.

6. On October 10, 1868, Carlos Manuel de Céspedes freed his slaves and proclaimed Cuba independent from Spain, thus starting the Ten Year War (1868–1878).

7. The United States declared war on Spain on April 20, 1898. Military operations ended on July 3, 1898.

8. *Napoleón: El faraón de los sinsabores* was also the first cartoon animated film in Cuba, released in August 1937. This two-minute piece filmed in black and white represented a huge effort as technology was very limited (Agramonte and Castillo 2012: 24).

9. For a biography and examples of his art, see Tebeosfera, www.tebeosfera.com/autores/orestes_suarez.html, accessed on April 13, 2016.

10. The Uruguayan Alberto Breccia was a master in the use of the expressive possibilities of black and white as seen in, for instance, *Mort Cinder* (1962–1964). The choice of

black and white is all too pertinent for page composition and stress effect reasons. In *El corazón delator* (1974), an adapted version from Edgar Allan Poe's tale, Breccia creates a somber atmosphere with the intense repetition of panels in the last page, also called modulated repetition by Daniele Barbieri (1991: 198), but most importantly for the use of black and white, with characters blending with the blackened background.

11. Merino makes an interesting point about the suture applied to the comic *Elpidio Valdés* by which the hero has no cultural heritage linked to Spain. The surname Valdés was the surname given to those who had no recognized father in Cuba and symbolically that represents autonomy for the hero from a Spanish identity (Merino 2003: 196). Merino is right in the sense that cultural, economic, and family ties between Cuban *criollos* and Spanish *peninsulares* are among some of the reasons for the belatedness in a strong independent movement. *Elpidio Valdés*, in its attempt to tell a story of good *mambí* guerrillas and bad U.S. imperialists and colonial Spaniards, manipulates history and neglects the complexity of the socioeconomic fabric in Cuba at the time.
12. "Power is everywhere; not because it embraces everything, but because it comes from everywhere" (Foucault 1990: 93).
13. However, reflecting on images and memory, historian Wulf Kansteiner has mentioned that, despite the evocative nature of images, words are equally necessary to provide them with a meaning. He discusses a "close relation between images and words in the making of collective memories, [which] can also be accessed and studied through their discursive and narrative foundations" (Kansteiner 2002: 191). This is particularly relevant for an examination of comics and collective memory. Scholars of comics, striving to define the medium, have generally pointed to the hybrid nature of comics, which combine words and images. This is true insofar as the majority of comics rely on both elements, but not all of them do so. In fact, narration can be developed using only images. Thus I do not support Kansteiner's claim, as images can convey meaning without the need of words. Comics are an example of this.

REFERENCES

Achugar, Hugo. 2004. *Planetas sin boca*. Montevideo: Trilce.

Agramonte, Arturo, and Luciano Castillo. 2012. *Cronología del cine Cubano II (1937–1944)*. Havana: Ediciones ICAIC.

Assmann, Jan. 1995. "Collective Memory and Cultural Identity." *New German Critique*, no. 65 (Spring–Summer): 125–33.

Barbieri, Daniele. 1991. *I linguagi del fumetto*. Milan: Bompiani.

Barnet, Miguel. 1995 [1966]. *Biography of a Runaway Slave*. Translated by W. Nick Hill. Willimantic, CT: Curbstone.

Barnet, Miguel. 1966. *Biografía de un cimarrón*. Havana: Instituto de Etnología y Folklore.

Basulto, Flora. 1963 [1954]. *Una niña bajo tres banderas*. La Habana: Editora juvenil.

Ben-Amos, Dan, and Liliane Weissberg, ed. 1999. *Cultural Memory and the Construction of Identity*. Detroit: Wayne State University Press.

Breccia, Alberto, and Juan Sasturain. 2014 [1985]. *Perramus*. Buenos Aires: Ediciones de la Flor.

Castro, Fidel. 1968. "Ceremony Marking Centennial of Cuba's Struggle." October 10. Online at http://lanic.utexas.edu/project/castro/db/1968/19681011.html. Accessed on July 15, 2013.

Castro, Fidel. 1959. "Fidel Castro Speaks to Citizens of Santiago." January 3. Online at http://lanic.utexas.edu/project/castro/db/1959/19590103.html. Accessed on August 30, 2013.

Congresos del PCC. 1980. "II Congreso del Partido Comunista de Cuba (Informe Central)." Online at www. http://congresopcc.cip.cu/congresos/ii-congreso-pcc. Accessed on September 3, 2013.

Cordoví Núñez, Yoel. 2012. *Magisterio y nacionalismo en las escuelas públicas de Cuba (1899–1920)*. Havana: Ciencias Sociales.

Domínguez, J. I. 1978. *Cuba: Order and Revolution*. Cambridge: Harvard University Press.

Eisner, Will. 2006. *Comics and Sequential Art*. Paramus, NJ: Poorhouse Press.

Fagen, Richard R. 1969. *The Transformation of Political Culture in Cuba*. Stanford, CA: Stanford University Press.

Foucault, Michel. 1990. *The History of Sexuality. Volume 1: An Introduction*. New York: Random House.

Funkenstein, Amos. 1989. "Collective Memory and Historical Consciousness." *History and Memory* 1, no. 1: 5–26.

Gillis, John R., ed. 1994. *Commemorations: The Politics of National Identity*. Princeton, NJ: Princeton University Press.

Gott, Richard. 2004. *Cuba: A New History*. New Haven: Yale University Press.

Guevara de la Serna, Ernesto. 2006 [1965]. "El socialismo y el hombre en Cuba." In *Cultura Cubana Siglo XX*. Volume 2. Edited by Sonia Almazán and Mariana Serra, 39–51. Havana: Félix Varela.

Halbwachs, Maurice. 1992 [1925]. *On Collective Memory*. Chicago: University of Chicago Press.

Hulme, Peter. 2011. *Cuba's Wild East: A Literary Geography of Oriente*. Liverpool: Liverpool University Press.

Iglesias Utset, Marial. 2008. "Cultura popular, choteo y nacionalismo en la primera intervención." *La siempreviva*, no. 4: 3–12.

Kansteiner, Wulf. 2002. "Finding Meaning in Memory: A Methodological Critique of Collective Memory Studies." *History and Theory* 41 (May): 179–97.

Kapcia, Antoni. 2009. *Cuba in Revolution: A History since the Fifties*. London: Reaktion.

Kapcia, Antoni. 2005. *Havana: The Making of Cuban Culture*. Oxford: Berg.

Kapcia, Antoni. 2000. *Cuba: Island of Dreams*. Oxford: Berg.

Landsberg, Alison. 2004. *Prosthetic Memory: The Transformation of American Remembrance in the Age of Mass Culture*. New York: Columbia University Press.

McCloud, Scott. 1994. *Understanding Comics: The Invisible Art*. New York: HarperCollins.

Medin, T. Cuba. 1990. *The Shaping of Revolutionary Consciousness*. Boulder, CO: Lynne Rienner Publishers.

Merino, Ana. 2003. *El Cómic Hispánico*. Madrid: Cátedra.

Mesa-Lago, Carmelo, ed. 1971. *Revolutionary Change in Cuba*. Pittsburgh: University of Pittsburgh Press.

Nora, Pierre. 1989. "Between Memory and History: *Les lieux de mémoire*." *Representations* 26 (Spring): 7–24.

Ortiz, Fernando. 1949. "Los factores humanos de la cubanidad." *Revista Bimestre Cubana* 15, no. 3: 161–86.

Padrón, Ernesto. 2012. E-mail interview with the author. September 12.

Padrón, Ernesto, and Orestes Suárez. 2009a. *La emboscada* [1982]. In *Historietas de Inés, Aldo y Beto*. La Habana: Pablo de la Torriente Editorial.

Padrón, Ernesto, and Orestes Suárez. 2009b. *Historietas de Inés, Aldo y Beto*. La Habana: Pablo de la Torriente, 2009.

Padrón, Juan. 2003 [1985]. *El libro del mambí*. La Habana: Casa Editora Abril.

Pérez Jr., Louis A. 1999. "Incurring a Debt of Gratitude: 1898 and the Moral Sources of United States Hegemony in Cuba." *American Historical Review* 104, no. 2 (April): 356–98.

Pérez Jr., Louis A. 1998. *The War of 1898: The United States and Cuba in History and Historiography*. Chapel Hill: University of North Carolina Press.

Pérez Firmat, Gustavo. 2010. *The Havana Habit*. New Haven: Yale University Press.

Roig de Leuchsenring, Emilio. 1975 [1950]. *Cuba no debe su independencia a los Estados Unidos*. Havana: Editorial Oriente.

Roig de Leuchsenring, Emilio. 1932. "En 1854 los EE.UU. anunciaron cómo se apoderarían de Cuba en 1899 y 1902." *Carteles* 18, no. 43 (October).

Sampayo, Carlos, and José Muñoz. 1975–1992. *Alack Sinner* in *Linus*. Milan: Baldini & Castoldi.

Samuel, Raphael. 1994. *Theatres of Memory, Volume 1: Past and Present in Contemporary Culture*. London: Verso.

Sherman, Daniel J. 1999. *The Construction of Memory in Interwar France*. Chicago: University of Chicago Press.

Shnookal, Deborah, and Mirta Muñiz. 1999. *José Marti Reader: Writings on the Americas*. New York: Ocean Press.

Soto, Lionel. 1977. *La revolución del 33*. Havana: Ciencias Sociales.

Tabares del Real, José A. 1975. *La revolución del 30: Sus dos últimos años*. Havana: Ciencias Sociales.

Torres-Cuevas, Eduardo, and Oscar Loyola Vega. 2006. *Historia de Cuba 1492–1898: Formación y Liberación de la Nación*. Havana: Editorial Pueblo y Educación.

Yates, Frances. 2007 [1966]. *The Art of Memory*. Chatham: Mackays of Chatham.

TWO

HOW TO MAKE A REVOLUTION WITH WORDS (AND DRAWINGS)

HISTORY, MEMORY, AND IDENTITY IN OESTERHELD'S COMICS

Edoardo Balletta

Héctor Germán Oesterheld is Argentina's most well-known comic scriptwriter, largely because of his *El eternauta*, widely considered to be his masterpiece. The final period of his production, however (from the late 1960s to his disappearance in 1977), is less well known.[1] This latter production was strongly influenced by Oesterheld's political radicalization and militancy in the Peronist guerrilla organization Montoneros. During these years Oesterheld's publications included some biographical graphic novels (*La vida del Che*, 1968; *Evita: Vida y obra de Eva Perón*, 1970), a new and more politicized version of the first part of *El eternauta*, its sequel (*El eternauta II*), and two comics that had been published serially in a daily paper and a weekly magazine connected with Montoneros: *Latinoamérica y el imperialismo: 450 años de guerra* and *La guerra de los Antartes*.[2] Even though these two stories have very different plots—the first a *graphic* history of Latin America and the second a dystopian science-fiction story of invasion—they do share some significant points of contact. Both comics were produced and published in the left-wing Peronist press during a dramatic period of Argentine history. This interval could be delimited by the election of Héctor Cámpora as the first Peronist president post-1955 in March 1973, and May 1, 1974, when Perón, after his return from exile, expelled left-wing Peronist militants from the Plaza de Mayo, (dis)qualifying them as "estúpidos imberbes."[3] In this context the two comics can be read as a strategy to interact with the pressing issues of the present by reappropriating the past. This process of constructing a cultural memory was the initial step in what would become the hegemonic force among the various "trends" of Peronism: by performing the past in the form of memory, the two comics also made something with it in the present and for the future.[4]

To analyze the role and importance of cultural memory in these two comics more effectively, I take it to be a *discourse* in which "present and past [interplay] in socio-cultural contexts" (Erll 2008: 2). This broad understanding of cultural memory has multiple advantages since it covers almost every aspect of what, in the present day, is empirically considered cultural memory itself. Moreover, this view outlines the tight connections that bind (in the discourse of memory) the present and the past, the key factor in my interpretation of the two Oesterheld comics examined. The frameworks of Aleida Assmann (2011 [1999]) and Jan Assmann (2011 [1992]) create some problems when opposing "cultural memory" to "communicative memory."[5] Jan and Aleida Assmann's concept of the "cultural," as stressed by Dietrich Harth (2008: 95), is influenced by the original German word (*kultur*), the meaning of which is not exactly the same as the English term "culture," the former being more strictly related to what is *high* culture. Therefore every discourse and social practice not part of *high* culture would be excluded from cultural memory.

A strict interpretation of the perspective of Jan and Aleida Assmann's perspective would imply, for example, that the remote past and origins of a group could be associated only with a highly formalized, institutionalized, and stable memory in the hands of a community of specialists in tradition (A. Assmann 2011 [1999]; J. Assmann 2011 [1992]), such as historians, cultural heritage workers, and so on. Power relations, in this context, tend to disappear from memory or, to be more precise, they stand watermarked in the opposition between "communicative" and "cultural" memory. Nevertheless, they are crafted in an asymmetric web of relations in which the agency of nonruling social groups is limited in space (communicative memory is based on everyday interactions), time (communicative memory has a range of eighty to one hundred years), and content. As pointed out by Theo D'Haen (2007), this framework does not fit when we come, for example, to subaltern or postcolonial studies. On the one hand, materials from the cultural memory archive—in A. Assmann's understanding (2011 [1999])—can be resignified as countermemories; on the other hand, communicative memories can serve as "cultural" and thus become institutionalized.[6]

If memory is a discourse (or a set of discursive practices), it can also be defined, from a critical discourse analysis perspective, as a social practice (Fairclough and Wodak 1997); as a result, a dialectical relation is established between a single discursive event (a chapter of a comic, in our case) and the social and political structures that frame it (such as the political culture of militants and adversaries). Thus cultural memory is not only socially conditioned (constituted) but also constitutive: it is shaped by social actors and institutions, but *dialectically* it also constructs "situations, objects of knowledge, and the social identities of and relationships between people and groups of people" (258). To put it another way, on the one hand, discursive events "play a decisive role in the genesis and construction of social conditions" (Barker and Galasiński 2001: 65), justifying and perpetuating (thanks to memorial discourses) the status quo but, on the other hand, they can also be instrumental in the transformation of the status quo. In this sense, one of the key features of memory should be considered *performativity*: cultural memory not only *represents* social past events but also shapes and modifies them and the way people act (Tilmans, Vree, and Winter 2010; Neumann 2007).[7]

From a similar perspective, in their key book on the discursive foundations of Peronism, Silvia Sigal and Eliseo Verón (1986: 25) have argued that Peronism should be considered primarily as an enunciative device (*dispositivo de enunciación*). This discourse-centred perspective, according to them, permits a closer understanding of the political process of 1973 and 1974.[8] Such an understanding should not be based only on Peronism's political-economic origins but also on its cultural dimensions, especially on "the particular reading of Peronism and, specifically, of Perón's political discourse implied by this position of the Juventud Peronista" (20).[9] On the one hand, Peronism should be considered as the "condition of production" of Montonero discourse; on the other hand, this discourse should be seen as the setting where a specific "configuration of effects" (from Perón's discourse) took place. Clearly, the question of power is not absent from this point of view: as Norman Fairclough (2003) has put it, discursive practices are social events that are produced and received by social agents that develop discursive strategies aimed at hegemonizing a sociopolitical or cultural field.[10] Memory, in this understanding, should not be referred to in the singular, as it is best described as a multiplicity of discursive practices targeted at the construction of a past as a means of intervening in the present and shaping the future (Neumann 2007: 307).

Returning to the performative and memory, it could be argued that before and after every memory there is a performative act. Memory is *performed* through discursive and/or sociocultural practices; it is also *performative* in the sense that it is a result or product of discursive practices and through the production of a discourse it constructs, "modifies," and interacts with our understanding. In this way, memory *materially* acts on society in the present and in the future. As Birgit Neumann (2007: 309) has argued, to speak of performativity of memory in this context means to consider the practice of interpreting the past as a socially binding action whose performative force resides in the intersubjective potential of a semiotic system. The two comics referenced at the outset of this chapter (*Latinoamérica* and *Guerra*) can thus be considered as part of a more general strategy developed by left-wing Peronist groups and their media to become the hegemonic group of the whole movement. In *Latinoamérica* and *Guerra*, this strategy is revealed by outlining several legitimation substrategies, such as highlighting group orthodoxy, loyalty to Perón and revolutionary faith, and reappropriating the past as a means of identity construction through memory.

LATINOAMÉRICA Y EL IMPERIALISMO: 450 AÑOS DE GUERRA

The comic *Latinoamérica y el imperialismo: 450 años de guerra* was published weekly in *El Descamisado* from July 1973 to April 1974. The first episode was preceded by a kind of anonymous prologue, which works as a statement neatly defining the aims and scope of the story that the public was about to read: "Now we are going to tell you about the history of imperialism so that all these questions and many more as well will be answered. *El Descamisado* will reveal the truth about our history. What our past was really like and what our present is really like. Because the history of imperialism is the history of the American continent—the Great Homeland—and the history of our homeland: four hundred and fifty years of war" (*El Descamisado* 10, July 24, 1973).[11]

The discourse is presented unequivocally and, by creating a space of veridiction ("the truth about our history"), it self-authorizes the enunciator's position: the voice of the Montoneros states that official history—the one taught in schools, which later is contemptuously defined as *mitrista*—is false.[12] As a result, the reader of *El Descamisado* will be offered a new, trustworthy version of history in which it will be undeniably clear that there is an enemy (imperialism and "puppet regimes") and that resistance to this enemy existed, still exists, and will continue to exist.[13] Underlying this clear and "solid" perspective on history, an against-the-grain reading of the text reveals other key aspects of Montoneros' discourse, offering quite a complete catalogue of the strategies and narrative practices of the comic itself. Throughout *Latinoamérica*—as in *El Descamisado* itself and various other militant publications—left-wing Peronism seeks to legitimize its revolutionary discourse and lay the foundations for the construction of a group identity.[14] All this is achieved by an operation of inclusion/exclusion in the field of history/memory and by attempting to create a clear ethical code for militants.

In terms of legitimation strategies, I focus on two key aspects: the double discourse construction as an ideological strategy and circularity as the way in which the comics (re)present history and construct memory. By *double discourse*, I mean the discourse resulting from the ambiguities and tensions arising from combining Peronist and left-wing ideology: the need for the legitimation of the movement necessitates the construction of a discourse aimed at trying to "harmonize" the left-wing Latin American vision ("la Patria Grande") with the more classical Peronist emphasis on the homeland. If Perón's iconographic image and his quotations are used as a source of authority, it is clear that the politico-cultural background of the comics, the authors, and the public should also be found in dependency theory.[15] This ambiguity, approached from enunciation theory, can be seen more as a "(failed) strategy to enter the enunciative device of Peronism" (Sigal and Verón 1986: 25) than as a reply to Peronist enunciation itself. Montoneros need to legitimate their discourse *without* exceeding the limits of Peronist orthodoxy and its patriotic rhetoric. Therefore the comic offers a double version of the homeland and constructs itself by pointing to the continuity of a tradition instead of a rupture. This continuity, in *Latinoamérica*, will help to solidify the connection between indigenous resistance, struggles for independence, and eventually Peronist (self-proclaimed) revolution. Another element contributing to the development of this legitimation strategy is the appearance of Perón himself three times in the comics: in the first chapter of *Latinoamérica*, Perón is shown in a photograph with a speech-balloon containing an anti-imperialist-like statement from one of his doctrinal works; while in the other chapters, the growing distance between Montoneros and Perón can be perceived, as Óscar Benítez (n.d.) has observed.[16]

Temporality is another interesting element in *Latinoamérica* and is conceived as a *circularity* where past and present evoke and mutually justify each other. This parallelism is strongly stressed on the opening page of the first chapter, where "tres ejemplos actuales del imperialismos dando zarpazos" (three contemporary examples of imperialism lashing out) (*El Descamisado*

10, July 24, 1973) are offered and, *immediately* after, when the Conquest is represented ("El ataque del imperialismo comienza cuando España llega a América") (The imperialist attack begins when Spain arrives in America). These examples are the Uruguayan *golpe* (June 27, 1973), the *tanquetazo* in Chile (June 29, 1973), and the Ezeiza massacre (June 29, 1973), which are clearly drawn and thus easily recognizable (figures 2.1 and 2.2). This strategy is replicated elsewhere in *Latinoamérica* through the logic of reiteration: "A history which continues to repeat itself, even today, but not for much longer

FIGURE 2.1. Three examples of present imperialism, taken from "La España Imperialista," *Latinoamérica y el imperialismo*: *450 años de guerra*. Courtesy of Doeyo y Viniegra editores.

FIGURE 2.2. Hernán Cortés slaughtering Indians, taken from "La España Imperialista," *Latinoamérica y el imperialismo: 450 años de guerra*. Courtesy of Doeyo y Viniegra editores.

[. . . the exploited] will no longer be cannon fodder. . . . They have learned that the 'Hail to our Nation!' of the past is today's 'Liberty or Death!'" ("El Ejército de la Patria Grande," *El Descamisado* 24, October 30, 1973).

Similarly, this parallelism reappears in the part devoted to the "traitor" Urquiza (*El Descamisado* 44–45, March 19 and 26, 1974): "The trees in San Benito de Palermo produced strange fruits. Fruits of people. There have always been martyrs who were willing to die for their country, who gave their lives for Perón, which is the same as saying for the people and their country. And there have always been generals like Valle capable of refusing to hand over their country to foreigners and of rejecting all lies, even if that meant ending up in front of the firing squad" ("La Traición de Urquiza," *El Descamisado* 44, March 19, 1974). The unsuccessful *contra-golpe* by Generals Valle and Tanco (June 9, 1956) is compared to the defection by Colonel Aquino's squads, harking back to an event that occurred almost one hundred years previously, to demonstrate that history repeats itself. Here is how the chapter ends:

> Buenos Aires: rich, powerful and permanently on sale to the highest bidder. And always flying in the face of history. At least as long as it was dominated by swindlers, oligarchs, *cipayos*, and all those on the payroll of English or Yankee imperialism . . . or even by the Brazilians. But it was when the people, the authentic people, elevated their own kind to power—men and women from the bosom of their own lives, their own roots, and not from the world where money reigned supreme—that the people became the driving force of history. Just like Rosas . . . and like General Perón in 1945.[17]
>
> ("Urquiza también perdió," *El Descamisado* 45, March 26, 1974)

In a 1975 interview Oesterheld himself explicitly refers to this need for circularity as one of the key guidelines for *Latinoamérica*: "I not only had to look for facts about the past but also to find connections with the present. This emerged as I was working, as I was writing. At the beginning it was not intentional. Gradually I got the hang of it and it remains one of the most original ideas in my comics" (as quoted in Trillo and Saccomano 2005: 28). This interweaving of past and present in the comics should be seen as another important tool in the construction of memory (and identity): by outlining a will for continuity, it suggests the idea of a *genealogy*.

The first step of *Latinoamérica*'s emphasis on origins is devoted to pre-Hispanic indigenous America and occupies the first two chapters of the comic, where a rather hurried panorama of the Conquest and the first

FIGURE 2.3. Tupac Amaru tortured by Spaniards, taken from "La Rebelión de Tupac Amaru," *Latinoamérica y el imperialismo: 450 años de guerra.* Courtesy of Doeyo y Viniegra editores.

indigenous riots are offered to the reader ("La Rebelión de Tupac Amaru," *El Descamisado* 11, July 31, 1973). The mythical foundation-line points to the Mayan, Tecun-Uman, and to the Inca, Tupac Amaru. In both cases, two elements are highlighted and praised as positive values: direct lineage and martyrdom (figure 2.3). Tecun-Uman is described as "our first martyr" and a "symbol of the *indios*" and his eyes as "the eyes of us all" ("La España Imperialista," *El Descamisado* 10), while Tupac-Amaru—nicknamed "the first Tupa" in clear allusion to the Uruguayan movement Tupamaros—is described as being still "among us, in the ongoing fight for liberation" (*El Descamisado* 11). This chapter ends with scenes of torture that the mythical cacique resists without betraying his comrades, obviously again hinting at a sort of ethical code for militants.

Following these initial identifications, which are meant to offer a kind of prehistory of the organization, the story focuses on the British invasions during the nineteenth century. Here, the dichotomy of the friend/enemy structure becomes more explicit: on the one hand, stand the "vendepatrias" (traitors of the nation), the "anti-nación," and, on the other hand, the foundational heroes. In both fields there are individual and collective actors. The alien enemy is British imperialism that has its "local" counterparts in

FIGURE 2.4. Rivadavia, Mitre, Onganía, Justo, Lanusse: the oligarchy of Buenos Aires through the ages, taken from "La Oligarquía Portuaria," *Latinoamérica y el imperialismo: 450 años de guerra*. Courtesy of Doeyo y Viniegra editores.

the "brilliant Illuminists," who are "completely estranged from the reality surrounding them (they are the far-left of the day)" ("La 'tercera' Invasión Inglesa," *El Descamisado* 15, August 28, 1973) who dream of an "unreal fatherland, soaked up from European authors" ("El '17' de los Orilleros," *El Descamisado* 16, September 4, 1973). Among this enlightened chorus of young intellectuals stands the future president, Bernardino Rivadavia, who is described in a chapter eloquently titled "Rivadavia: Garantía para los Ingleses" (*El Descamisado* 17, September 11, 1973). The great Argentine statesman is remembered here for his individual security bill and his overture to British monopolistic trade.

In both cases the text and images reveal, in parallel, the causes and effects of his political actions. Free trade, suggests the author's intervention, has resulted in poverty in the "interior" of the country, while the security bill is applied only to the "gente decente" (decent people), excluding the humble from constitutional rights. In parallel, the narrator's commentary brings the discourse back to the present: "[All this], then, goes back to the time of Rivadavia. One law for the 'decent people,' and another for the masses. Today, to search a home in the Barrio Norte you probably still need a warrant. To search a home in the shantytown, you only need to give the door a good kick" (*El Descamisado* 17, September 11, 1973). Apart from these cases, the enemy line is not developed much more, barring two other moments where a kind of past-to-present family tree is depicted: the political line runs from Bernandino Rivadavia and Bartolomé Mitre to Agustín Justo, Juan Carlos Onganía, and Alejandro Lanusse, who are represented on the same panel (*El Descamisado* 25, November 6, 1973) (figure 2.4).[18] Their economic counterparts are depicted through Rogelio Frigerio, Álvaro Alsogaray, and Adalbert Krieger Vasena ("La frontera" 38, February 5, 1974).

By contrast, the structure of the *friend-line* is developed further and can be subdivided into individual (the *próceres*) and collective heroes. Besides the indigenous caciques, the first line is constituted by José Artigas, Juan Manuel de Rosas, and Facundo Quiroga, while collective heroes are depicted thanks to a kind of symbolic name figure (Juan Cualquiera, Juan Paisano, Juan Esclavo) announcing the real heroes: "orilleros," "gauchos," "negros," "soldaderas," and, last but not least, "montoneras."[19] Clearly, the foundational mythology the comic seeks to reconstruct is *federal*, and to achieve this goal, it is necessary to subvert the official historical framework (*civilización/barbarie*) inherited from the nineteenth century and to reframe the historical narration so that it can effectively work in the double discourse that the Montoneros need to encourage (the Left *and* Peronism).[20] A narrative macrostructure will thus be constituted by an alliance between two actors: the brave, respected caudillo and the loyal *pueblada*, which is an obvious reference to the (claimed) idyllic relationship between the people and Perón.

The first great leader whom the reader encounters is José Artigas (*El Descamisado* 19–21), whose characteristics match those of the perfect caudillo: he is an "estanciero-trabajador," adored by his people because he is a "defender of the humble" who instead of "punishing them with blind justice, . . . understands and helps them." The narration of Artigas's political commitment is presented as a revolutionary epic that serves as an introduction to the main (and foundational) theme of the Montoneras ("Las Montoneras," *El Descamisado* 23). He is described as follows: "A great patriot of the Great Homeland. His ideal is unity forever, separation never" (*El Descamisado* 19, September 26, 1973). "Artigas pulsates with his people. He wants the independence of the great American nation and he wants it right away." Another significant Artigas portrait represents him dictating the "Reglamento Provisorio" in 1815, talking of giving away the confiscated Spanish properties "to the blacks, the *zambos*, the Indians, the poor creoles" (*El Descamisado* 21, October 9, 1973).

FIGURE 2.5. Fourth-estate Montoneras, taken from "Las Montoneras," *Latinoamérica y el imperialismo: 450 años de guerra.* Courtesy of Doeyo y Viniegra editores.

Juan Manuel de Rosas and Facundo Quiroga are portrayed in a very similar way. They are both part of a local tradition (versus European elite culture), and they constitute the real hope for the humble: "A worthy representative of the *estanciero-gaucho* before Paris appeared on our oligarchs' map, Rosas lives with tenant farmers; he works and spends his free time with them. The tenant farmers, as generous as always, offer him unconditional loyalty—'to the death.' [The people] understand that Rosas is fighting for the country of one and all, not for the country of a minority. For the Great Homeland" (*El Descamisado* 29, December 4, 1973). "[Quiroga] is the grand caudillo of the interior of the country, the right man to bring the long-awaited and long-desired unity of the nation to completion. He has enormous prestige. Excepting his physical stature, Quiroga is great in everything. He is great because he understands his people, because he defends them, because he fights for them. And his people feed his Montoneras and would follow him to hell itself. Because they know that he *is* the people. Much more than Rosas, Quiroga was the most authentic, concrete hope for national integration" ("La Muerte de Quiroga," *El Descamisado* 36, January 22, 1974).

Another key moment in the comic is the chapter devoted to "Las Montoneras," from which the later organization evidently took its name. After a splash page portraying a *montonera* in Fourth Estate fashion (figure 2.5), the narrator presents the idyllic life of gauchos before 1810 and the deterioration of their social conditions after the introduction of the "ley de vagancia" and free trade. These were the conditions, as the comic suggests, that led to the origin of the *montoneras*: "The underprivileged unite under the command of a man they know is capable of fighting. A man who is almost always a landowner and influential but with a heart to feel compassion for the misery in which the farmers live. And with the balls to put his life at risk for them without worrying about his own personal comfort. . . . that's how the Montoneras and the caudillo who leads them arise" ("Las Montoneras," *El Descamisado* 23, October 23, 1973).

This page is almost entirely occupied by war images, except for the last panel's caption, where the reader is led to establish an obvious parallelism:

> the same profound sentiments of freedom, justice and nationhood that twenty-eight years ago, on 17 October 1945, drove that other great Montonera rebellion to a splendid victory against imperialism. The same profound sentiments for a homeland that is just, free and independent and which gives

strength and courage to our last Montonera . . . that montonera forced to scatter and hide but that fought during the resistance and that triggered the Cordobazo uprising in an attack on the dictatorship which caused it to fall . . . and who, today, no longer dispersed, keeps careful vigil, ever ready to respond to the next blow. ("Las Montoneras," *El Descamisado* 23, October 23, 1973)

TODAY AS YESTERDAY

This discussion explicitly shows *circularity*: historical representation serves to create *exempla* from the past in order to explain the present and legitimize, through the construction of a countermemory, the discourse of the Montoneros. The opposite is also true: past events are understood and legitimized to form a part of the Montoneros' origins, thanks to a comparison between the present and the recent past. The two fundamental dates that appear in multiple passages of *Latinoamérica* are May 25, 1810, and October 17, 1945. Besides the differences, the structural composition of the two events in the comic leads to their consideration as an almost unique reality: on both occasions, "el pueblo [. . .] impone su voluntad" ("El '17' de los Orilleros," *El Descamisado* 16, September 4, 1973). The comic had already hinted at this confluence of dates before with reference to May 25. In the chapter that follows, on the reconquest of Buenos Aires led by Santiago de Liniers, the narrator explains: "The first English invasion has been defeated. Not thanks to the Spanish army. The professional army was a complete failure. And not thanks to the bureaucrats who did not hesitate to agree terms with the enemy in order to continue receiving their privileges. The first English invasion was defeated thanks to the people, who rose up in arms. It was a grassroots explosion which transcended its leaders. It was essentially the antecedent of '17 October' and a triumph over the foreign invaders" ("El '17' de los Orilleros," *El Descamisado* 16, September 4, 1973).

The discursive operation is evident but nonetheless less articulated. The Reconquista (the first Argentinean victory against invaders), which in this vision of history announces the second (the "Defensa") and the foundation of the independent country, is compared to October 17. In so doing, not only the chronology but also the value bestowed on the events becomes distorted: from this point of view, it is the foundational Peronist event that serves as a yardstick for those events in which the people impose their will and not (chrono)logically the opposite. The narration continues up to the proclamations of the Junta and, as usual, the narrator summarizes and comments on the event:

> 25 May 1810. The biased *cipayo*-oligarchic imaginary represented in school history books says that that was the day we achieved our Freedom. Just like that. With a capital "F" and forever. The cruel daily doses of reality in modern times, too, have clarified what that "glorious" 25 May really was: just a change of rulers. By making us believe that their fake "independent" government was real, England simply took Spain's place and sat down, right on top of us, for over a century. If only the splendid May sun of all those official speeches really had been shining on us! If it had, we wouldn't be here now, 150 years later, still facing the harsh iron-clad alternative of "Liberty or death." ("La Tercera Invasión Inglesa," *El Descamisado* 15, August 28, 1973)

The reader discovers that, in point of fact, May 25 *could have been* October 17, but these hopes were frustrated by "bureaucrats" and "traitors."

A similar parallelism reappears in the following chapter: "On 25 May 1810, the people stated their will only to see it completely ignored shortly thereafter. Just like on 25 May 1973, when the people wanted to establish the justicialist party line, their line for Argentina—the line that was swiftly neutered by the same old groups of bureaucrats and traitors" ("El '17' de los Orilleros," *El Descamisado* 16, September 4, 1973). Here, a second comparison is added: May 25, 1810, is *like* May 25, 1973, the day when Héctor J. Cámpora was appointed president only to resign shortly after (July 14, 1973). This means that if every successful event is a "verdadero 17 de octubre," every failure is a May 25, regardless whether it is 1810 or 1973. Hence, what remains is October 17, chosen to characterize the *orilleros* riot, whose representation is visually and textually styled on the *descamisados* in the Plaza de Mayo: "the authentic people. The grassroots base which foreshadowed another great popular revolution 130 years later" ("El '17' de los Orilleros," *El Descamisado* 16, September 4, 1973).

Other episodes can be read according to this same interpretive line. "La rebelión de Patricios y la Antipatria Fusiladora" (*El Descamisado* 18, September 18, 1973), for example, is an evident mix, where the events of the nineteenth century are textualized and represented from the perspective of contemporaneity. Starting from the title—which alludes to the "Fusiladora," as the Peronists called the (Revolución) Libertadora—the rebels are compared to the "martyrs of the José León Suárez, Trelew and Ezeiza massacres" ("La

Rebelión de Patricios y la Antipatria Fusiladora," *El Descamisado* 18, September 18, 1973). Another reference to Pedro Aramburu's coup can be found in the cited episode "Rivadavia: Garantía para los Ingleses" (*El Descamisado* 17, September 11, 1973), where the narrator recounts: "for the *gorila* [i.e., the anti-Peronist] back then, defeating the people—not the nation's enemies—was the only important thing. Just like the *gorila* on 16 September 1955; just like the *gorila* today."

It is noteworthy here that the past seems to have been legitimized by the present, which appears contrary to what I suggested was the Montoneros' main legitimation strategy (to legitimize the present through the past). These two opposite movements clearly exemplify *circularity*. Past and present are mutually constituted: on the one hand, this relation works as an ideological tool; on the other hand, it emphasizes the affective dimension of memory.

LA GUERRA DE LOS ANTARTES

The comic *La guerra de los Antartes* is science fiction. The comic relates how, in 2001, a "socialist and national" revolution triumphs in Argentina, when suddenly the world is invaded by aliens who land in Antarctica. The superpower leaders and diplomats make a pact with the invaders. If Latin America is sacrificed to the aliens, other countries will benefit from peace and fruitful trade with the newcomers. After discovering this betrayal, a resistance movement is formed in Buenos Aires. Here the story stops, as the newspaper *Noticias* in which the comic was being published was unfortunately shut down by the National Executive Power.

We are clearly dealing with a completely different story line from *Latinoamérica*. In *Guerra*, the reader participates in the creation of a utopic-dystopic future whose core elements are to be found in the present and recent past of the authors and readers. Nonetheless, the two comics share much in common; in fact, they complete one another. *Latinoamérica* acts as a pretext for *Guerra*: history in this comic is not a pivotal point of narration (as in *Latinoamérica*), but certain values and perspectives *on* history are implicitly taken as assumptions and they become a space for a shared memory. On the one hand, anti-imperialism and dependency theory is the general ideological frame; on the other hand, generational memory plays an important role when resistance to the enemy begins. In the first part of *Guerra*, for example, Lieutenant Sabino Torres (protagonist-narrator of this section), staring at Buenos Aires in ruins, draws a clear comparison between his own present and the Spanish Conquest: "like the Indios of the pampas when they saw the first Spaniards . . . when they heard a gunshot for the first time . . . that same terror" (Oesterheld and Trigo 1998: 32); after, when the Resistance is about to be launched, one of the leaders ("El Grone" Andrada) reminds the reader about the same genealogy of the enemy we read about in *Latinoamérica*: "actually, there's nothing new about this . . . imperialists were in power in the past too, Rivadavia, Mitre, Justo, Onganía, Lanusse" (78). *Latinoamérica* can thus be considered a kind of Montoneros archive ("stored memory" in A. Assmann's terms). Starting from that point—and with no need to repeat this historiographical perspective—*Guerra* creates a new discourse that is *projective*.

What I find more captivating in this second comic, partly as a consequence of its genre, is its temporal structure. We have a narrative time frame, which is divided into a present (2001) and a recent past, which cannot exactly be defined, although it could span from 1945 to 1974. The enunciator's (and reader's) temporality should also be taken into account: in this case, the present is 1973 and 1974 and the recent past extends again from 1945 to the present moment. The function of the narrative present is clear: it draws on two distinct (and opposite) possible scenarios for Argentine society (utopia and dystopia), the same scenarios that are echoed in the contemporary "Perón o muerte" slogan. The narrative past (which is also the enunciator's present), on the contrary, works as a stored memory for understanding the narrative present (2001) and constructing the identities in the story.

The remote past appears to be of no interest in *Guerra*. Apart from sporadic references, the comic focuses on an allegorical representation of first/third world dynamics.[21] Antartes invaders impose peace conditions, highlighting the privileges that the traitors will enjoy, thanks to the technical progress brought about by the invaders. After, the Antartes install phantom governments in conquered countries and the traitors (the United States and the Soviet Union) silence their opposition via political killings and censorship.[22] From cultural imperialism to coup d'état fostering and yankee neocolonialism, a large serving of items of the revolutionary Latin American leftist agenda is cleverly inserted throughout the story.[23] Readers are requested to decode these (evidently) allegorical sequences even though the key is highlighted in the text itself when comparing Antartes imperialism with the recent Pinochet *golpe*: "Without anyone finding out, the Antartes succeeded in carrying out a deep espionage operation . . . even before entering Plaza de Mayo, they knew exactly where and how to strike . . . they just copied what Pinochet did in Chile in 1973" (Oesterheld and Trigo 1998: 91).

The series of traitors is represented by underlining the hierarchic relation of political power, which is subject to economic supremacy. The division between "good" and "evil," as Irene Chauvin Depetris (2004) has pointed out, is graphically stressed thanks to the opposition of young-beautiful/mature-ugly, which recalls the predominantly generational character of the left-wing Peronist movements and organizations. On the opposite side stands third-world solidarity: the protests of Cuba, Peru, Uganda, and Zaire against treason. Zaire, because of its considerable technological development ("a flourishing country"; Oesterheld and Trigo 1998: 47), has a weapon that can destroy the Antartes basecamp, but the U.S. and Soviet ministers refuse to take the risk and instead bomb its capital city, killing the young, beautiful prime minister.

What remains of the past are dates (October 17, 1945, and May 25, 1973), sites (Plaza de Mayo), and narratives (the Peronist resistance) that can be considered the (ever)lasting myths and memories of the group. Torres's father recalls October 17 both as a foundational and personal memory ("I'd just been born"; Oesterheld and Trigo 1998: 71) and as a renewing force ("el nuevo 17 de octubre"; Oesterheld and Trigo 1998: 71). The day on which Cámpora was appointed president (May 25, 1973) is a beloved memory but also marks the remembrance of the defeat of the people's hopes and interests (as seen in *Latinoamérica*). In that "long time ago" ("hace mucho"; Oesterheld and Trigo 1998: 72), pronounced by Torres's father in 2001, both Oesterheld's and the militants' voices who in 1974 recalled Cámpora's appointment as a distant memory can be heard. In this general context, the Plaza de Mayo is a crucial (Von Sprecher 2007; Benítez n.d.) but also ambivalent scenario. It is the *lieu* (Nora 1984–1992) where the masses congregate in a remake of early Peronist imagery; being the centrifuge of new resistance, it is also where the people are slaughtered in an (eerie) recurrence of the Ezeiza Massacre.[24]

In these continuous shifts between the pessimism of intellect and the optimism of will, resistance becomes the discourse capable of aggregating and consolidating identities.[25] It is so *present* in collective (Peronist) memory that it does not need to be narratively justified. All elements are within reach. In a key moment, when Torres's father is at home, pondering with his family what to do, typical "Peronist" pickup trucks arrive with the "muchachos" brandishing "ferretería" (slang for "guns") and heading to Plaza de Mayo, conscious that they are risking their own lives. In this ambivalence of memory (myth/massacre), the backdrop of the disagreements, overt conflicts, and the final breakup of Montoneros and Perón can be glimpsed: harmony between the people and their leader is a distant memory that can be drawn only in the future where, in any case, the dreams of a recently born socialist homeland will be obliterated by a new enemy.

I have interpreted two comics written by Oesterheld by considering them as a fairly representative sample of the Montoneros' culture. The performativity of memory has been assumed to provide a general framework for understanding how their discourse on memory and identity was a means for participating—and triumphing—in the political struggle. Following John Langshaw Austin (1962), we can conclude that the Montoneros' discourse failed to establish *felicitous conditions* and therefore, along with more tangible reasons, the impact of the movement slowly decreased following Perón's return.[26] Our current concern is not the effects and materialization of their discourse but, rather, the ways in which the past was used (and operated) within the discourse itself. A pivotal element is the problem of the public use of history (Habermas 1988) and its relation to memory. In this context, Maurice Halbwach's legacy, which strongly opposes the two ways of conserving the past, should be discussed because, as Astrid Erll (2008: 15) has pointed out, "the whole question of 'history and/or/as memory' is simply not a particularly fruitful approach to cultural representations of the past," stating rather that memory and history should be considered two "modes of remembering in culture."

However, as Teresa Grande (2007) has argued, memory/history relations could be better described as a continuum ("field of tension") rather than an opposition. In our context a very poignant example of these multiple and entangled relations can be seen in the reaction to the episode entitled "El '17' de los Orilleros" (*El Descamisado* 16, September 4, 1973). Some readers disagreed with the comic's highly negative representation of the controversial politician and member of the first Argentine national council, Mariano Moreno, and wrote to the publication. Two of the letters received were published, in issue number 18 (by Norberto Galasso, September 18, 1973, 24) and number 20 (by Raúl H. Fenoglio, October 2, 1973, 31), together with the editorial committee's response. Both readers, who were very well-informed, criticized the episode and, in the case of Galasso, addressed the problem of historiographical sources with great precision: "I think that the origin of these errors is to be found in José María Rosa's books. But while Rosa may feel proud for having been honored by Stroessner's government or comfortable while sitting next to Sánchez Sorondo during a public ceremony . . . I believe that 'El Descamisado' should 'revise' this area too, and take into consideration not just the national revisionism of the right in the thirties but also the new contributions of those who, both in the past and today, are on the side of liberation and social nationalism." Galasso, who ten years earlier had published a study on *Mariano Moreno y la Revolución Nacional* (1963), is obviously not an impartial observer, yet he reveals the explicit connections between the historical narration in *Latinoamérica* and Argentine historical revisionism. What is at stake here, as Galasso indirectly points out, is the use of the past, which is the "common ground" between history and memory. There is no doubt that beyond *Latinoamérica*'s historical framework stands nationalist revisionism; what is less evident is how this mix became possible.

As Michael Goebel (2004 and 2011) has argued, the Peronism-revisionism connection is relatively recent and grounded in multiple factors, the most relevant being a "reversed appropriation" by Peronists of the anti-Peronist propaganda after the 1955 coup d'état. According to him, this perspective was slowly accepted by the Peronist resistance press (and Perón himself), culminating in a positive identification of Perón with Rosas, as presumed by *Latinoamérica*: "This is the same Rosas who gradually consolidated the National Government. The realistic politician who began to give substance to the concept of 'nation,' balancing it with contemporary reality. Only two other men in our history had as clear and lucid a sense of reality: José de San Martín and Juan Domingo Perón" ("Rosas. Primera Parte," *El Descamisado* 29, December 4, 1973). To understand this apparent incoherence, it might be useful to view it within the context of the left-wing culture of the late 1960s and early 1970s and its emphasis on "the new." As Hugo Vezzetti has argued (2007: 8), even though in Argentina "nobody talked openly of a *new Peronism*—novelty resided in a revision that aimed to unite old-style Peronism with Cuban socialism." This double discourse (the coexistence of Peronism and Cuban socialism) should be considered within a more general climate of cultural change that, under the influence of anticolonialist discourse, caused an inversion in the *civilización/barbarie* paradigm.[27]

With this backdrop in mind, I consider three different aspects while focusing on memory and the past in the two comics. Which cultural spaces are involved, which times and periods are presented, and how? The three elements are strictly intertwined. The latter trait—the "how"—has already been considered when talking about double discourse and circularity. The first refers to the Montoneros' location in two different (but still interconnected) cultural spaces, from which the distinct modalities of representing and remembering the specific periods and events are derived. This, in effect, determines the third element. Drawing a classical timeline that can describe the two comics' temporal representation—going beyond a mere surface description—would be a hard task. Periods come into focus if we assume an external position: a remote past (conquest and independence/state formation), a recent past (from 1945 to June 20, 1973), and the present (from Perón's return to the closure of the two periodicals). This tripartition could fit quite well Jan Assmann's conceptualization of "cultural" and "communicative" memory but, when trying to go beyond this first step into more articulated interpretative issues, things become more complicated. Actually, both remote past events and recent ones act as foundational myths, because of, at least in part, the *double* location that the Montoneros organization needs to occupy: a Latin American and a Peronist space, with all the ambiguities that this ideological mix brings.

As a consequence, it is necessary to reclaim two different origins: on the one hand, a Latin American foundation (in indigenous rebellions); on the other hand, a national (and more orthodox) myth. This second foundation is split into a Peronist myth (October 17, 1945) and what could be defined as a federal one, connected to historical revisionism. In both cases (Latin American and national) single events can be used as foundational myths because an operation has been carried out on the archive (stored memory, in Aleida Assmann's terms). In fact, the events that were selected in the comics to exemplify the conquest or narrate state formation (and the way in which these are interpreted) were not already part of official history (i.e., functional memory). This means that the memory of these events has been reactivated and transferred from stored memory to functional memory. Even though, in the case of federal myths, specialist intervention (A. Assmann 2011) could be envisaged, this does not hold true for Latin American and Peronist origins, which appear definitely as countermemories.

Shifting to the recent past, things become even more complex as, according to Aleida Assmann, we should not expect to find foundational myths (October 17, 1945, and the Peronist resistance) in this recent past. Using this framework, we would fail to inscribe these events into a single category, their contents being part of individual historical experience (communicative memory), but still constructing—and working as—foundational myth (i.e., cultural memory). Present events (1973–1974) work in different ways in the comics *Latinoamérica* and *La guerra*. In both cases, they are used as examples of the need for a revolution, but besides this general and obvious critical meaning, they possess slightly different functions. In *Latinoamérica* the present is a key to understanding the past—the opposite also being true, as we have seen. In *La guerra*, on the contrary, as the present becomes the narrator's recent past, it acts as an index to the present itself, as has been revealed. When, for example, the resistance is about to martial its forces, one of the characters makes a comparison between Antartes and Pinochet, obviously focusing on the reader's present.

Finally, even if the future does not properly fit into the time of memory, we can find a conglomeration of Montoneros' expectations, desires, and (dis)illusions. Utopian and dystopian narratives of the present and past are mixed in a relatively chaotic manner, which well represents the Argentine present of 1973–1974. Structurally speaking, the allegorical organization of this science-fiction comic allows the text to refer to the recent past and the present not only directly but also through allusions, as is the case with the final slaughter scene in the Plaza de Mayo (echoing the Ezeiza Massacre) or Torres' father's depiction, whose resemblance to Héctor "Tío" Cámpora is clear.

Iconic elements play an important role in the last part of *La guerra* and in *Latinoamérica*. Pictures of rallies, the Plaza de Mayo, and pickup trucks constitute the icons of the visual Peronist memory, but their impact on the reader appears to be quite different in the two comics. In one case, it is *epic*; in the other case, *melancholic*. In *Latinoamérica* these images form part of a general revolutionary rhetoric, while in *Guerra* they appear as a last (desperate) call to the rank-and-file leftist-Peronists. If *Latinoamérica* showed an evident *dialogic*—even if conflictual—strategy with the rest of the Peronist field, this purpose has almost completely disappeared in *Guerra*, where the discourse's focus is on the organization itself. Perón disappears from memory only to be replaced by the leader Eleuterio Andrada, whose nickname ("El Grone") can be seen as a tribute to José Sabino Navarro, an important Montoneros leader who had fallen in action three years earlier.

In *Guerra* memory withdraws in on itself. No longer a tool, it becomes a kind of talisman to shelter and protect, the founding memory of another (hi)story. After Perón expelled the Montoneros from the Plaza de Mayo on May 1, 1974, *Guerra*'s daily strips throughout June depicted the epics of resistance and the idyllic relation between the *pueblo* and the leader. What remains is desire: "El Grone" is what Perón should have been but is not. The Montoneros' discourse began trying to interact with and modify Peronist imagery and ended by constructing an imagined Peronism: the Perón-people-Montoneros triangle survives only on paper. The *Juventud maravillosa* was excluded from this love triangle, while the *burocrátas aprovechados* appeared as the real winners in this chess game with death. But that, of course, is another story.

NOTES

1. For further information on Oesterheld's life and works, see Merino (2001).
2. *El Eternauta*'s first version (1957) was illustrated by Francisco Solano López, while the second version (1969) was illustrated by Alberto Breccia. Even though it has basically the same plot, the second version is more graphically experimental and politically more explicit; *El Eternauta II* (1976) was also illustrated by Solano López; in this latter case it seems that Solano López disagreed with Oesterheld on some ideological aspects of the comic itself but, as Oesterheld was already living in clandestinity, Solano López couldn't discuss this with Oesterheld; see Von Sprecher (2005). *Latinoamerica y el Imperialismo: 450 años de Guerra* (*Latinoamérica . . .*) was first published in Montoneros' weekly magazine *El Descamisado* from issue 10 (July 24, 1974) through issue 46 (April 2, 1974) when the magazine was closed down by the government. *La guerra de los Antartes* (*Guerra . . .*) first appeared in *Noticias* on February 27, 1974, and ended on August 27, 1974, when the newspaper was also declared illegal by the National Executive Power.
3. For a further contextualization of Argentinean comics during the 1970s, see Ostuni, García, et al. (n.d.).
4. For more on these aspects, see Jelín (2002: 18): "El pasado que se rememora y se olvida es activado en un presente y en función de expectativas futuras."
5. For an insight into Jan and Aleida Assmann's framework, see Erll (2011 [2005]).
6. On power relations and memory, see Jedlowski (2007).
7. The concept of *performative/performativity* was introduced in linguistics by J. L. Austin in *How to Do Things with Words* (1962); contemporary critical discourse analysis moves toward a slightly different theorization, but Austin is important in having opened up the field of linguistics to *nonrepresentational* theories of language.
8. From cultural history, Matthew B. Karush and Óscar Chamosa (2010) have arrived at a similar account, arguing that novel interpretations of Peronism and its relations with Argentinean society can be achieved only by focusing on its highly discursive nature.
9. Unless otherwise indicated, all translations into English from the original Spanish sources are the author's.
10. Fairclough (2003), when introducing the concept of "hegemony," explicitly refers to Antonio Gramsci's conceptualization in his *Prison Notebooks* (New York: Columbia University Press, 1992).
11. *Latinoamérica y el imperialismo* (the book edition by H. G. Oesterheld and L. Durañona [2004]) is unpaginated; for this reason I refer to the issue number and date of *El Descamisado* in which each chapter first appeared.
12. "The 'official' *mitrista* [from Bartolomé Mitre, the father of Argentine liberal

historiography] version of history deliberately lied for more than a century; it proclaimed its lies in schools, universities, newspapers, and magazines. May Juan Manuel de Rosas be loathed and abhorred for all eternity! That damned tyrant does not deserve even two meters of Argentine soil . . . our real history is very, very different" ("Rosas. Primera Parte," *El Descamisado* 29, December 4, 1973); see also "Rosas. Cuarta parte," *El Descamisado* 32, December 24, 1973): "A dishonest history that has disguised itself and that continues to deceive us today: with the pretense of appeasement, local historians like Félix Luna equate San Martín with Rivadavia, Rosas with Urquiza and with Mitre . . . with this kind of standardizing criteria, Perón ends up lumped with Lanusse, Onganía, Krieger 'Deltec' Vasena and Alsogaray."

13. For a broader discussion of historical revisionism in revolutionary Peronism, see Goebel (2011) and Cristiá (2011).
14. For a discussion on Montoneros' visual propaganda strategies, see Reati (2009).
15. From the mid-1960s to the early 1970s, the most important socioeconomic books on dependence theory were accessible in Argentina: Celso Furtado's *Desarrollo y subdesarrollo* (first edition; Buenos Aires: Eudeba, 1964); Fernando H. Cardoso and Enzo Faletto's *Dependencia y desarrollo en América Latina* (first edition; Buenos Aires: Siglo XXI, 1969); Gunder Franck's *Capitalismo y subdesarrollo en América Latina* (first edition 1965; Argentinean edition: Buenos Aires: Signos, 1970); Theotonio Dos Santos's *Dependencia y cambio social* (1970; Argentinean ed: Buenos Aires: Amorrotu, 1974). In this context, Ariel Dorfmann and Armand Mattelart published the famous analysis of Disney comics and colonialism (*Para leer el pato Donald: Comunicación de masa y colonialismo,* 1971, Buenos Aires: Siglo XXI, 1972); this perspective was also shared and made popular by Eduardo Galeano's best seller *Las venas abiertas de América Latina* (1971) and by Fernando Solanas's documentary *La hora de los hornos* (1968) with which *Latinoamérica* had much in common. For a comparison between *Latinoamérica* and *La hora de los hornos*, see Cristiá (2011).
16. "[The scourge of imperialism which] deprives nations of their basic freedoms by eradicating their self-determination and economic independence" (*El Descamisado* 10, July 24, 1973); see Perón (1953: 17).
17. *Cipayo* is slang for a politician or soldier serving foreign interests as in, for example, *sepoy* soldiers in the British Indian Colonial Army.
18. This same lineage is repeated in *La guerra de los Antartes*.
19. For example: "and that's how Juan Whosoever dies, defending his country. Fighting against imperialism, just like so many other 'Juan Whosoevers' who will come after him. Juan, the warrior of Güernes, Juan Moreno of Sanmartín, Juan Mazorquero, Juan the Revolutionary of 1890, Juan of the Resistance, Juan Montonero" (*El Descamisado* 13, August 14, 1973). On the representation of indigenous people, Afro-Americans, and women in *Latinoamérica*, see Héctor Fernández L'Hoeste

(2011). The abundance of collective heroes, besides being a classical element in Oesterheld's comics, is related to the need for heroes by the movement, which lacked public and official monuments.

20. The terms *civilization* and *barbarism*, as set out by future Argentine president Domingo Faustino Sarmiento in the nineteenth century, refer to the tension he perceived between the modernizing metropolis of Buenos Aires with its European cultural heritage and Argentina's rural interior, which he saw as backward and uncivilized.
21. "The Spanish conquest of South America is what made the Industrial Revolution in England possible. . . . The reconquest of South America by the Antartes opened up unforeseen possibilities for the U.S. and Russia" (Oesterheld and Trigo 1998: 62).
22. The agreement between the United States and the Soviet Union can be seen as an overlap between Perón's *tercera posición* and the nonaligned movement of which Argentina had become a member in 1973.
23. See, for example: "If the Antartes really adopt a peaceful approach, humanity will be able to enjoy enormous progress under their leadership! They have a far higher level of development than we do." The invaders' rhetoric mimics this sentiment: "We Antartes bring peace and prosperity! Our technology is significantly more advanced than yours and it will be used to improve conditions here on Earth!" (Oesterheld and Trigo 1998: 58).
24. The second scene of the massacre in Plaza de Mayo was originally published in *Noticias* (204, June 21, 1974), an issue that commemorated the Ezeiza Massacre on its front page.
25. On the Peronist resistance myth, see Gillespie (1982) and James (1988).
26. According to Austin (1962), a performative utterance is neither true nor false but (un)felicitous depending on specific conditions, such as appropriateness of context and participants' or speaker's authority/ability to formulate a particular utterance for a specific statement ("I now pronounce you man and wife" is "felicitous" only if the speaker is entitled to marry people).
27. An example of this change in literature is Germán Rozenmacher's short story "Cabecita Negra"; see Avellaneda (2002).

REFERENCES

Assmann, A. 2011 [1999]. *Cultural Memory and Western Civilization*. Cambridge: Cambridge University Press.

Assmann, J. 2011 [1992]. *Cultural Memory and Early Civilization: Writing, Remembrance, and Political Imagination*. Cambridge: Cambridge University Press.

Austin, J. L. 1962. *How to Do Things with Words*. Oxford: Clarendon Press.

Avellaneda, A. 2002. "Evita: Cuerpo y cadáver de la literatura." In *Evita, mito y representaciones*. Edited by M. Navarro, 43–64. Buenos Aires: Fondo de Cultura Económica.

Barker, C., and D. Galasiński. 2001. *Cultural Studies and Discourse Analysis: A Dialogue on Language and Identity*. London: Sage.

Benítez, O. N.d. "Historietas montoneras: Imaginario social de la izquierda peronista 1973–1974." Online at http://historiapolitica.com/datos/biblioteca/benitezl.pdf. Accessed on September 15, 2012.

Cristiá, M. 2011. "Falsa la historia que nos enseñaron." Argumentos visuales, sensibilización y revisión de la historia desde el peronismo revolucionario (Argentina, 1966/1976). In *VIII Jornada Internacional de Historia de las Sensibilidades. Historias e historiografías de la subversión en las Américas: Dinámicas narrativas, dinámicas políticas, dinámicas historiográficas*. L'École des hautes études en sciences sociales (EHESS), Paris, March 23, 2011. Online at http://nuevomundo.revues.org/61131?lang=en. Accessed on September 15, 2012.

Depetris Chauvin, I. 2004. "Historieta, memoria e identidad política: 'La guerra de los Antartes' de Oesterheld en Noticias, 1974." *Anuario Escuela de Historia* 20: 97–117.

D'Haen, T. 2007. "Memoria culturale e studi postcoloniali." In *Memoria e saperi: Percorsi transdisciplinari*. Edited by E. Agazzi and V. Fortunati, 625–36. Rome: Meltemi.

Erll, A. 2011 [2005]. *Memory in Culture*. Basingstoke, Hampshire: Palgrave Macmillan.

Erll, A. 2008. "Cultural Memory Studies: An Introduction." In *Cultural Memory Studies: An International and Interdisciplinary Handbook*. Edited by A. Erll and A. Nünning, 1–15. Berlin: de Gruyter.

Fairclough, N. 2003. *Analysing Discourse: Textual Analysis for Social Research*. New York: Routledge.

Fairclough, N., and R. Wodak. 1997. "Critical Discourse Analysis." In *Discourse as Social Interaction*. Edited by T. A. van Dijk, 258–84. London: Sage.

Fernández L'Hoeste, H. 2011. "Del nacionalismo como treta de la imaginación identitaria en 450 años de guerra contra el imperialismo, de Héctor Germán Oesterheld y Leopoldo Durañona." *Revista Iberoamericana* 234: 41–57.

Gillespie, R. 1982. *Soldiers of Perón: Argentina's montoneros*. Oxford: Oxford University Press.

Goebel, M. 2011. *Argentina's Partisan Past: Nationalism and the Politics of History*. Liverpool: Liverpool University Press.

Goebel, M. 2004. "La prensa peronista como medio de difusión del revisionismo histórico, 1955–1958." *Prohistoria*, no. 8: 251–66.

Grande, T. 2007. "Memoria, storia e pratiche sociali." In *Memoria e saperi: Percorsi transdisciplinari*. Edited by E. Agazzi and V. Fortunati, 31–47. Rome: Meltemi.

Habermas, J. 1988. "Concerning the Public Use of History." *New German Critique* 44: 40–50.

Harth, D. 2008. "The Invention of Cultural Memory." In *Cultural Memory Studies: An International and Interdisciplinary Handbook*. Edited by A. Erll and A. Nünning, 85–96. Berlin: de Gruyter.

James, D. 1988. *Resistance and Integration: Peronism and the Argentine Working Class, 1946–1976*. Cambridge: Cambridge University Press.

Jedlowski, B. 2007. "Memoria e interazioni sociali." In *Memoria e saperi: Percorsi transdisciplinari*. Edited by E. Agazzi and V. Fortunati, 31–47. Rome: Meltemi.

Jelín, E. 2002. *Los trabajos de la memoria*. Madrid: Siglo XXI.

Karush, M. B., and O. Chamosa. 2010. *The New Cultural History of Peronism: Power and Identity in Mid-twentieth-century Argentina*. Durham, NC: Duke University Press.

Merino, A. 2001. "Oesterheld, the Literary Voice of Argentine Comics." *International Journal of Comic Art* 3, no. 2: 56–69.

Neumann, B. 2007. "La performatività del ricordo." In *Memoria e saperi: Percorsi transdisciplinari*. Edited by E. Agazzi and V. Fortunati, 305–22. Rome: Meltemi.

Nora, P. 1984–1992. *Les lieux de mémoire*. Paris: Gallimard.

Nünning, A., and A. Erll, eds. 2008. *Cultural Memory Studies: An International and Interdisciplinary Handbook*. Berlin: de Gruyter.

Oesterheld, H. G., and L. Durañona. 2004. *Latinoamérica y el Imperialismo: 450 años de guerra*. Buenos Aires: Doeyo y Viniegra Editores.

Oesterheld, H. G., and G. Trigo. 1998. *La Guerra de los Antartes*. Buenos Aires: Colihue.

Ostuni, H., F. García, et al. N.d. "Politics, Activism, Repression, and Comics in Argentina during the 1970s." Online at http://www.camouflagecomics.com/pdf/03_bordel_en.pdf. Accessed on September 15, 2012.

Perón, J. D. 1953. *Política y estrategia (no ataco, critico)*. Reprint 2006. Buenos Aires: Instituto Nacional Juan Domingo Perón.

Reati, F. 2009. "Argentina's Montoneros: Comics, Cartoons, and Images as Political Propaganda in the Underground Guerrilla Press of the 1970s." In *Redrawing the Nation: National Identity in Latin/o American Comics*. Edited by H. Fernández L'Hoeste and J. Poblete, 97–110. New York: Palgrave MacMillan.

Sigal, S., and E. Verón. 1986. *Perón o muerte: Los fundamentos discursivos del fenómeno peronista*. Reprint 2008. Buenos Aires: EUDEBA.

Tilmans, K., F. V. Vree, and J. M. Winter. 2010. *Performing the Past: Memory, History, and Identity in Modern Europe*. Amsterdam: Amsterdam University Press.

Trillo, C., and G. Saccomanno. 2005. "El (¿último?) gran reportaje." In *Oesterheld en primera persona*, 13–33. Buenos Aires: La Bañadera del Comic.

Vezzetti, H. 2007. "Conflictos de la memoria en la Argentina: Un estudio histórico de la memoria social." In *Historizar el pasado vivo en América Latina*. Edited by A. Pérotin-Dumon. Online at www.historizarelpasadovivo.cl/downloads/vezzetti.pdf. Accessed on September 15, 2012.

Von Sprecher, R. 2007. "Discurso montonero en las historietas de Héctor Germán Oesterheld." *Revista Astrolabio*, 04. Online at www.astrolabio.unc.edu.ar/articulos/filosofiasocial/articulos/vonsprecher.php. Accessed on September 15, 2012.

Von Sprecher, R. 2005. "Las transformaciones en la construcción de la subjetividad de los personajes de Héctor G. Oesterheld desde El Eternauta a la Guerra de los Antartes." In *Las (trans)formaciones de las subjetividades en la cultura contemporánea: Reflexiones e intervenciones desde la comunicación*. By various authors. Villa María (Córdoba): Red nacional de investigación en Comunicación.

THREE

MAFALDA

TALISMAN OF DEMOCRACY AND ICON OF NOSTALGIA FOR THE 1960S

Isabella Cosse

"If Quino were still drawing her, Mafalda would now be among the thirty thousand disappeared in Argentina."[1] With this 1988 headline, the Spanish magazine *Cambio 16* placed the creation of Quino—the pseudonym of Joaquín Salvador Lavado—at the heart of the crisis faced by Argentine society after the violation of human rights carried out during the 1976–1983 military dictatorship. In the years that followed, the comic would become part of the social processing of that recent, painful, and unresolved past. Only *Mafalda* could fulfill such a role because the strip was already a social phenomenon, surpassing individual experiences and subjectivities to engage with collective identities and sociopolitical realities within and beyond Argentina.[2]

When Quino created Mafalda, he never imagined such a future for his cartoon. He first sketched *Mafalda* for an advertising campaign for electrical appliances. The agency that commissioned him was hoping to produce a subliminal effect, and it asked him to draw an "average" family similar to those in the popular U.S. strips *Dagwood* and *Peanuts*. For reasons that had nothing to do with the comic, the campaign went no further. Quino reworked the idea, however, and began to publish the strip in the magazine *Primera Plana*, focal point of the journalistic revival of the 1960s, which set out to create a new modern elite of executives, professionals, and intellectuals. In the pages of *Primera Plana*, Mafalda—the "intellectualized girl"—embodied the destabilization of gender roles and generational hierarchies: she adopted traits and attitudes traditionally associated with men and challenged her parents from the very first strip. Quino used Mafalda to push his irony and ingenuity to their limits. With inferred references, implicit speech, and open endings, his humoristic strategies played with the increasingly blurred boundaries between the public and the private, an effect of bourgeois modernity, by throwing light on the political via the family and vice versa. The comic began to be published in the newspaper *El Mundo*. With the demands of daily submissions, Quino added new child characters, including Susanita (the "housewife") and Manolito (the immigrant who aspires to climb the social ladder). Tapping into different social stereotypes made the story line more complex. A sense of belonging quickly formed around the comic since it enabled readers to process the tensions generated by sociocultural modernization and the frailties of Argentine democracy (Cosse 2014a).

The comic's political meaning had a "real" presence beyond the frames: the character Mafalda embodied the identity of a progressive middle class person, and the comic strip in its entirety expressed the heterogeneous composition of a middle class marked by cultural and ideological differences. Its sociopolitical importance was highlighted when one image, published on the same day as the military coup led by General Juan Carlos Onganía in 1966, became an antiauthoritarian emblem expressing the desire for democracy. In the years that followed, Quino condemned political repression under Onganía and in 1970 created the character of Libertad, a symbol of the politicized youth. As the degree of political polarization and violence increased, Mafalda was caught in the crossfire, labeled as subversive by the conservative right and as a member of the petite bourgeoisie by the revolutionary left. Given this panorama, in 1973 Quino decided to stop creating new strips. There was no longer any place for a comic in which ideological and cultural disputes (such as those constantly expressed by the disagreements between Mafalda and Susanita) sat alongside each other in harmony. Symbolically, Quino's characters said goodbye to their readers on the very same pages that were reporting the "massacre at Ezeiza," the violent attack by the Peronist right on the Peronist left on the occasion of Juan Domingo Perón's return to Argentina from exile. This event resulted in dozens of deaths and demonstrated the bloody fashion in which Argentine society would now process its differences (Cosse 2014b).

By saying farewell, *Mafalda* altered the pact it had established with its readers. Broken were the close ties between the strip's fictional world and the everyday context that it represented. Its readers could no longer demand that the strip's characters offer their take on the surrounding political landscape. The end of *Mafalda* meant that it was protected from the controversies that such views might have generated in what was an increasingly turbulent social reality. In 1973 the importance of Quino's decision was not immediately evident but, over time, it helped the more atemporal meanings of the comic, as well as the new meanings created by the manner in which the strip was constantly being reworked and brought up to date, to endure. As a result, Quino unwittingly breathed fresh life into his creation. The updated pact with its readers meant that *Mafalda* began to evoke meanings tied to the time of its creation and daily publication (the 1960s), mobilizing the history of the strip itself and its relationship to the lives of individual readers. It began, in short, to speak to the relationship between past and present. *Mafalda* was located in the sphere of collective memory.

There are numerous studies of *Mafalda*. One line of research has approached the strip by analyzing it in terms of social communication, linguistics, semiotics, and the graphic image (among the most important of which are Steimberg 1977: 174–76 and Latxague 2011). Other studies have taken an entirely different approach, looking at the social and the political within the strip by putting the comic in dialogue with its political context and with such issues as the relations between generations, transformations in family life, and Argentine national identity (Sasturain 1995: 167–77; Foster 1980 and 1989; Wainerman 2005: 69–71; Fernández L'Hoeste 1998). This chapter, part of a larger study situated between these approaches, takes a more markedly historical approach (Cosse 2014a). More specifically, I address the new meanings attributed to *Mafalda* during the 1980s and 1990s when the strip was located in the field of collective memory and disputes over the recent past. I take memory, following Maurice Halbwachs (2004 [1925]), to be a social product that involves a process of selection and, as a result, of memories and forgetting in which different groups and actors intervene according to their own interests and present values.

In Argentina and Latin America more broadly, such productions of memory have had considerable political and social significance in the debates over the most effective ways to safeguard democracy, over determining responsibility for human rights violations, and, more recently, over grasping how in previous decades such acts of violence could have come about. In that sense my analysis draws together two lines of inquiry. On the one hand, it is linked to memory studies that have demonstrated the complexity and density of the debates over the ideas, representations and understanding of state terrorism and human rights violations.[3] On the other hand, it is tied to those studies of recent history that, focusing on the 1960s, have taken great strides in understanding a period marked by social, cultural, and political radicalization and by the rise of violence and authoritarianism.[4] *Mafalda* therefore offers a bridge between those studies rooted in the memory of repression and the more recent research into the period of the comic's creation.

I aim to understand the meanings attributed to *Mafalda* in the 1980s and 1990s, when it was positioned in the field of social memory. The way its meaning was located in the present was tied to events that shook Argentine society and everyday life across Latin America and beyond, namely the trials of those who had violated human rights, debates over the 1960s and 1970s, and the rise of neoliberalism. Within this context, both the comic and the character became image, object, and mode of questioning the past but always in relation to the realities and struggles created by the crisis in the sense of belonging that it had fomented. These questions over the past, facilitated by *Mafalda*, allow us to assess how a certain progressive sensibility addressed, during the 1980s, political debates over human rights and the political violence of the 1970s and in the 1990s the abandonment of social utopias and the triumph of neoliberalism.

MAFALDA IN THE FIELD OF MEMORY DURING THE RETURN TO DEMOCRACY

In Argentina the return to democracy in 1983 was dominated by the legacies of the dictatorship: economic crisis and human rights violations. In response, the government of President Raúl Alfonsín created an investigative commission of dignitaries, which would subsequently produce the *Nunca Más* report. The commission revealed, in the authoritative voice of its members, the terrible violence carried out by state terrorism and the scale of the disappearances (Crenzel 2008). Soon after, the government set in motion the trial of the former leaders of the military dictatorship, which represented an affirmation of democracy and a victory for the human rights movement. Nevertheless, military unrest increased and the threat of military uprisings demonstrated the intent of the armed forces.

Within that context the government put forward the Punto Final Law, approved by Congress in December 1986, which put a time limit of sixty days for new cases to be brought against perpetrators of human rights violations. Rejected by the human rights organizations, the law resulted in around three hundred court summonses in the early months of 1987. The military response was swift. During Easter week in April 1987 a group led by Aldo Rico took over the military base of Campo de Mayo. Civil protests, encouraged by the president, filled public squares, while government-led negotiations brought about the group's surrender. In the midst of the uprising, Quino lent his support to democracy by sending a picture of Mafalda to the president. Looking at the viewer and seated in her little chair, she said: "What a mess, don Raulito! . . ." "But you can count on us," "Democracy! Justice! Liberty! Life!" (Quino 1993b: 41–43). Quino himself explained that he had sent the drawing after reflecting critically on the role that humor had played in the ridiculing of the radical president Arturo Illia in 1966, when jokes about the inefficient nature of his government increased support for a coup, one that eventually arrived and brought General Juan Carlos Onganía to power.[5] *Mafalda* participated, in this way, in mobilizing vast sectors of society, including an intellectual middle class, who came out to defend democracy and human rights.[6] The comic strip's affinity with the democratic creed gave it unprecedented recognition.

In 1988 the celebrations for the twenty-fifth anniversary of *Mafalda* helped the comic to be brought up-to-date and placed definitively within the field of collective memory. A retrospective exhibit that included unpublished strips was held as part of the celebrations in the prestigious San Martín Theatre, a place associated with the democratization process as a result of its liberal programming and because it was there that the commission investigating the disappearances had held their meetings. The exhibit was visited by thousands of people, and its content was published as a book, *Mafalda inédita* [Mafalda unpublished]. Quino contributed to both the exhibit and the book, as did the publishing house Ediciones de la Flor, which had been publishing the strip in Argentina since the 1970s; Alicia and Julieta Colombo, Quino's wife and niece and also his representatives, who compiled the texts; and Sylvina Walger, who undertook journalistic research (Quino 1988).

Both the exhibit and the book were a huge success, appealing to a public loyal to the strip and who would likely be interested in the offcuts of a work that, as tends to happen with classics, had increased in standing as time passed. In the Buenos Aires Book Fair, *Mafalda* was an explosive and irrefutable success story, and the long queues to get books signed were formed by grandparents, parents, and children. The book's publishers, encouraged by the teenage son of its owners, distributed a questionnaire among the public that was completed by thirty-five hundred "experts," those able to remember such details as Mafalda's age or Manolito's surname.[7] The comic, according to the editors, had by that point sold some six million copies worldwide.

Memory lay at the heart of these events, which stirred up the subjective

However, he did agree to bring Mafalda back to life, using her symbolic force, to defend democracy. He drew her for a poster used by the Ministry of Foreign Affairs after a half-decade of democracy. When presenting a new book with unpublished strips to Raúl Alfonsín, Quino included a dedication that read: "To the president capable of showing that what they teach us in school can be true!" (Quino 1993b: 37). His words echoed the famous strip, published the day of the coup that brought Onganía to power, in which Mafalda wonders about what she is being taught at school—a reference to the content of the democratic education that ironically had been introduced by the government that had ousted General Juan Domingo Perón in 1955. Quino thus attempted to exorcise a past marked by coups d'états by using the symbolic force of *Mafalda*.

Nevertheless, the hopes placed in democracy by vast sectors of Argentine society were quickly dashed, buried in the ruins of the economic, social, and political crisis. In the midst of the economic downturn, with a wave of strikes brought about by a fall in wages and inflation, the military threats increased. An uprising toward the end of 1988, led by Colonel Mohamed Alí Seinaldín, who was demanding amnesty for the Armed Forces and their vindication, was put down but it still demonstrated the weakness of the government. The political scene was further complicated a month later with the assault on La Tablada barracks by a group of armed left-wing militants. In May 1989 the victory of the Peronist leader Carlos Saúl Menem in the elections sealed the end of Alfonsín's government. Amid hyperinflation and supermarket sackings, the increasingly fragile president handed power over early to Menem.

The new government quickly offered a pardon to those members of the military who had been convicted for carrying out repressive activities during the dictatorship and to those who had been members of the guerrilla organizations. A year later, the measure was extended to include the members of the military juntas and the leaders of the guerrilla organization Montoneros. In Italy for Mafalda celebrations, Quino stated to the magazine *L'Espresso* that "reprieves dent democracy," a phrase that took up once again, albeit with a new twist, the metaphor that he had created three decades earlier with the "little club for denting democracy."[11] In the latest context, the "little club" alluded to the reprieve that let the repressors go free, perpetuating the legacy of those who had repressed ideas twenty years earlier. In this way the scene prior to the dictatorship was tied to its aftermath via the demand for justice and democracy. In turn, the fresh meanings given to the strip would be characterized by the rise of neoliberalism.

THE LEGACY OF THE 1960S IN THE NEOLIBERAL ERA

Placing Mafalda in the field of memory meant tying her to debates over human rights violations in Argentina and also, in a broader sense, to debates over the 1960s that were taking place within the context of the ideological and economic rise of neoliberalism. In 1988 and more or less simultaneously across several continents, the celebrations for the twenty-fifth anniversary of *Mafalda* favored this particular contextual reading of the comic. The feedback created by international press agencies, with the multiple impact of news stories about the anniversary, the celebrations, and the history of the strip, provided a certain unity to rereadings of the comic among its public in, among other places, Italy, Spain, and Mexico—three of the strip's most important markets as a result of the comic's immense popularity in those countries during the 1970s (see Cosse 2014b).

On an international level, the twentieth anniversary of the 1968 student uprisings stimulated debate about the 1960s. As so often happens, the aura of the round number encouraged reevaluations of the past and projections about the future. To different degrees in each country, the 1960s generation remained at the center of public opinion and political debate. As a result, controversies over the legacy of the conflictive nature of that past, and over the political meaning that it had in the present, intensified. The debates took place in a divided ideological field in which socialism was in crisis—the Berlin Wall came down in 1989—and the right was on the rise. Some critiqued "the fabrication of the sacrosanct generation" and the "melancholy reassessment of the *gauchiste* adventure" (Nora 1996: 500). Others, by contrast, were ready to defend the "spirit" of 1968 by celebrating collective action, the libertarian ideal, and the utopian imagination.

It was in that context that, in 1988, the twenty-fifth anniversary celebrations for *Mafalda* were held. In Spain they began with the publication of *Mafalda inédita* [Mafalda unpublished] and with a retrospective exhibition. According to an article in *Cambio 16*, the comic stirred up opinions about the generation of the 1960s and 1970s. Mafalda was "an early feminist, television critic, concerned by ecology, the future of Humanity and the yellow peril." The journalist remembered a strip in which the "intellectualized girl" recognized that "if you don't hurry up and change the world, soon the world will change you." The same caustic irony was evident in the Spanish testimonies, collected by the journalist, that projected onto Mafalda critiques of the former rebels of 1968. One interviewee, for example, imagined that Mafalda would have become a "conservative liberal" in much the same way as those "who were involved in the events of May 1968 were now yuppies."[12]

The anniversary triggered memories in those who had been young in the 1970s when the comic was part of anti-Franco cultural expression. Censorship meant that *Mafalda* had been banned for those underage and the comic carried a warning to that effect on its album covers. But censorship also encouraged the identification of the comic with a public keen to make fun of the tiresome obscurantism of the regime, turning it into a best seller. Its conceptual humor was in tune with those who were used to reading between the lines and who lived in a climate of repression. For those readers, *Mafalda* returned them to the sensitive and personal backbone of that period, that of their youth, a time when they were leading the struggle against Franco and participating in the cultural fervor that came with the transition to democracy. The comic allowed them to recover the certainty of a better future in which the collective and the personal, the political and private, were intertwined. The longevity of the comic's success, which continued to sell as well as it had in its "golden period" when "that Argentine girl was considered to be a genuine figure of rebellion," meant it could participate in the critique of the neoliberal order. Such a viewpoint could be found in the conclusion to another article published in the newspaper *ABC*: "We hope that, even if only in Quino's memory, that girl . . . carries on thinking that the Beatles could have been the best presidents of the world."[13]

It was not possible for that past to return. Not even *Mafalda* could come back to life, as Quino stated again and again. Therein lay the appeal of the game of imagining what its characters would be like as adults. In that sense, *Mafalda inédita* restored the pleasurable experience of coming across unknown strips and bringing the social act of their reading up to the present. It reinstalled a community of belonging among those who shared a sufficiently in-depth knowledge of the comic to be interested in a cult publication but who also shared an ideological space that gave meaning to its reading. As a result, the comic could be tied to other cultural expressions, handed down by the 1960s, that symbolized the belonging to a space on the left, one that was progressive and allied in its resistance to the rise of neoliberalism. That link, for example, was referred to in *El País*, which reported that the book included a drawing of Mafalda that had been intended for the album *El Sur también existe*, recorded by Joan Manuel Serrat and with poems by Mario Benedetti, but which in the end had not been included in the disk.[14] There had been "a misunderstanding between a Catalan and an Andalusian," as Quino himself put it—an anecdote that revealed the sensibility that emerges from artistic and ideological empathy. It is not by chance that during this period *Mafalda* began to be published in *La Vanguardia*, the historical Catalan newspaper affiliated with the Socialist Party, which included the strip on the back cover of its magazine as part of its 1989 redesign.[15]

In Italy the launch of *Mafalda 25*, a compilation with unpublished drawings released by the publishing house Bompiani, made the comic visible to the public. In the country where Quino continued to spend long periods of time, the strip was still being published in the newspaper *Il Messagero* and Mafalda was enshrined as "the rebel par excellence." As *L'Unitá* had suggested earlier, the protagonist was considered to be a "small feminist witch," born in the midst of the women's movement and an "enfant terrible" who, located in a "normal family," had turned into a bomb ready to explode. It was for that reason, the paper maintained, that the comic's creator had had to silence her in 1973.[16] When the book with the unpublished drawings was published, the press included declarations by Quino himself who, after remembering that his creation was a child of the era of the Beatles, "Che" Guevara, and the decolonization process in Africa, said: "All that no longer means anything. Now all people want to do is to earn the biggest amount of money possible in the shortest period of time. There's no room for childhood dreams and my viewpoint is increasingly innocent and naïve."[17]

Mafalda enabled a rereading of the 1960s in Latin America. In 1988, Quino took *Mafalda inédita* to the Guadalajara Book Fair. On that occasion the magazine *Plural*, edited by left-wing intellectuals, put into circulation a large number of the unpublished drawings by including them as part of a long article. As the columnist explained, in Mexico, just as in other countries, *Mafalda* "satisfied those varied readers who identified with its rebellious attitude towards the spheres of the family and school, and in its judgments and assessments of the state of the world." The ideological meaning of that position was reinforced at the end of the article where Quino confessed his unease and expressed his political position with a directness not seen in public up to that point, but which would be increasingly evident in the future: "I think capitalism is shit, I think it's the worst of systems, but the socialist countries are taking a step backwards in terms of their orthodoxy. . . . With leaders like 'Che' Guevara, Ho Chi-Minh, Mao, Pope John XXIII gone, I'm very lost."[18]

In 1988 the celebrations for *Mafalda* brought back to life a legacy that, with varying local manifestations, reintroduced the validity of the ideals of political commitment and social change dating from the 1960s that were increasingly meaningful in the context of the rise of ideological and social neoliberalism. The circulation of unpublished drawings revitalized the story of the comic's origins by broadening its circulation and contributing anecdotes to a narrative about the social meaning of the past. Reading *Mafalda* enabled people to return to collective events that were part of their own memories and to use them to give meaning to the present. As a result, the public never tired of seeing *Mafalda* in the media. Memory awakened feelings of nostalgia.

GENERATIONAL NOSTALGIA

In 1995, Eric Hobsbawm (1995: 10) considered it inevitable that his history of the twentieth century, written at the start of the 1990s, would end with a "view into obscurity." He thought that the magnitude of the crisis was not only a result of the collapse of the world economy or of the collapse of the socialist block but of the loss of beliefs and humanist and rationalist principles. But his diagnosis was even more serious. The backward steps in the foundation of modern civilization—taken by both liberal capitalism and communism—were tied to a crisis in "the historic structures of human relations." That is to say, in his terms, the collapse affected all possible ways of organizing society (11). His unease was not the result of the irritated viewpoint of an obstinate Marxist historian; it expressed a climate that colored the reflexions of those who, with varying ideological standpoints, were not prepared to resign themselves to the end of a historical period marked by faith in humanity and the utopia of a better world.

That climate took on specific characteristics in Argentina. The government of Carlos Saúl Menem refashioned the Peronist leadership by distancing it from the party's historical principles of state interventionism and a politics of welfare and social inclusion. It privatized public entities and fired thousands of public employees, and the indiscriminate freedom given to the economy affected large sectors of the working and middle classes, who watched as the material and symbolic place they had held in the past came apart at the seams.[19] Such measures resulted in the emergence of a new cycle of social protests that drew on certain slogans and methods used by human rights organizations (Filc 1998). Indeed, in the midst of the 1990s and particularly around the time of the commemoration of twenty years since the 1976 coup, new debates about dictatorial repression emerged that placed memory and the role of the 1960s generation center stage (see, among others, Lorenz 2002).

In this context the comic became part of the cultural expressions that confronted the rise of neoliberalism and the showbiz style and frivolity of

Menemism. Mafalda provided a space for outright opposition, bringing together ideology, aesthetics, and subjectivity as part of a process that was giving renewed importance to the legacy of the 1960s generation. The strip was in tune with those groups—new social movements, intellectuals, and a progressive public opinion—that were demanding the importance of political commitment in the public sphere and the ideals of equity and social integration. Such expressions were particularly meaningful because they flew in the face of a certain naturalization of the legitimacy that was being given to the logic of economic profitability and to the supposed diagnosis of the end of history that was dominating the cultural and political field.

That meaning was fomented by the celebrations for thirty years of *Mafalda*. The year 1993 saw the publication of *Toda Mafalda* [Complete Mafalda] (Quino 1993b), which contained for the first time all the strips in one book, and the inauguration of the exhibit of Quino's work titled "Páginas de Humor" [Funny pages], which opened in the Centro Cultural Recolecta, in Buenos Aires, a leading art space.[20] At this time, Menem's government was reinforcing its power base after electoral triumphs that boosted plans for the presidential reelection campaign. *Mafalda* revived a middle-class identity that had been eroding for some time but which Menemism had ferociously assaulted. The government was not only destroying the material foundations that supported that identity, but it was also encouraging a culture of an internally divided middle class. In a symbolic way, this middle class was abandoning the urban grid (the neighborhood, the square, the public school) that the comic itself had exalted, in favor of the culture of the suburban country club, the shopping center, and the private bilingual school.[21] The reviews of the launch of *Toda Mafalda* described the strength of that threatened identity that seemed to want to sustain itself via the durability of threatened cultural principles: parents who took their children to a bookshop; children interested in asking questions; teachers who remembered playing at identifying the Manolitos and Mafaldas among their new students. As well as demonstrating admiration, that kind of folklore validated an Argentina that had formed a powerful middle class but that had also praised state intervention to prevent social inequality.[22]

"Menem and Quino" was the title used by *Página 12*, at the time the leading opposition newspaper, for the article that reported on the retrospective exhibit of works by Quino but that did not include *Mafalda*. In honor of the person he regarded as his mentor, Miguel Rep, a humorist of the new generation, stirred up the symbolic confrontation between those two Argentinas: "Argentina is indeed a strange country, capable of giving us and the world a refined man, more sensitive than anyone else, producer of the most intelligent graphic humor. Such is the nature of this inexplicable nation that it can create Quino on the one hand and so much arrogant tack on the other. Today you should go and see the genius from Mendoza, Quino, touch him, have a glass of wine with the maestro, see the light that he emanates and look at his humorous pages, cut yourself off for a moment from everything that surrounds us, and then come back, but slightly changed. Quino is exhibiting from today, and it's a miracle. Menem creates an exhibit almost every day." The conflict of sensibilities could not have been clearer. The cultured, European, intelligent, and witty country was facing the high-handedness and bad taste of a character whose "type"—unworthy of being Argentine—needed no explanation for readers.[23]

The event demonstrated the coming together of that besieged country. One young man, surprised by the presence of Alfonsín, said to the press: "Here there are old people, children, those in the middle and presidents, everyone." Seemingly, *Mafalda* was the only absence but its presence became inevitable, not just because the gathering was interceded by its social meaning—that of the Argentine "melting pot," proud of its middle class—but also because the readers brought the strip with them.[24] They took the recently published *Toda Mafalda* for Quino to autograph. The press registered its presence in even more symbolic fashion. The correspondent from *Clarín* saw an enfant terrible playing with a ball by the entrance to the Cultural Centre. Her father told her off using her name: "Mafalda!" According to the journalist, she had been named after the 1960s child.[25]

Such an interpretation was present in other interventions that used the comic to refer to the latest social processes that Argentine society was experiencing. In this vein, Jorge Schvarzer, in *Página 12*, took the strip to be a symbol of a middle class fractured by successive economic crises. *Mafalda* looked back to the "idyllic world" of equitable social distribution that had collapsed. According to the author, one part of that middle class—its "backbone," comprised of teachers and public employees—was getting poorer, while another sector got rich on the back of speculative investments and new "niches" in the market. No one was better placed to express such divisions as Mafalda. Once again, Manolito was bitter because his parents' grocery store had gone bankrupt while Susanita was coming back from Disneyland. Scholar Luis Alberto Quevedo saw the same phenomenon: "Mafalda demonstrated the virtues and miseries of a class that had been living its best moment" but that was "taking its summer holidays on the patio."[26]

The celebrations demonstrated the all-encompassing nature of the generational renewal. At the Book Fair, held in the Centro Municipal de Exposiciones, more than one hundred children had come to get the artist's signature, in addition to hundreds of adults who wanted an autograph for themselves or for children or grandchildren. A conversation between Quino and twenty children was organized at the stand of the Unión de Trabajadores de Prensa de Buenos Aires (Press Workers Union of Buenos Aires).[27] New merchandise such as Mafalda figurines began to be sold to a younger audience. The sugar confectionery company Lipo launched a chewing gum whose slogan—"At last! . . . a gum for thinking"—was illustrated with Mafalda, and school folders and sheets of paper with drawings of the characters were sold.[28] There was, as a result, a generational broadening of the reading public.

The anniversary updated the social and political meaning of the comic. The appropriations created a dialogue with the social processes that affected Argentine society and, in particular, large sectors of the middle classes that, with economic crises and neoliberal economic adjustment, had been ejected from their former social and symbolic positions. The comic even supported academic interpretations into this process of social, political, and symbolic fractures. The admiration for *Mafalda* helped support an identity wounded by economic impoverishment that was at odds with a modern, altogether different middle-class culture. The crisis gave increased meaning to the comic and to associated cultural practices like going to exhibits, visiting the Book Fair, and buying books. Acquiring the comic itself expressed resistance to the liberal order on the part of that sector of the middle class.[29] The collection of the original books of the comic had sold, according to the calculations of Daniel Divinsky, the cofounder of Ediciones de la Flor, some twenty million copies: *Mafalda inédita* (published in 1988) had sold out its 115,000 copies and *Toda Mafalda*, released the previous year with 650 pages and quality binding, had sold 55,000 copies with another 15,000 being printed.[30] But the number of readers was even greater. Paradoxically, the introduction of convertibility, which pegged the Argentine peso 1:1 with the U.S. dollar, with its temporary economic boom, helped the process of obtaining production rights for a strip in conflict with the ideology that sustained that very model. As a result, the comic was reproduced in numerous newspapers in the interior of Argentina.[31]

Outside the country, the anniversary came at a point when the comic had gained greater visibility. In Italy it revived Quino's intellectual and artistic standing. The celebration, held in Il Circolo de la Stampa in Milan, included the participation of figures of considerable standing such as Umberto Eco, whose reading of the comic had been extremely important. On this occasion, Eco imagined an encyclopedia edited in 2040 in which the entry for Quino would read "twentieth-century cartoonist and moralist." Almost simultaneously, in the children's book fair held in Bologna, homage was paid to the comic with the presentation of *I Pensieri di Mafalda*, an edition of the strips organized thematically (everyday life, economics and politics, pessimism and optimism, Mafalda and company) and *Il Mondo de Mafalda*, published the previous year (Quino 1993a and 1994).[32]

Quino, on his part, said that he was not concerned about the anniversary of the comic but about Berlusconi's Italy and the "centennial celebrations" of the right across the world.[33] The declaration implied a clear identification with the left and, as such, with the utopias of the 1960s. The same happened with Mafalda's appearances in the mass media. In 1991, for example, a television programme entitled "Mafalda," which paid homage to the character, had managed to get an audience of almost six million viewers, promising them a "provocative and transgressive" key for understanding women in the workplace. As Neva Kohman—Italian librarian—remembered, many girls in the 1970s saw themselves in Mafalda not just because of her qualities ("woman," "rebel," "incomparable") but also because of her struggle against injustice and her love of humanity (Quino 2010: 587). Quino explained that "Mafalda wanted to change the world. Young people today just think about getting a job" and he added: "There are more Manolitos and Susanitas than Mafaldas and Felipes."

In Spain, the thirty-year anniversary saw the social game of imagining the destiny of characters reaching fever pitch. *El País* recognized with some irony that, with a certain lack of ideological belief, comics had replaced the heroic figures that had fallen along with the Berlin Wall. But it also used Susanita to highlight the hypocrisy of the European societies that gave prizes to photographs of poverty in Rwanda but which kept their imperial designs.[34] Quino had given form to social archetypes that, three decades later, had become metaphors that could be richly adapted for understanding the dilemmas produced by the crisis created by neoliberalism.[35] Interpretations of the strip continued to be hugely diverse but even within that diversity one key thread was that which, against the grain of the period, defended social utopias in the same fashion as Mafalda. Quino tended to explain, with some bitterness, that the comic maintained its contemporaneity because the problems that it had originally critiqued had not disappeared. But at the end of the 1990s he clarified his position: "The world is in a worse place since at the time of

Mafalda there were the Beatles, the Vietnam War, May '68. All of that went to hell. The lasting nature of the character is a result of nostalgia for the ideals of my generation. . . . You might say that we are nostalgic for the 1960s."[36]

In 1973, Quino stopped publishing new strips of *Mafalda* and changed the reading pact with his public. The link between the world of fiction and its everyday surroundings was broken. The readers could no longer hope that the characters would refer to and intervene into reality. Quino sheltered the comic from the controversies that the characters' opinions might have stirred up in the stormy political and social reality of the mid-1970s. But he also helped the strip's more atemporal meanings to endure, and he validated the process of constantly bringing the strip up to date, giving it fresh meanings and interpretations. That breathed modern life into the creation and helped create a new reading pact that located it in the field of collective memory. This chapter has analyzed the relationship between the comic, memory, and the recent past. I want to summarize the different movements and implications brought about by the installation of the comic in that field.

First, with the return to democracy Quino modified the relationship between the comic and political commitment. Aware of the antagonistic role played by political humor during the later years of the dictatorship, he brought his creation back to life and placed it explicitly and directly in the service of the forces of democracy and the government itself, threatened by the economic crisis and military uprisings. The link between the strip and the democratic creed, which large sectors of society were supporting, renewed the popularity of *Mafalda*. That recognition was tied to the strategies for celebrating the strip's twenty-fifth anniversary—the exhibit and the edition with unpublished strips—that helped a reinterpretation of the strip in terms of a rereading of the 1960s and 1970s. In that context, a game developed in newspapers comprised of imagining what would have happened to each character had they carried on growing up. It was Quino himself who suggested that Mafalda might have been one of the disappeared. The interpretation was readily taken up, as it allowed for a continuation of the tragic past that the rebellious generation, symbolized by the "intellectualized girl," had experienced. It allowed for a recovery of the legacy of the young "rebels," in tune with the conceptualization rooted in the notion of the victim, without having to open up the debate about left-wing armed violence.

Second, the comic was interpreted as a legacy of the 1960s in terms of the victory of neoliberalism and the collapse of the Soviet bloc. It revived a sensibility that appeared to be defeated by the pragmatic severity of economic adjustment plans and discourses of individualism. That resignification was at its strongest in connection with the impoverishment of the middle class brought about by Menemism and with the cultural and symbolic confrontation with that political force. From that angle *Mafalda* became part of the efforts by different actors to sustain an identity wounded by economic decline that was at odds with a new, altogether different middle-class culture. But it was also part of that confrontation. It was a symbol that defended political commitment, collective action, and social utopias in opposition to the praise of individualism, capitalism, and the "end of history."

Third, this rereading mediated a nostalgic take on the past; that is to say, a vision of the past as a golden era that had been eclipsed by an economic and individualistic logic that represented a historical step backward. That nostalgia, expressed in the form of criticism and vindication, characterized the rhetoric of a wide range of actors who, in the following decade, ideologically and symbolically defended the lasting importance of social utopias, political militancy, social commitment, and a middle class that was integrated into Argentine society. Indeed, that position would acquire its real value a decade later when Argentina, in the depths of crisis, needed to find an alternative to neoliberalism.

In each of these steps, Mafalda helped to produce different ways of interpreting the past in which it had first emerged and, by doing so, its relationship with the reading public was located in the relationship between personal/family memory and political disputes over the collective past. The "intellectualized girl" was, in the 1980s, a symbol of the "rebellious" generation in an association so firmly interlinked that it seemed possible to see in Mafalda the destiny of the young people of the 1960s and imagine her as one of the disappeared. That perception was supported, in the 1980s, by the conceptualization of the disappeared purely as victims, which avoided the contentious debate about armed left-wing struggle. In the years to come, that vision existed alongside a use of the strip that challenged the rise of neoliberalism and Menemism. It allowed for a sensitive revaluation of the 1960s and helped restore one core element for a group of readers who had themselves suffered the defeat of social utopias and who had been shaken by economic crises and the dismantling of state politics. For them, *Mafalda* became a vehicle for memory because it gave meaning to the past and allowed them to recover the values transmitted to subsequent generations, those who would come to define the "us" of social belonging.

NOTES

This chapter was translated from the Spanish by James Scorer. I would like to thank Paulo Drinot and James Scorer for their comments on an earlier version of this chapter.

1. Unless otherwise noted, all translations into English from the original Spanish sources in this chapter are the author's. Norma Morandini, "Los 25 años de Mafalda," *Cambio 16*, no. 862 (June 6, 1988): 203–4.
2. I follow here and elsewhere in this chapter the line I developed in Cosse (2014a, 2014b).
3. For an overview of this impulse in memory studies, see Jelin (2002).
4. For a review of this period, see Franco and Levín (2007). For a perspective on the social history of this period, see Cosse (2010) and Cosse, Felitti, and Manzano (2010).
5. On humor and dictatorship in broader terms, see Burkart (2011); also Levín (2013).
6. On the middle class and Alfonsín, see Adamovsky (2009: 414–21).
7. Carlos Ulanovsky, "Mafalda, una pasión argentina," *Clarín*, November 4, 1988, p. 19.
8. Norma Morandini, "Los 25 años de Mafalda," *Cambio 16*, no. 862 (June 6, 1988): 203–4.
9. Eduardo Blaustein, "Nena qué va a ser de ti," *Página 12* (October 19, 1988): 10–11.
10. "Quino," *Revista Confederal* (September 1988): 4–5.
11. "El indulto abolla la democracia, dijo Quino," *Nuevo Sur* (November 8, 1989): n.p. Article from the *Clarín* newspaper archive.
12. Norma Morandini, "Los 25 años de Mafalda," *Cambio 16*, no. 862 (June 6, 1988): 203–4.
13. Mar Correa, "El regreso de Mafalda," *ABC*, March 31, 1989, p. 91.
14. Carlos Ares, "Mafalda cumple 25 años," *El País*, November 2, 1988, pp. 42–43; Javier Coma, "Menores de edad, mayores de mente," *El País*, November 2, 1988, p. 43; and Horacio Eichelbaum, "Mafalda nos hace cosquillas," *El País*, November 2, 1988, p. 43.
15. "Mafalda por Quino," *La Vanguardia*, October 3, 1989, p. 15.
16. Giusi Quarenghi, "Così ho ucciso a Mafalda," *L'Unitá*, December 8, 1984, p. 15.
17. "Italia también festeja los 25 años de Mafalda," *Nuevo Sur*, December 12, 1989, p. 19.
18. Mauricio Ciechanower, "Mafalda, esa famosa y tremenda criatura," *Plural*, no. 209 (February 1, 1989): 62–73.
19. On this process of impoverishment, see Minujin and Kessler (1995); Svampa (2001).
20. "Mi temática es siempre la lucha entre débiles y poderosos," *La Maga*, October 20 1993, p. 16; Diego Fischerman, "De qué se ríe Quino," *Página 12*, October 15, 1993, p. 27.

21. See Guano (2002) and Adamovsky (2009: 421–38), in addition to the texts cited earlier.
22. See, among others, Carolina Muzi, "Mafalda, según pasan los años," *Clarín*, April 26, 1993, pp. 14–15, and "Mafalda y compañía," *Noticias*, December 13, 1992, p. 28.
23. Miguel Rep, "Menem y Quino," *Página 12*, October 12, 1993, p. 26.
24. See Garguin (2007).
25. Carolina Muzi, "Con ojos de Quino," *Clarín*, October 15, 1993, p. 15.
26. Luis Alberto Quevedo, "Ahora veranean en el patio," *Clarín*, September 28, 1994, p. 19.
27. "Quino que se vengan los chicos," *Clarín*, July 22, 1994, p. 15.
28. "Mafalda," *Clarín*, c. November 1994, n.p. Illegible date, from the *Clarín* archive.
29. Daniel Samper Pizano, "Aguante, Mafalda," *Clarín*, May 16, 1993, pp. 32–35.
30. "Mafalda: La genia del genio," *Revista Viva*, October 2, 1994, pp. 17–24.
31. Advertisement "Hola Córdoba!," *La voz del Interior*, September 20, 1995, p. 13. The strip began to be published the following day. See also the author's interview with Alba Lampón, Buenos Aires, August 23, 2012.
32. "Quino, a la Feria de Bolonia," *Excélsior*, April 6, 1994, n.p. *Excélsior* newspaper archive.
33. Karmentxu Marín, "Mafalda," *Clarín*, April 1, 1994, n.p. *Clarín* newspaper archive.
34. Manuel Vicent, "Imágenes," *El País*, July 31, 1994, n.p.; and Ángel de la Peña Tejerina, "Hipocresías," *El País*, August 10, 1994, online at http://elpais.com/diario/1994/08/10/opinion/776469604_850215.html, accessed on October 10, 2012.
35. "Quinosofía. Personajes / Joaquín Lavado," *El Clarín*, October 24, 1993, p. 20.
36. Roque Casciero, "Somos nostálgicos de los 60," *Página 12*, September 22, 2000, p. 25.

REFERENCES

Adamovsky, Ezequiel. 2009. *Historia de la clase media argentina: Apogeo y decadencia de una ilusión, 1919–2003*. Buenos Aires: Planeta.

Burkart, Mara. 2011. "Humor: La risa como espacio crítico bajo la dictadura militar, 1978–1983." PhD dissertation, Facultad de Ciencias Sociales, Universidad de Buenos Aires.

Cosse, Isabella. 2014a. *Mafalda: Historia social y política*. Buenos Aires: Fondo de Cultura Económica.

Cosse, Isabella. 2014b. "Mafalda: Middle Class, Everyday Life, and Politics in Argentina (1964–1973)." *Hispanic American Historical Review* 94, no. 1: 35–75.

Cosse, Isabella. 2010. *Familia, sexualidad y familia en los años sesenta*. Buenos Aires: Siglo Veintiuno Editores.

Cosse, Isabella, Karina Felitti, and Valeria Manzano. 2010. *Los sesenta de otra manera: Vida cotidiana, género y sexualidades en la Argentina*. Buenos Aires: Prometeo.

Crenzel, Emilio. 2008. *Historia política del Nunca Más*. Buenos Aires: Siglo XXI.

Fernández L'Hoeste, Héctor D. 1998. "From Mafalda to Boogie: The City and Argentine Humor." In *Imagination beyond Nation*. Edited by Eva P. Bueno and Terry Caesar, 81–106. Pittsburgh: University of Pittsburgh Press.

Filc, Judith. 1998. "La memoria como espacio de confrontación política: Los relatos del horror en Argentina." *Apuntes de investigación del CECYP* 2, no. 2–3 (November): 37–53.

Filc, Judith. 1997. *Entre el parentesco y la política: Familia y dictadura, 1976–1983*. Buenos Aires: Editorial Biblos.

Foster, David William. 1989. "Mafalda: Ironic Bemusement." In *From Malfada to Los Supermachos: Latin American Graphic Humor as Popular Culture*. Pp. 53–64. Boulder, CO: Lynne Rienner Publishers.

Foster, David William. 1980. "Mafalda: An Argentina Comic Strip." *Journal of Popular Culture* 14, no. 3: 497–508.

Franco, Marina, and Florenica Levín, eds. 2007. *Historia reciente: Perspectivas y desafíos para un campo en construcción*. Buenos Aires: Paidós.

Garguin, Enrique. 2007. "'Los argentinos descendemos de los barcos': The Racial Articulation of Middle Class Identity in Argentina (1920–1960)." *Latin American and Caribbean Ethnic Studies* 2: 161–84.

Guano, Emanuela. 2002. "Spectacles of Modernity: Transnational Imagination and Local Hegemonies in Neoliberal Buenos Aires." *Cultural Anthropology* 17, no. 2: 181–209.

Halbwachs, Maurice. 2004 [1925]. *Los marcos sociales de la memoria*. Barcelona: Anthropos.

Hobsbwam, Eric. 1995. *Age of Extremes: The Short Twentieth Century, 1914–1991*. London: Abacus.

Jelin, Elizabeth. 2002. *Los trabajos de la memoria*. Madrid: Siglo XXI.

Latxague, Claire. 2011. "Lire Quino: Poétique des Formes Brées de la Littérature Dessinée dans La Presse Argentine (1954–1976)." PhD dissertation, L'Université de Grenoble, Université Stendhal–Grenoble 3.

Levín, Florencia. 2013. *Humor y política en tiempos de represión*. Buenos Aires: Siglo XXI.

Lorenz, Federico. 2002. "¿De quién es el 24 de Marzo? Las luchas por la memoria del golpe de 1976." In *Las conmemoraciones: Las disputas en las fechas in-felices*. Volume 3. Edited by Elizabeth Jelin, 53–98. Colección Memorias de la Represión. Madrid: Siglo XXI.

Minujin, Alberto, and Gabriel Kessler. 1995. *La nueva pobreza en la Argentina*. Buenos Aires: Planeta.

Nora, Pierre. 1996. "Generation." In *Rethinking the French Past: Realms of Memory.* Volume 1. Edited by Pierre Nora, 498–531. New York: Columbia University Press.

Quino. 2010. *Tutto Mafalda.* Milan: Salani.

Quino. 1994. *Il mondo di Mafalda.* Milan: Bompiani.

Quino. 1993a. *I Pensieri di Mafalda.* Torino: Lo scarabeo.

Quino. 1993b. *Toda Mafalda.* Buenos Aires: Ediciones de la Flor.

Quino. 1988. *Mafalda inédita.* Buenos Aires: Ediciones de la Flor.

Sasturain, Juan. 1995. *El domicilio de la aventura.* Pp. 167–77. Buenos Aires: Colihue.

Steimberg, Oscar. 1977. *Leyendo historietas: Estilos y sentidos en un "arte menor."* Buenos Aires: Nueva Visión.

Svampa, Maristella. 2001. *Los que ganaron: La vida en los countries y en los barrios privados.* Buenos Aires: Biblos.

Wainerman, Catalina. 2005. *La vida cotidiana en las nuevas familias: ¿Una revolución estancada?* Buenos Aires: Lumiere.

FOUR

COMICS IN A REVOLUTIONARY CONTEXT

EDUCATIONAL CAMPAIGNS AND COLLECTIVE MEMORY IN SANDINISTA NICARAGUA

Christiane Berth

After the Sandinista revolution in July 1979, the new government was faced with one great challenge: How could it convey its political messages to a population with high degrees of illiteracy? Images soon came to play a central role in revolutionary propaganda, which is why posters, murals, and billboards filled streets and public places of Nicaraguan cities. As the writer Sergio Ramírez (2007: 20) has argued, political posters became a new form of mobilizing and motivating people. To stress that visual communication was far more successful than written texts in striking a chord with the Nicaraguan people, Ramírez in his essay referred to the frequent saying, "A picture is worth more than a thousand words." During the Sandinista insurrection, graffiti had been an important medium to communicate political slogans and visual icons in support of the revolutionary struggle. In 1984 former Sandinista leader Dora María Téllez (1984: 87–89) characterized graffiti as an expression of the masses against the dictatorship and stated that Nicaraguans had a high affinity toward graphic expressions. After the revolution, political slogans and revolutionary heroes continued to occupy an important space in Nicaraguan public life. Especially during the political transition, images offered a modern set of visual representations to support the identification with the revolutionary process. Key elements were the Sandinista flag and such revolutionary heroes as Augusto César

Sandino and Carlos Fonseca. They became inscribed in Nicaraguan collective memory and are still present in today's political iconography (Richter 2007: 47; Medina 2010).

Here I focus on how the Sandinistas used comics as part of their political and educational campaigns. Before the revolution there was only a weak tradition of comics and political caricatures in Nicaragua. Beginning in the 1930s, Nicaraguan newspapers regularly published U.S. comics. The first Nicaraguan satirical weekly, the anti-Somocista *Los Lunes de la Nueva Prensa*, was founded in the 1940s, followed by *Semana cómica* in the 1950s and 1960s (*Barricada*, August 21, 1987, p. 9). The two main newspapers in the 1960s and 1970s each employed a caricaturist. One of them was Alberto Mora Olivares (AMO), who criticized the Somoza regime in his *Nicasio* stories in *La Prensa* (Mora Olivares 1975). He was an exceptional case, as his influence was so strong that other caricaturists described Olivares as the "thorn in the flesh of the dictator Somoza" (*La Prensa*, June 26, 1993, p. 16). Foreign comics reached Nicaragua mostly through the distribution channels of other Latin American countries, especially from Mexico and Colombia. In addition, the daily newspapers *La Prensa* and *Novedades* published such U.S. comic strips as *Mutt and Jeff* or the *Katzenjammer Kids* (Pérez Yglesias 1985: 182–85; Whisnant 1995: 134–36). Another reason for the weak presence of comics in Central America was a slower urbanization and industrialization than in the rest of Latin America. As the urban readership increased only gradually, national comic industries developed later and thus experienced more competition from other new media, mainly television (Fernández L'Hoeste and Poblete 2009: 7). After the revolution, comics and political caricatures gained more presence, however. The young caricaturist Róger Sánchez Flores regularly published his political caricatures and comic strips, titled *Muñequitos del pueblo*, in the Sandinista newspaper *Barricada*.[1]

The Sandinista mass organizations began to use comic strips for their political campaigns. Different ministries promoted their aims by publishing comic booklets and short comic strips in daily newspapers. The Christian weekly *El tayacán* and the satirical weekly *Semana cómica* published comic strips. Topics were broad, ranging from the economy, infrastructure, defense, elections, and shopping to public transport. This chapter is based on more than 120 educational comic strips published during the 1980s in the Sandinista newspaper *Barricada* as well as a small selection of comic books edited by different Nicaraguan government institutions. In the case of the booklets, their length varies from twenty to forty pages; in the case of the comic strips, their length differs between short strips of three panels and longer ones filling up to four pages. In many instances the author remains unknown because the comic strips lack individual signatures.[2]

Educational comics contributed in a significant manner to the formation of collective memory in Nicaragua during the political transition period. Sandinista planners used the medium to diffuse the importance of collective action and their vision of a new revolutionary society based on responsible subjects doing everything to support the revolutionary project. As the comics were used for popular education and discussed in workshops of Sandinista mass organizations, they introduced Sandinista values and fresh historical narratives in a collective setting. Many comics addressed two main historical topics: the revolutionary uprising and the past of the Somoza dictatorship. This first part of this chapter focuses on comic booklets' narratives of insurrection, arguing that they utilized the special advantages of the comic genre to involve their readers in the military side of the insurrection. As an innovative feature, they included the masses as an actor in the comic stories. In the second part of the chapter, I analyze the educational comics dealing with health and economic subjects that juxtaposed the Sandinista reforms with the social inequality during the dictatorship. Their contribution to collective memory lies in the denunciation of the Somoza past, introducing to their readers the visual icon of a ludicrous figure. Although they embraced important elements of the comic genre, some of the comics missed out on the chance to reach an illiterate audience by strongly relying on the information in the text boxes. Below is a brief introduction into the role of visual memories and popular education in political transition periods. I look at similar examples in other Latin American countries, especially in Cuba and Chile.

MEMORY, POLITICAL TRANSITION, AND THE ROLE OF COMICS

In Nicaragua the revolutionary government promoted a fresh national identity based on Sandinista ideology. With its political campaigns, the government aimed at diffusing revolutionary values represented by the ideal of the "hombre nuevo"—the ideal of a new man transformed through the revolutionary process. The latest historical narratives focused on the importance of mass struggle in Nicaraguan history. The Nicaraguan historian Margarita Vannini (2011) has identified three main subjects in Sandinista memory politics: the anti-imperialist character of the struggle of the Nicaraguan people; the establishment of Sandino as a national hero; and the leading role of the FSLN (Frente Sandinista de Liberación Nacional) in the fight against the dictatorship. All three subjects were illustrated with a different assortment of images, such as mass meetings, Sandino's silhouette, or the visual representation of FSLN leaders during revolutionary struggle. In the years after the revolution, education became an important area of memory politics. The central actors were state institutions on the one hand and the thousands of volunteers participating in the popular education campaigns on the other hand. The government also instigated oral history projects, published interviews with Sandinistas, and renamed streets and public places (Vannini 2011).

The sociologist Maurice Halbwachs (1985) has characterized memories as reconstructions influenced by present conditions. He distinguished between individual and collective memories, both of which are always influenced by the four different frameworks of language, time, space, and experience. Different social groups form different collective memories, according to Halbwachs, which means that they share a common version of historical events within their group building the framework for group communication. The relationship between individual and collective memory is a process of interaction, as individuals appropriate collective memory and by doing so develop their own viewpoint. In general, each individual has a singular relationship of different, overlapping collective memories depending on the social groups he or she belongs to (Wetzel 2009: 61–84; Halbwachs 1985). Thanks to illustrated print media, film, and television, visual elements became crucial for memory in the course of the twentieth century. People increasingly relied on images provided by mass media to remember historical events; such images arguably can be characterized as "visual sites of memory" (Paul 2013: 635). Visual elements played a central role in the political campaigns in Sandinista Nicaragua. As a consequence, visual factors influenced memory in a particular way.

The need to relate images and memory was established by ancient philosophers and rhetoricians who invented different mnemotechnic methodologies to link content with images. According to their writings, the connections between memory and image were most successful when visuals fulfilled two criteria: they had to be linked with the content to be memorized, and they had to be emotionally impressive. Later on, this connection was reaffirmed by art historian Aby Warburg, who also insisted on the necessity of figurative images (Yates 1990; Paul 2013: 637–38). Popular education projects in different parts of the world utilized these findings and incorporated visual material as the main constituent into their educational efforts. By and large, comics apply the following techniques to stimulate identification and imagination of their readers: First, they draw on heroes or familiar protagonists easy to identify with. Second, they have a dramaturgy of action, making recipients curious and eager to follow the next installment of the series, which is supported by onomatopoeic elements, symbols, and emanata. Third, visual elements appeal to the viewers' emotions, encouraging them through different visual perspectives to identify with the protagonist. Finally, the gutters—as comic theorists call the spaces between each panel—open up a space for the recipients' imagination. Readers must imagine what happened between two panels to make sense of the story (Grünewald 2000: 40–42). Consequently, the understanding of comics requires "active, interpreting reading with imaginative combination" (42).

The comics on Nicaraguan history contributed in particular ways to the formation of collective memory of the Sandinista revolution because they encouraged the historical imagination of the transition period and raised issues the Sandinista leaders considered as important for the revolutionary project. For the most part, the comics emphasized again and again the importance of collective subjects for Nicaraguan history by highlighting moments of successful resistance against U.S. imperialism and authoritarianism. The historical comics focused strongly on insurrection, while the comics on health and economy addressed the lived experiences of Nicaraguan people. The Sandinista leader Omar Cabezas highlighted in 1984 another advantage of political caricatures that is also applicable for the comic genre: "The caricature has, as a consequence, turned into an invaluable weapon, as it reaches an audience straight away. It is immediate. Society that reads books is more limited, whereas it is easier for millions of people to see a caricature. It is almost like an intravenous, intracerebral education. . . . It is almost a traveling, daily university of plastic art. Humor achieves a subversive character as it mobilizes promptly. It can, in certain cases and situations, be explosive, as it directly impacts the brain whereupon and thus people either identify with the situations or reject them" (TANA 1984b: 10). This statement adds two important insights to the advantages of the comic genre: They spread their messages immediately and achieve with humor a direct emotional involvement of their recipients. Shortcomings in the conception of some of the educational comics weakened their success, however.

COMICS AS A MEDIUM FOR POPULAR EDUCATION IN LATIN AMERICA

Before the Nicaraguan revolution, other left-wing governments in Latin America had made use of comics for political education. In the early 1970s the Unidad Popular government in Chile became worried about the strong influence of U.S. comics. A study conducted in 1972 revealed that 87 percent of all comics published in Chilean newspapers were of foreign origin. By contrast, Chilean comics were only dominant in the socialist and communist newspapers. As the government realized that comics were popular, especially in working-class families, they developed a new strategy to break the dominance of foreign comic books. As a first step, members of the state-run editorial house Quimantú interviewed workers to find out about their preferences. As a second step, they decided to maintain the format and techniques of the foreign comic books but to change their content. The situation is similar to Nicaragua, where government representatives and campaign strategists intended to transform values and attitudes with their publications.

One important principle was that comics should relate to the current Chilean situation by including special episodes on the agrarian reform and illiteracy. The characters in these episodes were of working-class origin and lived in the fictitious neighborhood "Lo Chamullo." Another strategy consisted in substituting U.S. superheroes with Chilean social heroes—a transfer that became possible when Quimantú acquired several licenses of foreign comic books. The art historian David Kunzle has characterized the Quimantú comics as "a curious mixture between the old and the new" (Kunzle 1978: 123). He raised concerns about prevailing sexual stereotypes embraced by the authors to increase the reader's emotional involvement in the comic plots. Yet the success of the fresh strategy was limited: the political left still perceived comics as a capitalist genre and remained critical. Besides, interviews with workers corroborated that they disliked the dominance of political subjects in the comic books. Chilean politicians and editors had to accept that foreign comics still gained a larger audience than their Chilean counterparts (Rinke 2004: 459–66; Soto G. 2003; Woll 1976; Kunzle 1978).

Parallels can also be drawn to the Cuban case, where the government after the 1959 revolution undertook a literacy campaign and broad adult education programs. The Nicaraguan literacy campaign was heavily based on the Cuban example from 1961, as use of the same symbols reveals: both campaigns used the open book as an icon and declared a region as "free" or "victorious" territory after a successful alphabetization, which was indicated by the display of red and black flags (Musset 2005: 22). In Cuba the CDR (Comités para la Defensa de la Revolución) played an important role for the educational campaigns, with a membership of 1.5 million to 2 million people contributing to different government campaigns and revolutionary vigilance.

They served as a model for the Nicaraguan CDS (Comités de Defensa Sandinista), which had approximately six hundred thousand members mainly in urban areas who were essential for popular education (for Cuba, see Fagen 1969: 69–96; for Nicaragua, see Utting 1992: 125–26).

However, there are differences as well. Cuba had a strong comic art tradition, with several satirical magazines dating back to the beginning of the twentieth century. The 1960s and 1970s witnessed controversial debates on comics, with Cuban intellectuals denouncing comics as part of imperialist mass culture whereas art professionals insisted on their potential. The graphic artists' aim was to create a national Cuban comic industry that would contribute to the strengthening of revolutionary values and working discipline as well as to discredit the revolution's enemies (Catalá Carrasco 2011; Merino 2003: 153–93; Lent 2009b). In both countries, parallels to Nicaragua exist. Like Chilean comics, the Nicaraguan ones combined traditional elements of the comic genre with new components that sometimes hampered their appeal. The Cuban government utilized the educational comics for similar objectives as its Nicaraguan counterpart. In Cuba and Chile, however, comics had a stronger tradition, allowing campaign strategists to count on an audience already familiar with the genre.

OBSERVATIONS ON THE RECEPTION OF EDUCATIONAL COMICS

The historian Wulf Kansteiner (2002) raised as a methodological concern to collective memory studies that reception is often left out in the analysis; this omission can lead to wrong conclusions as media representations do not necessarily enter collective memories. The recipients are an important group of actors: they can change the historical versions offered by memory makers and give them their own meaning. But the recipients also have the power to ignore and forget. In his publication on the power of images historian Gerhard Paul has established three criteria for images to enter collective memory: first, they need to be present on a mass scale, which is generally reached by the second factor, their distribution by mass media. Third, recipients have to use the images frequently (Paul 2013: 640–41).

As there is, unfortunately, little information on comic reception in Nicaragua, I will synthesize the extant evidence. Most of the educational comics were published in the early years after the revolution, with editions varying between five thousand and fifty thousand copies. It is likely that they were each read by several people and distributed by the Sandinista mass organizations. According to the numbers given by educational researcher Ronald Arnove (1986), these organizations had a broad distribution network in the mid-1980s, influencing more than 190,000 persons (48–49). *Barricada* reached editions of up to one hundred thousand copies in the first half of the 1980s, which gave comics strips a wide dissemination (Mattelart 1986: 9). Róger Sánchez Flores recalled in an interview that *Barricada* readers from workers' districts always demanded more caricatures—in fact, more than he was able to produce (Sánchez 1985: 116). Sánchez's comic strips and caricatures were so successful because they could be understood without having to read the texts. An administrative employee interviewed after Sánchez's death in 1991 remembered the combination of humor and information in his works: "The *Muñequitos del pueblo* depicted the difficult situation faced by the people, we learned to laugh about our lives and problems. Humor is the most beautiful thing in life, it makes us forget the troubles, and what was significant about Róger was the knowledge he transmitted" (*Barricada*, November 5, 1991, p. 1B).

These statements indicate the positive reception of comic strips and caricatures. Whether this is also true for the text-loaded advertisements published by the ministries (the governmental administrations issuing them) seems doubtful because illiterate recipients could rely only on their visual impression or had to ask for the help of others. Political scientist Adam Jones concluded in his investigation on the history of *Barricada* that the newspaper mainly had an impact on middle- and upper-class readers, as it was a relatively expensive medium (Jones 2002: 231). Rural people, it is fair to assume, were reached more easily by radio announcements than by press campaigns. However, the case of the health pamphlets might be different, as they were discussed collectively during workshops in the communities where literate recipients were able to help illiterate persons and different interpretations could be discussed. Nonetheless, we should keep in mind the influence of workshop leaders, which might have suggested a particular interpretation. For a more precise analysis, research on the realities of popular education and the reactions to the pamphlets would be necessary, but sources on the contemporary reactions of Nicaraguans to the comics are difficult to locate.

All the propaganda of state institutions was coordinated by the national advertising system, headed by the Nicaraguan poet Gioconda Belli from 1985 on. In an interview published the same year, she lamented that most advertisements had too many slogans and repeated the same rhetorical elements, which audiences found boring. Once the Nicaraguan people became used to the political messages, they did not pay attention anymore (Mattelart 1986: 20–21). The educational comics in general relied on the same narrative structure: they introduced a problem, explained the reasons, and appealed to Nicaraguan people to change their behavior, either by reducing consumption, increasing production, or avoiding strikes.

The particular feature of comic reception is that readers have to fill in the spaces between the panels with their own imagination. If the panel order avoids leaps in time, spaces can be filled in more easily, which was especially true for the comics dealing with the insurrection period as they closely followed the events. Other educational comics required more abstraction and relied more strongly on the textboxes. The reception also depended on the knowledge and visual repertoire of each person (Grünewald 2000: 38; McCloud 2004: 74–77). Certain symbols or historical facts might have been familiar to residents of an urban district in Central Nicaragua, for example, but totally alien to people living in a rural community along the Atlantic Coast. The German comic author Harald Juch worked for several years in Nicaragua and related in his account that he once went to a rural cooperative to draw some comics on reforestation. A member of the Movement for Rural Cultural Entertainment (Movimiento de Animación Cultural Rural, MACRU) saw his early drawings and judged they were suitable only for Managuan middle- and upper-class people (Juch 1989: 8–9). The same problem may have occurred with other educational comic strips drawn by authors with a foreign or urban background. Stereotypes about the uneducated rural population might have prevailed among the Sandinista planners with an urban background, making them underestimate the educational level and reception capacities of rural people.

Given the limited scope of this information on circulation and reactions of Nicaraguan people, the reception of the educational comics is difficult to assess. Consequently, I concentrate here on the intentions of Sandinista planners and authors who employed comics as an element of memory politics and as a medium for revolutionary identity construction. The educational comics demonstrate how the Sandinista planners molded the ideal new revolutionary man in the Nicaraguan society. They introduce a historical narrative of the insurrectional period to strengthen the identification with the collective struggle. The visual elements comic authors embraced reveal their political priorities and their target audiences. Below I introduce the basic concepts and strategies characterizing Sandinista mass education as a framework for the analysis of educational comics.

EDUCATION IN SANDINISTA NICARAGUA

Education became an important priority for the Sandinista government and one of its most popular projects was the literacy campaign of 1980. Within a year the campaign reduced the illiteracy level from more than 50 percent to 23 percent (Arnove 1986: 27).[3] More than one hundred thousand young participants had been involved in the campaign, spending several months in remote areas of the country. The literacy campaign gained a great importance in Nicaraguan collective memory, as reflected in several monuments and the success of the traveling exhibition "Tren cultural" shown across the country in 2006. Turning to the subject of methodology, the Sandinista education introduced new, participative approaches. Theoretically, it relied on the method of the Brazilian educator Paulo Freire, who considered active learning as an important principle. At the different educational levels, every lesson should have a concrete result and enable the students to put the ideas into practice. To diffuse the contents, the Ministry of Education relied on such Sandinista mass organizations as the CDS, the Nicaraguan women's association (Asociación de Mujeres Nicaragüenses Luisa Amanda Espinoza, AMNLAE), and the Sandinista Workers' Central (Central Sandinista de Trabajadores, CST).

The idea was to train a small group of disseminators in Managua who would then pass the information to the local committees and units. As a result, in mid-1984 already 17,000 educational collectives had been formed that reached up to 195,000 people (Arnove 1986: 48–49). These collectives for adult education employed the mass media, incorporating visual elements into their campaigns. The Sandinista newspaper *Barricada* supported the educational campaigns with special features in plain language. The didactical material utilized by the popular educators contained local references, thus making the messages easier to understand for the Nicaraguan audience. The books included easy texts, comic strips, games, and photo stories. Of particular importance were the symbols employed in the campaigns, such as the Nicaraguan flag and the icons of revolutionary heroes (Lacaze 2012a; Arnove 1986: 52–53).

Although the educational campaigns achieved some spectacular successes, Robert Arnove also mentions problems related to education in Sandinista Nicaragua. Despite their high degree of enthusiasm, popular educators were often poorly trained. Because of the war and individual economic hardships, there was a high level of fluctuation among the educators. Lack of preparation, combined with didactic material that did not stimulate critical thought, led sometimes to indoctrination instead of the intended critical reflection (Arnove 1986: 53). Arnove observed during a CDS meeting in Managua:

> It is not uncommon for those attending meetings to be lectured for an hour or more by different FSLN representatives. After sitting through such a CDS meeting in a working-class neighborhood of Managua, a staff member of the national office of the CDS observed enthusiastically, "You can see there is a lot of participation." What I had observed was some 30 people sitting for about 45 minutes in fold-up chairs in the early evening dusk while three different FSLN spokesmen read to them the nationally-prepared statements on the causes of the economic problems in the country; there had not been a single question or comment from the group assembled in the street. (Arnove 1986: 66)

The danger of boring the audience with repetitive propaganda and moral appeals also prevailed in the comics on economic topics (discussed later in the chapter). Next I reveal how the government used historical comic booklets as a means to construct a memory politics of the insurrectional period. Campaign strategists designed the booklets as a "martial documentary" to involve secondary witnesses in the military confrontations of 1978 and 1979.

COMMEMORATING INSURRECTION ON THE FIRST ANNIVERSARY OF REVOLUTION

Assembled around a large fire, a Matagalpan revolutionary exclaimed: "Debemos de luchar compañeros por una Nicaragua liberada, libre de todo vestigio de corrupción con que nos ahoga esta sangrienta tiranía" ("we have to fight for a liberated Nicaragua, comrades, free from all vestiges of the corruption in which this bloody dictatorship is drowning us").This introductory scene to the comic *Matagalpa: Insurrección de agosto!* is dominated by the bright fire symbolizing the illumination of Nicaraguan people by revolutionary ideas in August 1978. Most of the audience lacks individual characteristics and appears as a blue and green crowd against a yellow sky background. At the top of the page, the Sandinista flag with Sandino's hat on it overlooks the scene, thus establishing continuity between the Sandinista revolution and Sandino's struggle in the 1930s (Ministerio de Cultura de Nicaragua 1980b: 1).

FIGURE 4.1 Introductory scene to the comic *Matagalpa: Insurrección de agosto!* Source: Ministerio de Cultura 1980b, p. 1.

In July 1980 the Ministry of Culture started a series of educational comics to commemorate the first anniversary of the Sandinista revolution by retelling the story of the insurrection in different parts of the country. Though information on the edition and circulation of these comics is unavailable, they provide important clues to the historical narratives in comics. The educational comics on insurrection have been analyzed by scholar Bram Draper (2009), who argues that Nicaraguan comics were written in the tradition of U.S. adventure stories but lack the typical monsters or heroes. The first comic in the series, *Heroic Cities*, dealt with the revolutionary struggle at the end of August 1978 in Matagalpa in northern Nicaragua and was produced by a group of artists at the local Popular Center for Culture. The second comic in the series was dedicated to the uprising in Estelí and was billed as a "military documentary," indicating the strong focus on the armed confrontation. This coincided with similar tendencies in early testimonial literature at the beginning of the 1980s that tried to build up heroic narratives of the revolutionary process.

The notion of a documentary laid claim to authenticity while also making reference to the proximity of the comic genre to moving images in films. The series relied on some traditional comic techniques to capture its audience, such as a dramaturgy of action, which in this case is focused on the insurgency in Matagalpa and supported by strong colors and onomatopoeic elements. By zooming in on different actors, the authors aspired to allow readers greater insight into the struggle and to involve them emotionally at the same time. For instance, the brutal National Guard soldiers should provoke disgust and hatred. However, the authors refrained from focusing on one revolutionary protagonist the recipients could identify with. Instead, the comic concentrates on mass action and introduces the following revolutionary symbols: the Sandinista flag, the silhouettes of Sandino and Carlos Fonseca, and the clenched fist.

The spontaneous uprising of armed youth became known in Nicaragua as the "insurrección de los muchachos." In Matagalpa a monument in the city center, the "Monumento a los héroes y mártires de la revolución," recalls the event indicating its importance for collective memory. The young revolutionaries succeeded in taking control of the city for a few days until they were finally defeated by the National Guard. The event preceded the insurrection planned by the FSLN in several Nicaraguan cities on September 9, 1978. The comic portrays the struggle as a prelude to successful revolution, although it ends with the withdrawal of the insurgents. It has a strong focus on the military confrontations but refrains from portraying individual heroes in the struggle, with the exception of the very first Matagalpan martyr. On the regime's side, the National Guard soldiers in their green uniforms come across as aggressors, described by such expressions as "beasts" or "rabid dogs" (Ministerio de Cultura de Nicaragua 1980b: 3). They are constantly attacking the city until they suffer a temporary defeat after which the former repressors seem vulnerable soldiers losing their helmets and weapons. They have to retire to their cartels, where they are humiliated by their commanders, thus showing the viewers that the powerful army can be defeated.

On the revolutionaries' side, the gender politics of the comics tended to be more traditional than the actual events portrayed in them. For instance, the comic portrays the students who gain support of the local population as mostly male. When women do appear, it is as supporters of men, either providing them with food or helping them produce arms. The absence of women reflects male opposition toward women participating actively in the revolutionary mass organizations (Montoya 2003: 62–63). During the entire 1980s, *Barricada* published only one comic strip dealing explicitly with women's role in Nicaraguan society, but ironically women are almost absent in this comic (*Barricada*, November 2, 1986, p. 6). By assigning traditional female roles to women and by ignoring real involvement of women as subjects of the revolutionary process, the comics missed the chance to provide an alternative vision for gender relations. This phenomenon is largely congruent with the general tendency of Latin American comics to address mainly male recipients (Fernández L'Hoeste and Poblete 2009: 9). Consequently, the educational comics reached out mainly to the collective memories of male Nicaraguans in central Nicaragua as being active in one of the Sandinista mass organizations.

Halfway through the comic, the main plot's action is interrupted to provide some historical background information. In several longer text boxes, the authors narrate the historical events leading to the insurrection and present the assassination of Pedro Joaquín Chamorro as the main driver for mass opposition. This interpretation is supported by the visual arrangement of the comic panel, where Chamorro appears in the center as the dominating figure accompanied by the revolutionary masses in the background. This scene constructs a direct relationship to Augusto César Sandino, whose silhouette appears on the Sandinista flag flying above the scenery. The panel appears like a historical collage, bringing different events and symbols together (Ministerio de Cultura de Nicaragua 1980b: 7). Before switching back to the regional level, the comic mentions the attack on the National Palace on August 25, 1978, and the general strike as events undermining the dictatorship's stability. This is illustrated by the triumphal image of the Sandinista leaders with raised fists and guns, being celebrated by the masses (11).

Back in Matagalpa, the first victim is murdered by the National Guard, a local student named José Alberto Chavarría. His assassination is only shown in a small panel, where recipients see him fall down after the National Guard has opened fire. The scene shows only his back, making it impossible to glimpse his face. Instead of focusing on Alberto Chavarría's death and suffering, the comic highlights the reactions of the local population. His funeral became the trigger for the insurrection in Matagalpa and mobilized thousands of people to go out on the streets shouting such slogans as "Down with the dictatorship!" or "People unite!" Finally, the comic retells the military confrontations with the National Guard. One central scene

FIGURE 4.2 Central scene of the comic *Matagalpa: Insurrección de agosto!* Source: Ministerio de Cultura de Nicaragua 1980b, p. 18.

titled with the radical slogan "Patria libre o morir" describes the victory against an attack by the National Guardia, illustrated by a colorful image where weapons and exploding bombs intermingle with the soldiers' bodies (Ministerio de Cultura de Nicaragua 1980b: 18).

In these scenes the aim of a martial documentary seems to be accomplished: Recipients perceive combat scenes accompanied by frequent onomatopoeic elements, providing them with an impression of the war's soundscape. Planes, tanks, and helicopters appear on the scene, illustrating the regime's technological supremacy, whereas the insurgents are running out of munitions and decide finally to leave Matagalpa. The final panel shows their departure into the mountains, singing the hymn of the FSLN while leaving a crying crowd behind. The text box urged the recipients to render honor and glory to the revolutionary martyrs. On the last page of the comic, we see the group walk toward us with their rifles in their hands, overseen by a gigantic silhouette of Carlos Fonseca. In this way, the comic relates the insurrection to the struggle of revolutionary martyrs.

The series intended to diffuse and preserve the history of insurrection in different Nicaraguan regions, as also attempted in other Sandinista memory projects. For example, an oral history project formed part of the literacy campaign to document the memories of the revolution in different areas of the country.[4] The comics' focus on collective subjects in revolutionary action coincides with similar tendencies in early testimonial literature published after the revolution. Its didactical-propagandistic messages promoted unity as a necessary element for the victory against the Somoza dictatorship and consequently utilized the collective "we" instead of an individual voice. By contributing to the creation of revolutionary legends and heroes, they provided role models for the new political order and can be read as symbolic texts of the new political power (Mackenbach 2004: 82–96). Cultural anthropologist Bradley Tatar (2009) has convincingly argued for the case of Monimbó (Masaya); the FSLN eliminated contradicting versions from its narrative of the insurrectional process to establish the party members as vanguard group. If similar rewritings have taken place in the Matagalpan case, this would have to be established by comparing different historical and testimonial accounts of the events, which is beyond the scope of this chapter.

HISTORICAL COMIC STRIPS IN THE SANDINISTA NEWSPAPER

During the entire decade of the 1980s, *Barricada* published only two comic strip series dealing with historical topics: the first series on Sandino and the second one on FSLN activities in 1978. The Somoza regime had made an effort to eliminate the memory of Sandino completely and discredited him as a "bandit." In opposition, the Sandinistas restored Sandino's role as a fighter against U.S. imperialism and formed his image according to their political necessities (Whisnant 1995: 356–63). One example of this intent is the *Barricada* comic series that highlights the initial phase of guerrilla struggle in 1927, beginning with the battle of Ocotal. To attack the city, Sandino had mobilized farmers from the surroundings and captured the town. In the end he was defeated by the air force, but news of resistance against the U.S. intervention spread throughout Latin America (69–71). The comic strip contains several battle scenes illustrated with onomatopoeic elements. Sandino is generally characterized as a human leader willing to pardon his enemies and to protect women and children. The series title *History of*

Dignity is contrasted with a box titled "History of Infamy" in the comic strip that includes historical information on U.S. activities and the Nicaraguan government (*Barricada*, February 25, 1984; March 5, 1984; March 10, 1984). As a result, readers would identify with the historical struggle of Sandino and condemn U.S. interference.

The second series, focused on the December 1978 events, is titled *Diciembre victorioso*. As in Matagalpa, these events are depicted as a predecessor to the successful revolution. On the one hand, the comic concentrates on the repression of the Somoza regime, denouncing the ongoing U.S. support for the dictatorship. On the other hand, it highlights the leading role of the FSLN during the insurrectional process. Most of the comic panels emphasize only one detail, such as risen fists, a revolutionary slogan, or a boot of a National Guard soldier (*Barricada*, December 1, 1984; December 8, 1984; December 15, 1984). As in *La insurreción de Agosto*, the author frequently presents scenes of military confrontations illustrated by onomatopoeic elements. Although the time lapses between the comic panels in *La insurreción de Agosto* are short, the sequences in the *Barricada* series leave a lot of space for readers' imagination to fill in the gaps, which might be a result of the limited space available in the newspaper. Consequently, the panels required more creativity and active commitment from the recipients.

Both *Barricada* series on historical events were soon abandoned, however. Thus they had no deeper impact on collective memory. However, they shared the central aims of the series on *Heroic Cities*: the use of the comic genre to focus on armed struggle and revolutionary mass action. They lack individual protagonists easy to identify with and hence lack an important feature of the traditional comic genre. It is questionable if the anonymous masses of the Sandinista comics managed to fulfill this vacuum with the same positive emotional appeal. By and large, the comics on insurrection represented a series of extraordinary feats performed by the revolutionaries and tried to communicate them to secondary witnesses. The narrative concentrates on the revolutionaries' bravery and willingness to sacrifice, leaving out other war experiences such as fear, injuries, deaths, and grief.

THE USE OF COMICS IN SANDINISTA HEALTH CAMPAIGNS

A young boy with a three-wheeler decorated with a "Sandinista Revolution" flag appears on the scene, driving away an old representative of the Nicaraguan bourgeoisie wearing a top hat and smoking a large cigar. The legend says that the revolution is taking measures to eliminate exploitation and improve living conditions in Nicaragua. Next, the three-wheeler directly drives into another scene showing a large group of people laughing, shouting slogans, and carrying signs with such important Sandinista reform projects as the literacy campaign, the agrarian reform, and the cooperatives. The revolutionary movement driving away the past—this is the introduction to one of the pamphlets edited by the Ministry of Health promoting as its central message that the mass movement induced political change in Nicaragua (Donahue 1986: 72).

The Ministry of Health relied on public campaigns to increase knowledge on health problems and change certain unsanitary habits. In April 1980 it created a Division of Education and Popular Communication to organize the campaigns; it also formed local health centers for the rural communities, each of which was supposed to have a health educator responsible for information dissemination and the organization of workshops. The campaigns aimed at improving popular knowledge about a variety of health problems; they were intended to stimulate activities contributing to their solution. To encourage group discussions, the ministry distributed pamphlets on more than twenty different health subjects, such as diarrhea, breastfeeding, and vaccination. Most were illustrated with comic strips. The participants were expected to look at the illustrations, answer the questions, and reflect on their learning process. In addition to the pamphlets, the Ministry of Health regularly published comic strip series on health topics in *Barricada*. As a sign of solidarity with the revolution, caricaturists from other Latin American countries participated, such as Eduardo del Río "Rius" (Mexico) and Miguel Marfán (Chile) (Donahue 1986: 63–69). Arguably, their participation indicates the weak local comic tradition. In Mexico, Rius had invented a sui generis genre of didactical comic books and composed more than one hundred books on topics like Marx, Che Guevara, religion, Mexican politics, and nutrition. They have been translated into several other languages and gained a broad audience (Merino 2003: 236–38; Hachfeld 1997). Given his left-wing political orientation, Rius's participation in the Nicaraguan educational campaigns is not surprising, taking into account that several of his educational books deal with Nicaraguan topics (see, for example, Rius 1983).

The Nicaraguan government considered its political campaigns as part of the fight against the social and political legacy of the Somoza regime by drawing attention to its repression and social exclusion. It made an effort to portray Somoza and the National Guards as symbols of the past, as backward, reactionary, exploitative, and cruel. In the comic strips the dictatorship is typically personified by three characters: Somoza himself, members of the National Guard, and the Nicaraguan bourgeoisie. One important act at the beginning of the revolution was the destruction of the Somoza monument near the National Stadium in Managua. The physical destruction of the monument was accompanied by an effort to wipe out the power of the dictatorship's visual symbols. The educational comics contributed in this effort by ridiculing Somoza's image, which can also be interpreted as an attempt to substitute his image in collective memory.

Research on memory in Nicaragua has mainly focused on memories of the revolution and memory politics dealing with revolutionary events and heroes. By contrast, the memory of the dictatorship period has not been studied systematically until now, even though Victoria González-Rivera (2010) recently analyzed the history of Somoza's female supporters. Exploring how the period of the dictatorship is addressed in Sandinista educational campaigns can contribute to the history of its collective memory, as the educational material promoted the government's vision and was a precursor to later interpretations. During the political transition process, the memories of the former oppressed were recognized for the first time and could be communicated without fear of repression. The references in the comics opened up a space for reflection and discussions in the popular education workshops. Take the case of the health comics, which demonstrated to their readers how the health system worked before the revolution by underlining the lack of preventive medicine and denouncing the fact that patients had to pay for basic health care. In one pamphlet the recipients see a medical office where the doctor attends only patients with sufficient income (Donahue 1986: 76). By mentioning these experiences, the comics connected to the experiences of people who had suffered during the Somoza regime. They now found that their memories were mobilized as elements of the government campaigns and may have felt encouraged to share their experiences during the discussions on the health workshops.

Again and again, Somoza appears in the pamphlets as a negative symbol. In several comics, bacteria with a human face, the face of Somoza, are attacked by the immune system, depicted in form of the Sandinista army. In a comic on trash, Somoza appears again, on this occasion raising his head out of a garbage bin. The strip explains the need to close garbage bins and, in the end, we see a young boy shutting the bin with a loud noise, explaining simultaneously: "Like that, the garbage does not get out any more" (Donahue 1986: 121). Undoubtedly, the comic refers to the need to control Somoza supporters and counterrevolutionary forces in Nicaragua. Emphasizing a sharp dichotomy between the old and the new regime, the comic authors contributed to constructing the collective memory of the Somoza past. Their interpretation highlighted the regime's negative aspects and portrayed it as a dark chapter of Nicaraguan history—a chapter that the Sandinista government wanted to be closed.

Ultimately, the special contribution of the comic strips is a visual one: they expose Somoza to ridicule by giving him the face of a bacteria or showing him in loser situations (such as being encased in a garbage bin). Instead of remembering the president's representative photos, recipients of the comic strips now could refer to another visual collection of Somoza images and laugh together at the former dictator. The frequent use of military references reflects the history of the guerrilla war and the start of the Contra war. For example, in one comic the human immune system is likened to a group of the popular militia. In another, bacteria (represented by the National Guard) attack the defense system of the human body (represented by an armed Sandinista group). The pamphlet explains that the immune system saves an image of the aggressor while the drawing shows a popular militia member holding a "Wanted" sign with the bacteria. When the same bacteria attack again, the human body recognizes it and starts its defense measures, symbolized in the comic by an armed Sandinista group (*Barricada*, February 4, 1982, p. 9).

In one health pamphlet the authors linked the human immune system directly to the struggle of popular militia in northern Nicaragua: "In the Popular Militia of our country, we are currently preparing to defend our revolution. This has mainly been a reaction to the Somocist gangs, invading across the northern border. These gangs are like the virus of Somocism's disease. As we want neither this illness to return nor any other kind of intervention, we have to knuckle down and organize our defense: the Militias.

FIGURE 4.3. Educational comic for the vaccination campaign.
Source: *Barricada*, February 4, 1982, p. 9.

These Militias are like the antibodies our body builds up when we are vaccinated" (Jornadas Populares de Salud 1981: 6). While Somoza is a frequent symbol of the negative, the positive heroes of the revolution remain absent in the health pamphlets. In contrast to the literacy campaign where Sandino and Carlos Fonseca were omnipresent, the health campaigns did not rely on revolutionary heroes. Instead, the pamphlets promote the idea of collective action and preventive measures. For example, in one drawing a member of a Sandinista health council in a Superman uniform appears saying that health was not the work of a superhero but of the Nicaraguan people. As a symbol for the campaigns to improve hygienic conditions, he holds a broom in his arm, whereas the Superman symbol on the uniform is substituted by the abbreviation CDS (Donahue 1986: 83).

Rius argues in the same vein in a comic strip published for the first anniversary of the *Jornadas Populares de Salud.* The protagonist is a Mexican singer wearing a sombrero visiting revolutionary Nicaragua. He refers to the depressing hygienic conditions and frequent illnesses present a year ago and then tells his audience about the successful health campaign. His Nicaraguan interlocutors explain that the success was accomplished by the Nicaraguan people. In the captions Rius uses the metaphor of a battle to describe the struggle between health and illness, visualizing the latter as a small snake. He emphasizes the increased democratic opportunities of Nicaraguans and argues that the first important step of prophylaxis against authoritarian regimes was the expulsion of Somoza from Nicaragua. The last panel of the comic strip relates to the enemies of the revolution and ends with the militant slogan: "No pasarán" (*Barricada*, May 28, 1982, pp. 8–9).

Another comic booklet dealing with fruit consumption introduces a hero from a Sandinista mass organization, in this case the EPA (Ejército Popular de Alfabetización). The young and always smiling protagonist visits the Nicaraguan countryside and proposes the vision of Nicaragua as a "paradise of fruit" to the recipients. He warns of the dangers of deforestation and denounces "yankee imperialism" as its historical cause, personified by an iconic Uncle Sam with stars and stripes on his hat. Together with Somoza and the local bourgeoisie, they appear as owners of "Nicaragua Company," which exploited the country's natural resources until 1979 (Ministerio de Cultura de Nicaragua 1980a). The comic also includes trees and animals as popular figures and is thus quite illustrative for the recipients. The health comics sought to establish new heroes in collective memory: everyday people and members of the mass organizations.

FIGURE 4.4. Educational comic for the promotion of fruit consumption blaming the Somoza regime for natural resource exploitation. *Source*: Ministerio de Cultura de Nicaragua 1980a, p. 3.

One important element of the health comics was their reference to local cultural codes. For example, several of the illustrations include baseball scenes, as in one comic strip on breastfeeding where the two protagonists eliminate old traditional beliefs by destroying them with a ball. Baseball, at that time, was the most popular sport in Nicaragua. As another local reference, local food such as *tiste* (a Nicaraguan corn drink) or tortillas (Donahue 1986: 73) appears in the drawings. For the most part, the comic strips in the pamphlets contain funny illustrations to make their readers smile, thus fulfilling one important criteria for being remembered: creating emotional involvement. Visual elements as narrative boxes and motion lines facilitate the understanding of the action while the text is limited to the most important information and short comments by the protagonists. The comics give advice on what to do in case of illness or on how to store food more hygienically by very simple visual instructions. These directives increased their practical use for the health projects. Although most health comic strips were not understandable without the content of the narrative boxes and speech balloons, they attracted recipients by funny illustrations, familiar references, and a dramatic composition.

Despite these successes, other Sandinista educational comics lacked important elements to enthrall their audience and to communicate their message successfully to illiterate people. To demonstrate, I analyze three educational comic strips on economic policy. Since April 1981 the protagonist Compa Clodomiro was introduced in the comics on economic topics, but in contrast to the health comics' protagonists, he lacks characteristics permitting an easy identification. Clodomiro is a young party member with a seldomly changing expression. Although his clothing sometimes changes, assigning him with different social roles, the rolled-up arms of his shirt indicate Clodomiro's energy. He was assigned to present the new economic program in 1981 to Nicaraguan people. On the whole, the economic policy strips were unlikely to win their audience: visual illustrations such as Nicaraguan people or landscapes nearly disappear among the large text boxes. Coming back to the initial example, Clodomiro introduces as a central message the need to raise production and limit consumption by referring to the structural problems and the external dependence of the Nicaraguan economy. He concludes the argument by presenting long statistics of several pages with goals for agricultural and industrial production (Ministerio de Planificación 1981). In other words, there is no stirring dramaturgy leading to the main message.

In the comics on supply problems, the protagonists are generally ordinary Nicaraguan people discussing their daily difficulties. One story begins with a group of women asking what the origins of the problems were. In his answer the protagonist lists several reasons, such as production problems, climatic conditions, war, and speculation, but speech balloons in this strip are so text-heavy that protagonists seem to vanish from view (*Barricada*, January 4, 1984, p. 8).

This is also true for another comic dedicated to the explanation of inflation. By using the example of tortillas, it illustrates the process of a currency losing value and ends with a militant statement. The protagonist shouts that

FIGURE 4.5. Text-loaded educational comic on economic policy. Source: *Barricada*, January 4, 1984, p. 8.

Nicaragua will never succumb to U.S. imperialist pressure and argues for raising production, fighting speculation, and reducing government spending (*Barricada*, March 6, 1985, p. 4), but again speech balloons dominate the entire plot. This reflects that the Sandinista planners', and the comic author's thinking was focused on texts to explain economic issues, probably a result of inexperience with visual expressions for complex topics. The characters have no names and seem to be exchangeable, which made them easier to forget and might have led to their nonconsideration in collective memory.

Educational comics in a revolutionary society fulfill a special function for political communication. They serve as a medium of revolutionary identity construction, memory politics, and give practical advice in everyday life situations. In the case of Sandinista Nicaragua, visual expressions had played an important role during the insurrectional period. After the revolution visual media remained important for the communication of political messages as Sandinista politicians and planners were faced with a high percentage of illiterate people. Inspired by popular education projects in other Latin American countries, these leaders introduced a participative methodology and new didactical material into the education sector. Comics were one important piece in the ensemble of different media used to communicate the government's messages. The different revolutionary mass organizations formed a central space of communication where the educational material was discussed.

The comics contributed in an active way to collective memory formation during the political transition period. They opened up spaces for the recipients' historical imagination and for the debate on the political transformation in a collective environment. By introducing new narratives on insurrection and the Somoza period, these comics were a precursor for later historical interpretations. They also give us an insight into the messages the government wished to inscribe into collective memory. In the comics on insurrection, announced as a "martial documentary," viewers should be involved at an emotional level in the military confrontations and identify with the masses as agents for change. At the same time, the comics rely on the revolutionary icons to demonstrate a continuity with earlier anti-imperialist movements. In contrast to U.S. comic strips, superheroes and romantic adventures are absent in these stories but other typical elements of the comic genre support the dramaturgy. Finally, the comics provide us with an understanding of the Sandinista planners' visions for the revolutionary society. By portraying responsible, organized revolutionary subjects prepared to sacrifice their individual aims for the revolutionary process, they established an ambitious role model.

The comics on health topics demonstrate that the educational material was designed in a creative way. Their strength lies in their humorous approach combined with visual metaphors to explain basic health subjects. Although not central to the stories, a historical narrative is inherent, making a sharp dichotomy between the past of the Somoza regime and the revolutionary present. Visually, they replace the image of the powerful dictator with a ludicrous figure, which is their particular contribution to collective memory and relates to earlier satirical traditions in political caricatures. By contrast, the comics on economic issues show that the reliance on texts still dominated the planners' didactical approach. They also reflect the weak tradition of comics in Nicaragua and a lack of qualified authors who could transform tedious contents into attractive comic plots. Although some of the advantages of the genre were utilized, educational comics lacked a thrilling dramaturgy and familiar protagonists to identify with. These comics addressed such unpopular topics as the need to reduce consumption or avoid strikes. Their repetitive structures and strong moral arguments posed the risk of boring and indoctrinating the audiences. Finally, the comic authors focused mainly on the experiences of male, urban people in central Nicaragua and thus missed the chance to offer a more inclusive picture of Nicaraguan society.

Most of the comics were produced during the early years of revolution, the period of political transition when the need to establish revolutionary ideals and historical narratives was especially high. After the spectacular success of the literacy campaign, illiteracy rose again from the mid-1980s as a result of the Contra war and economic difficulties. Consequently, the need for visual educational material was still there, but resources continuously diminished. With the ongoing war, supply problems for printing materials and paper increased. The memories of Harald Juch (1989), sent to Nicaragua by the German Development Service (Deutscher Entwicklungsdienst, DED) in 1987, also indicate a decline in government's interest. After three years of nearly useless efforts to establish a comic series on vegetable cultivation for the National Food Program, Juch left the country disillusioned in 1989. Róger Sánchez died at the age of thirty-one in November 1990, and soon after *Semana cómica* ceased publication. With the electoral loss of the FSLN in 1990, the tradition of educational comic strips was abandoned.

NOTES

This chapter forms part of the Swiss National Science Foundation Project Nr.PP00P1_123471, "Recipes for Modernity: The Politics of Food, Development, and Culture Heritage in the Americas," principal applicant Professor Corinne A. Pernet, PhD, University of Basel. I appreciate the comments and suggestions made by Corinne Pernet, Heike Wieters, Ana Merino, and the participants of the Saint Gallen colloquium on Latin American studies who kindly read different versions of the chapter. I would also like to express my gratitude to the anonymous peer reviewers. Unless otherwise noted, translations in this chapter from their original-language sources into English are that of the author.

1. Born in 1960, Róger Sánchez joined *Barricada* after breaking off a technical career at the university in the 1980s. Collections of his work have been translated and published in the context of the international solidarity movement (Sánchez 1985).
2. In general, it is difficult to locate the educational comics of the revolutionary period in Nicaraguan archives and libraries, although they were distributed in relatively high editions in the early 1980s. A selection of the health pamphlets was published by J. Donahue (1986: 71–131). In addition, the International Institute of Social History (based in Amsterdam) holds a small collection of Nicaraguan comics.
3. The official statistics claim a reduction to nearly 13 percent, but they exclude a group of 130,000 people considered as "unteachable" (Arnove 1986: 27).

4. The recordings realized by the Brigada de Rescate Histórico Germán Pomares Ordóñez are kept in the collections of the Institute for Nicaraguan and Central American History in Managua.

REFERENCES

Arnove, R. F. 1994. *Education as Contested Terrain: Nicaragua, 1979–1993*. Boulder, CO: Westview Press.

Arnove, R. F. 1986. *Education and Revolution in Nicaragua*. New York: Praeger.

Austin, J., and J. Fox. 1985. "The Role of the Revolutionary State in the Nicaraguan Food System." *World Development* 13, no. 1: 15–40.

Barbosa, F. J. 2005. "July 23, 1959: Student Protest and State Violence as Myth and Memory in León, Nicaragua." *HAHR* 85, no. 2: 187–221.

Catalá Carrasco, J. 2011. "From Suspicion to Recognition? 50 Years of Comics in Cuba." *Journal of Latin American Cultural Studies* 20, no. 2: 139–60.

Donahue, J. M. 1986. *The Nicaraguan Revolution in Health: From Somoza to the Sandinistas*. South Hadley, MA: Bergin & Garvey.

Draper, B. 2009. "Sandino and Other Superheroes: The Function of Comic Books in Revolutionary Nicaragua." *International Journal of Comic Art* 11, no. 2: 136–75.

Fagen, Richard R. 1969. *The Transformation of Political Culture in Cuba*. Stanford, CA: Stanford University Press.

Fernández L'Hoeste, H., and J. Poblete. 2009. Introduction. In *Redrawing the Nation: National Identity in Latin/o American Comics*. Edited by H. Fernández L'Hoeste and J. Poblete, 1–16. New York: Palgrave Macmillan.

González-Rivera, V. 2010. "Gender, Clientelistic Populism, and Memory: Somocista and Neo-Somocista Women's Narratives in Liberal Nicaragua." In *Gender and Populism in Latin America: Passionate Politics*. Edited by K. Kampwirth and K. Weyland, 67–90. University Park: Pennsylvania State University Press.

Grünewald, D. 2000. *Comics*. Tübingen: Niemeyer.

Hachfeld, R. 1997. "RIUS für Anfänger." *Ridiculosa* 4: 188–200.

Halbwachs, M. 1985. *Das kollektive Gedächtnis*. Frankfurt/Main: Fischer Taschenbuch.

Jones, A. 2002. *Beyond the Barricades: Nicaragua and the Struggle for the Sandinista Press, 1979–1998*. Athens: Ohio University Press.

Jornadas Populares de Salud. 1981. *Primera Movilización Vacunación Antipolio: Documento 1*. Managua.

Juch, H. 1989. "Unser revolutionärer Alltag: Teil 2. Tagebuch Comics Zeichnungen Fotos." Unpublished manuscript.

Kansteiner, W. 2002. "Finding Meaning in Memory: A Methodological Critique of Collective Memory Studies." *History and Theory* 41, no. 2: 179–97.

Kunzle, D. 1998. "Róger Sánchez's 'Humor Erótico' and the *Semana Cómica*: A Sexual Revolution in Sandinista Nicaragua?" *Latin American Perspectives* 25, no. 4: 89–120.

Kunzle, D. 1978. "Chile's La Firme versus ITT." *Latin American Perspectives* 5, no. 1: 119–33.

Lacaze, C. 2012a. "Construcción de un héroe nicaragüense: Augusto 'César' Sandino." *Revista de Historia 28*. Instituto de Historia de Nicaragua y Centroamérica.

Lacaze, C. 2012b. "El FSLN y la iconografía de Augusto 'César' Sandino." *Caravelle, Cahiers du Monde hispanique y lusobrésilien* 98: 59–75.

Lent, J. A. 2009b. "Cuban Cartoonists: Masters of Coping." In *Redrawing the Nation: National Identity in Latin/o American Comics*. Edited by H. Fernández L'Hoeste and J. Poblete, 81–95. New York: Palgrave Macmillan.

Mackenbach, W. 2004. *Die unbewohnte Utopie: Der nicaraguanische Roman der achtziger und neunziger Jahre*. Frankfurt/Main: Verveurt.

Mattelart, A. 1986. "Communication in Nicaragua between War and Democracy." In *Communicating in Popular Nicaragua*. Edited by A. Mattelart, 7–27. New York: International General.

McCloud, S. 2004. *Comics richtig lesen*. Hamburg: Carlsen.

Medina, J. 2010. "Caricatura del sandinismo y de la Resistencia en mutación." *Istmo 20*. Online at http://istmo.denison.edu/n20/articulos/3-medina_julia_form.pdf. Accessed on September 15, 2013.

Merino, A. 2003. *El cómic hispánico*. Madrid: Ediciones Cátedra.

Ministerio de Cultura de Nicaragua. 1980a. *La fruta es nuestra ¡Aprovechémosla! O la manera de sembrar la nueva Nicaragua para nuevos Nicaragüenses*. Managua: Taller de Artes Gráficas.

Ministerio de Cultura de Nicaragua. 1980b. *Matagalpa . . . Insurección de agosto! Un recorrido al valor de un pueblo heroíco*. Managua: Ministerio de Cultura.

Ministerio de Planificación. 1981. *Clodomiro y el programa 81*. Managua: Centro de Publicaciones Silvio Mayorga.

Montoya, R. 2003. "House, Street, Collective: Revolutionary Geographies and Gender Transformation in Nicaragua, 1979–99." *Latin American Research Review* 38, no. 2: 61–93.

Mora Olivares, A. 1975. *Nicasio* 2. Managua: La Prensa.

Musset, A. 2005. *Hombres nuevos en otro mundo: Nicaragua de 1980 en los diarios de la Cruzada Nacional de Alfabetización*. Managua: Institute for Nicaraguan and Central American History (IHNCA) / Universidad Centroamericana (UCA).

Paul, G. 2013. *BilderMACHT: Studien zur Visual History des 20. und 21. Jahrunderts*. Göttingen: Wallstein Verlag.

Pérez Yglesias, M. 1985. "RicaSUPERTIÑOSA ayuda a LOS AGACHADOS . . . ¿Qué pensará MAFALDA? Historiar la historieta: ¿Un proyecto académico y/o político?" *Anuario de Estudios Centroamericanos* 11, no. 2: 157–93.

Ramírez, S. 2007. "Fenster mit Ausblick: Ansichten einer Revolution." In *Die Revolution ist ein Buch und ein freier Mensch: Die politischen Plakate des befreiten Nicaragua 1979–1990 und der internationalen Solidaritätsbewegung*. Edited by O. Bujard and U. Wirper, 18–20. Cologne: PapyRossa-Verl.

Richter, B. 2007. "Gewehr und Taube: Bildgeschichte und Symbol." In *Die Revolution ist ein Buch und ein freier Mensch: Die politischen Plakate des befreiten Nicaragua 1979–1990 und der internationalen Solidaritätsbewegung*. Edited by O. Bujard and U. Wirper, 40–53. Cologne: PapyRossa-Verl.

Rinke, S. 2004. *Begegnungen mit dem Yankee: Nordamerikanisierung und soziokultureller Wandel in Chile (1898–1990)*. Cologne: Böhlau.

Río, Eduardo del "Rius." 1983. *Hallo Nicaragua*. Dortmund: Weltkreis.

Sánchez, R. 1985. *Karikaturen aus Nicaragua*. Edited by Richard Grübling. Wuppertal: Edition Nahua.

Soto G., A. 2003. "Caricatura y agitación política en Chile durante la Unidad Popular, 1970–1973." *Bicentenario* 2: 97–137.

TANA (Tribunal Antiimperialista de Nuestra América). 1984a. *El humor como arma de la lucha ideológica: Primer concurso de la Caricatura Antiimperialista 1983*. Managua: TANA.

TANA (Tribunal Antiimperialista de Nuestra América). 1984b. *El humor como arma de la lucha ideológica No. 2: Segundo Concurso de Caricatura Antimperialista "Sandino Vive."* Prologue by Omar Cabezas. Managua: TANA.

Tatar, B. 2009. "State Formation and Social Memory in Sandinista Politics." *Latin American Perspectives* 36, no. 168: 158–77.

Téllez, D. M. 1984. "También las paredes se insurreccionaron." In *Pintas y graffiti de Nicaragua: La insurrección de las paredes*. 87–94. Managua: Editorial Nueva Nicaragua.

Utting, P. 1992. "The Political Economy of Food Pricing and Marketing Reforms in Nicaragua, 1984–87." *European Journal of Development Research* 4, no. 2: 107–31.

Vannini, M. 2011. "Memoria e imagen: Políticas públicas de la memoria en Nicaragua (1979–2010)." Ponencia, Segundo Seminario Internacional Memoria, Cultura y Ciudadanía 7.9.2011, Instituto de Historia de Nicaragua y Centroamérica (Managua). Online at www.ihnca.edu.ni/SSIDOS_imagen_memoria_MV. Accessed October 9, 2012.

Wetzel, D. J. 2009. *Maurice Halbwachs*. Konstanz: UVK Verlagsgesellschaft.

Whisnant, D. E. 1995. *Rascally Signs in Sacred Places: The Politics of Culture in Nicaragua*. Chapel Hill: University of North Carolina Press.

Woll, A. L. 1976. "The Comic Book in a Socialist Society: Allende's Chile 1970–1973." *Journal of Popular Culture* 9, no. 4: 1039–45.

Yates, F. A. 1990. *Gedächtnis und Erinnern: Mnemonik von Aristoteles bis Shakespeare.* Weinheim: VCH, Acta Humaniora.

FIVE

CYBER-CUY

REMEMBERING AND FORGETTING THE PERUVIAN LEFT

Paulo Drinot

In this chapter I examine comments attached to the online version of *El Cuy*, the Peruvian comic strip (in Spanish, *tira*) that Juan Acevedo, one of Peru's foremost artists, began in the late 1970s and early 1980s. The eponymous Cuy is not a "gopher," as scholar David William Foster (1989: 103) has suggested, but rather a guinea pig, a rodent ubiquitous in the Andes, and an important source of protein in the Andean diet. In Euro-American society, of course, it is also a pet.[1] In Peru the guinea pig is an animal identified with Andean Peru rather than with coastal Peru, and therefore with the indigenous rather than the "creole" or Europeanized population. Using a metonymic device also found in Art Spiegelman's *Maus* (1986 and 1991) and, perhaps most famously, in George Orwell's *Animal Farm* (and of course in many more comics and graphic novels, not least those populated by such Disney characters as Mickey Mouse, Goofy, Donald Duck, and so on), in this comic strip Acevedo represents Peruvian society in the early 1980s as constituted by guinea pigs, dogs, pigs, rabbits, and rats/mice. These animals are stand-ins, in very broad strokes, for social classes, although the relation between animal and class is not always straightforward. The comic strip was originally published in a weekly, *La Calle*, in 1979 and subsequently in *El diario de Marka*, a left-wing daily, in 1980 through 1981.[2] Much of the comic was published in book form in 1981 as *¡Hola Cuy!* (Acevedo 1981). A more recent edition,

El Cuy tira, was published in 2011 (Acevedo 2011). But this chapter focuses on *El Cuy*'s cyber-existence as a blog.

In September 2008, Juan Acevedo started a blog titled *El diario del Cuy*.[3] He updates this blog regularly and has been uploading both the *El Cuy* strip sequentially as well as other material that he has produced over the years. Like most blogs, Acevedo's has a comment function that allows visitors to leave comments and interact with one another and, indeed, with Acevedo, who regularly contributes to discussions. This chapter is based on an analysis of these comments. In particular, it explores what these comments tell us about the collective memories that *El Cuy*, in its cyber-reincarnation, helps to mobilize.[4] In this sense, along the lines put down by scholar Marianne Hirsch (1992–1993) in her reading of *Maus*, I approach Acevedo's blog as a memory site; what historian Pierre Nora has famously called a *lieu de mémoire* or, perhaps to be more precise, as a website of memory.[5] I am particularly interested in examining how *El Cuy* the blog (as opposed to *El Cuy* the comic strip) elicits collective memories of the Peruvian Left, and through such memories, how it contributes to constituting particular epistemologies of Peruvian history and politics. I approach Acevedo's blog as a technology of memory (Sturken 2008) through which to study how Peruvians remember and forget the history of the Peruvian Left at a particular critical historical juncture: the late 1970s and early 1980s. In so doing, I participate in an exercise that Acevedo himself begins to recognize as an important potential of his blog: "to remember, to reflect, to share with today's youth, could be an interesting task for those who lived through those years. The publication of these comic strips is Cuy's grain of sand."[6]

I first discuss *El Cuy* in its original context, the late 1970s and early 1980s. Although Acevedo returned to *El Cuy* in the mid-1980s and occasional strips have appeared since, including some that have appeared for the first time on the blog, I concentrate here on the comic strips that appeared in *La Calle* and *El diario de Marka* (the ones that Acevedo has also uploaded on his blog, which are eliciting comments from visitors) from 1979 through 1983.[7] Though many read *El Cuy* in these newspapers, others came across the comic first in the 1981 book *¡Hola Cuy!*. Either way, for many Peruvians who lived through the 1980s, *El Cuy* was a key cultural and political referent, as it was for many who did not live through the 1980s but who share what scholar Alison Landsberg (2004) has called a prosthetic memory of that period with those who did. As Acevedo himself notes in response to a post from a visitor to the blog who asks for help in identifying where he has seen a particular sequence of the comic strip before: "Perhaps you saw it in the book *¡Hola*

Cuy!, or perhaps you didn't see it and it just sounds familiar, because, I presume, these comic strips are in the Peruvian imaginary of those years (and they continue to shape it)."[8]

Later in the chapter I analyze some themes that emerge in the comments. I focus particularly on how the blog mobilizes memories of the Peruvian Left and of the rise of the insurgent Maoist group Sendero Luminoso (Shining Path) and the early years of Peru's internal armed conflict. However, it is worth stressing that *El Cuy* touches on many other interesting themes, including machismo, feminism, abortion, and racism, which elicit comments from posters to the blog.[9]

FROM DICTATORSHIP TO DEMOCRACY

El Cuy first appeared in Peru during a period of transition from dictatorship to democracy that was shaped by the emergence of an unprecedentedly powerful but divided left.[10] The "Peruvian Experiment" of the Revolutionary Goverment of the Armed Forces, led by General Juan Velasco Alvarado, consisted of heterodox and progressive reforms, including a sweeping agrarian reform and policies that favored popular mobilization. By the mid-1970s, the "experiment" had reached a bottleneck.[11] The regime of General Francisco Morales Bermúdez, who took over the reins of the military regime in 1975 after a palace coup, rolled back some of Velasco's reforms and reverted to orthodoxy in the style of military rule and economic policy. It also initiated a transition to democratic rule. This occurred in the context of, and to some extent was a consequence of, the emergence of a number of social movements, particularly labor unions but also peasant leagues, women's groups, and urban squatters, which mobilized against the military regime. Two major general strikes in 1977 and 1978 paralyzed the country.[12] This popular mobilization, largely a response to the dire economic situation the country faced and to the military regime's economic policies (seen to be impacting particularly negatively on the poor), was channeled more or less effectively by political parties of the left.[13]

These transition years were the heyday of the Peruvian Left, particularly of the so-called New Left. The origins of the Peruvian Left can be traced back to the formation, in the early 1930s, of both the Peruvian Communist Party (PCP) (largely coopted by successive governments and perceived as a spent force by the 1960s) and the Alianza Popular Revolucionaria Americana (APRA) of Víctor Raúl Haya de la Torre, which veered sharply to the right in the 1950s, and to a lesser extent Luciano Castillo's short-lived Socialist

Party. The New Left, which broke from the traditional left in the 1960s, was a reaction to the status quo in the country and within the left more specifically. The New Left was born in the wake of the Cuban Revolution as young militants left the PCP and APRA (and also Acción Popular, known as AP, the populist party vehicle established by President Fernando Belaúnde, 1963–1968 and 1980–1985) to form new parties, often sectarian and insurrectionary, that aligned along Guevarist, Maoist, and Trotskyist lines. The New Left was also a response to pressure from below, exemplified by the peasant uprisings and land occupations that shook the east of Cuzco province (*departamento*) in the early 1960s and brought to prominence Hugo Blanco, a Trotskyist and perhaps the left's most charismatic, if not necessarily most influential, leader. In the mid-1960s the military quickly and violently repressed Cuban-inspired guerrillas formed by the Movimiento de Izquierda Revolucionaria (MIR) and the Ejercito de Liberación Nacional (ELN). Although they failed to generate a *foco* in the Andes, these guerrilla movements were directly, if not exclusively, responsible for the military's decision to take power in 1968.[14]

In addition to benefiting from the tacit support of the Moscow-leaning Peruvian Communist Party, the Velasco regime actively coopted important cadres of the New Left, including some of those who had led the guerrilla movements of the mid-1960s. These cadres, such as Carlos Franco and Héctor Béjar, would play a key role in giving shape to the political project of the Revolutionary Government of the Armed Forces, particularly in the context of the regime's popular mobilization programmes or SINAMOS (the acronym stands for National System of Support for Social Mobilization but can also be read as "sin amos," meaning "without masters"). Nevertheless, an important sector of the New Left, both of the Guevarist persuasion and particularly of the Maoist tendency, rejected cooption and constituted a left opposition to the military. As is well-known, Shining Path began around this time to organize in Ayacucho in preparation for armed struggle (Stern 1998; La Serna 2012). It would initiate its "popular war" spectacularly on the day of the 1980 general elections by burning the ballot boxes in the village of Chuschi.

Overall, however, the New Left was weakened by the experience of the Velasco regime. Confronted by an authoritarian government that was actively implementing what to many looked like socialist policies, including a popular agrarian reform, but also orchestrating a transition to democracy in which the left could participate openly, the left, divided over whether to follow the route of electoral politics or armed insurrection, splintered and weakened. As political scientist Philip Mauceri has noted, the transition to democracy was not welcomed by the left, whose objective, at least as far as a majority of militants was concerned, was not procedural democracy but radical social change. For the left, the transition was "a step backward, away from reform and toward the return of conservative elites" (Mauceri 1997: 25).

The divisions within the left and the problems that the transition to democracy raised for the left were explored in great detail in Acevedo's strip, which appeared from 1980 on in *El diario de Marka*, the main left-wing daily in Peru in the early 1980s, and a singular experiment in the history of the Peruvian press, because of its ownership structure and because it attempted to represent the whole of the left.[15] The debates at the heart of the Peruvian Left, in particular the debates between more radical and more reformist wings, and the constant factionalism of the left, constituted a key theme in *El Cuy*. They were reflected in the discussions between the more impulsive Cuy and the more restrained or conciliatory Humberto, his sidekick. Yet even Cuy was easily outflanked by more radical groups on the left, such as the Juventud Roedora Revolucionaria (Revolutionary Rodent Youth) critical of Cuy's "emburguesamiento."[16]

Another key theme reflected in the comic strip was the belief on the left that Peru could very easily succumb to a Southern Cone–type dictatorship. This anxiety was expressed through the Videchet (Videla/Pinochet) character, a rat with close links to right-wing and unscrupulous antidemocratic elites represented by such characters as Doña Rancia and Doctor Chancho and by the regular presence of soldiers, depicted as pigs in uniform, in several strips. Finally, around 1982, the comic strip began to address the rise of Shining Path and the left's reaction to the insurgency. I focus on the memories elicited by these three broad political issues as reflected in the comments attached to the blog.

To be sure, political and social commentary has been present in Peruvian comics or comic forms since the late nineteenth century (Lucioni 2005; Sagástegui 2009). However, *El Cuy* represented a departure in terms of the extent to which politics, and more specifically the politics of the left, dominated the comic strip. Like no other comic strip of the time, *El Cuy* in effect expressed in comic strip form the political issues (on both Peruvian and international affairs) that appeared elsewhere in *El diario de Marka* (and within editorial meetings) and, more generally, the political debates that raged in the late 1970s and 1980s within the left.[17] As some of the comments suggest, for some readers the comic strip format of *El Cuy* made those political debates accessible and attractive (if not necessarily any easier to comprehend). *El Cuy* was a channel for, or a conduit to, a political education, an *aggiornamento* on the left, a way to develop and make your own a left critique of Peru's political and social order. It was also a subtle commentary on the left or, more precisely, on Peru's many leftist factions.[18] Acevedo's own position can be discerned at times from the way in which the arguments and positions of different sectors of the left are depicted in the comic. In this sense, *El Cuy* was both a channel through which the debates of the left could resonate to a broad (and often, if not exclusively, youthful) audience and an active interlocutor. It proved to be an influential voice that, unlike the left, continues to resonate widely today.

REMEMBERING THE LEFT

The formative role of the strip in one's personal identity and in a personal history shaped by being on and of the left or, more often, being the children of left-wing parents is one of the themes that comes through quite early in the blog comments, when Acevedo first began to upload new and old strips of *El Cuy*.[19] Several posters express this idea in remarkably similar ways. Alvaro, for example, writes that he began reading *El Cuy* when he was five or six years old. His father, "an old man of the left," gave them to Alvaro to read and he would read them along with the comic *Mafalda*: "I always recall with nostalgia the *Cuy* strip and supporting the United Left. Long live the militant and revolutionary Cuy!!!"[20]

The recollection of having been initiated into the pleasures of reading *El Cuy* by relatives, and typically by relatives identified as being of the left, is recurring. Ivonne, now thirty, remembers reading *El Cuy* from the age of eight or nine because her parents bought *El diario de Marka* and *Sí/No* (a satirical magazine): "I am of a generation of left-wing youths who had fun reading your stories (perhaps only understanding about half of it because we were so young)," she tells Acevedo.[21] For some, this experience was not only pleasurable, it was also didactic. Akane writes: "I learned to write with *El Cuy*!"[22] Edgar Vilca Figueredo approaches the issue of identity from a different perspective: "When I read *El Cuy*, I felt represented, just like the Argentines with *Mafalda*. A great way to do politics."[23] *El Cuy*'s success, this suggests, owed to some degree to its perceived "Peruvianness." It was a comic strip made by a Peruvian for Peruvians, unlike so many other comics that were published at the time in Peruvian newspapers.

For many readers, the identity that *El Cuy* helped to constitute, with its political and national dimensions, was also generational; it expressed a commonality derived from having lived a shared experience. As Lukysh puts it, Cuy, his childhood hero, represents a whole period of history for his generation.[24] Jairo, who read *El Cuy* so many times as a child that he knew portions of it by heart, similarly states: "*El Cuy* represents so much of what we are, our questions and our explorations, sometimes mistaken, but always trying to be sincere."[25] This positive recollection of *El Cuy* in terms of one's own personal history and the development of a distinct generational identity stands in stark contrast to the negative recollection of the period in which these contributors first encountered *El Cuy*, the 1980s—a time of fear as scholars Deborah Poole and Gerardo Rénique (1992) have called it, a lost decade, when little that was positive happened. Maykolt writes: "I was born in the 1980s . . . now that I am almost thirty, when I read these strips I am transported to those days, to that chaos which occupies so much space in my memories."[26] Similarly, Emilio Salcedo recalls that he was ten years old when he read *El Cuy* and *La Araña No* (another of Acevedo's comic strips): "Although I tried, I didn't understand them very well. To remember this, one of the few good things about that period of history, fills me with nostalgia."[27]

In reminiscing about *El Cuy*, several commenters remark on the ways in which the comic strip offered them a new way to understand and to think about this particularly difficult time in Peruvian history but also about Peruvian society more generally. Miguel Plá states, for example, that what attracted him to *El Cuy* was the fact that it "analyzed reality from the point of view of the excluded" and that it became a tool through which "to appreciate what is ours."[28] Javier expresses the same sentiment, noting that he found Cuy's social commitment to others sincere, and that he liked the fact the Cuy would gnaw lightly on some issues, "leaving it to us to chew on the matter (in order to understand it)."[29] Similarly, Emilio articulates how, even at a very young age, *El Cuy* offered him a fresh political perspective on the world that other comics simply did not provide. At the time, he was eight years old and read only comics that his mother bought him, such as *Little Lulu*, *Archie*, and *Donald Duck*, but *El Cuy* "gave me a broader understanding of what could be done and transmitted through comics."[30] In a different post, Emilio points to how effective the metonymic or metaphoric strategy of *El Cuy* was in unveiling the tensions at the heart of Peruvian society. He always understood that Acevedo had set out to portray a metaphor of Peruvian society: "In these comics Juan showed the racism and self-racism in the world of rodents. . . . An allegory of what happened (and still happens) in Peruvian society."[31] In this sense, many posters agree with David William Foster's (1989: 104) suggestion that Acevedo's purpose is "not to diffuse a humble regional product as merely another trivial imitation of the cultural dictates of the vias of international consumption, but to metamorphize the treacherous and dominating icons into referent signs of local values whose merit consists of not competing with, but referring to, more global and popular cultural systems and their traditional meaning."

As the comments on the blog make clear, *El Cuy* not only helped the posters make sense of the world around them. It also enabled them to acquire a left-wing view of the world and even played a role in their decision to "militar"—that is, to become a militant in one of the political parties of the left. Patricia Temple Arciniega writes, for example, that it was thanks to Cuy and his dialogues with Humberto that she took her first steps in developing an interest in politics.[32] Similarly, José associates his reading of Cuy with a process of personal development that resulted in joining the left: "This is very moving! I still remember the first time I read *El Cuy*. It was in *La Calle* magazine, now no longer published (like so many others). It was a time of Cold War and soldiers in government. In that time, to be of the left was practically an obligation, a sign of improvement, a natural consequence of an honest life." However, José adds a note of sadness: "I don't know when our hopes ended or when the enormous disappointments that we experienced later [began] to undermine such sentiments."[33] Elsewhere, in a comment to a sequence on Cuy's emerging romance with Pericotita (Cuy's love interest and future wife), José writes: "I remember this sequence very well. I was eleven and I was very moved by the idea of being a left-wing guinea pig. Not only because of the social consciousness that this implied, but also because it could help to attract the sensitive little mice [*las pericotitas sensibles*] who were strolling around the hen coop. How times have changed! Now the little mice are great big rats! [*ahora las pericotitas son unas ratazas!*]."[34]

For José, and for many others, being of the left at the time of *El Cuy*'s original publication was both a natural political decision and a lifestyle option that was highly desirable and could be rewarding. But, as he indicates, this situation soon changed. As other posters confirm, the left lost its way after an initial period in the 1980s. Commenting on a scene in which Cuy's daughter, Anita, confronts her father and accuses him of being machista and "adultista" while making ironic comments about his claim to be a leftist, Carlos el baterillero recalls a better time, when being of the left had real and positive consequences. In particular, he recalls the electoral success of Alfonso Barrantes, who as the United Left candidate won the mayoral elections in Lima in 1984.[35] That moment, it is implied, has gone. As César Flores Huallpa explains, in response to Carlos el baterillero's comment, the collapse of the Soviet Union and the Eastern Bloc in the 1980s and Shining Path atrocities "ended up by screwing the Left, which today only survives recycled as defenders of the few Indians that survive, as environmentalists or nationalists."[36] Writing in September 2011, following both the unexpected election of Susana Villarán to the post of mayor of Lima on a left-of-center agenda and of Ollanta Humala to the presidency, also on a broadly left-of-center agenda (later largely abandoned), César Flores Huallpa adds: "Now that the left has come to power with Susana Villarán and Ollanta Humala, I hope it will do a better job than it did back then."[37]

The idea that the left lost its way is expressed most clearly in response to a sequence of strips that refer explicitly to the first electoral campaign of Alfonso Barrantes, leader of the United Left, known affectionately as "frejolito" (little bean), in the 1980 mayoral election. Several contributors express a clear nostalgia for Barrantes himself. Rafael Vega Llallapasca recalls "the times of Alfonso, one of the few decent politicians in the history of our country."[38] Luis Ramírez, similarly notes, in allusion to Ollanta Humala, Peru's recently elected president at the time of writing, "today cases of corruption are so common. . . . Let's hope that Ollanta will remind us of 'frejolito.'"[39] This is a theme reprised by Acevedo himself, who repeats the idea that Barrantes was one of the few decent politicians: "That is why we still remember him fondly."[40]

José expresses a similar view with an even stronger dose of nostalgia: for him, it was always a pleasure to see and listen to "dear uncle frejolito." Few politicians today have the same charisma, he suggests. This is the reason, José claims, that he no longer goes to political rallies. When he went to see Susana Villarán address a crowd in Lima's Campo de Marte, where, he adds, he ran into Juan Acevedo, he was moved by the situation: "That night I had a knot in my throat because my parents are now dead and I felt that at that moment I went back in time/space and I became again that child who went to see his uncle frejolito . . . whose life was an example of simplicity and humility that I do not perceive in our politicians. At least, this is how I will remember him, with fondness, until the day I die too."[41]

Yet alongside this nostalgic and even romantic view of a left represented by the figure of Alfonso Barrantes, the posters also express a far more critical perspective on the left, which focuses on its "errors," its sectarianism, and its failure to distance itself and openly condemn Shining Path. The left's sectarianism, alluded to in a sequence of strips in which Cuy decides to establish an "izquierda sabroza" (a "tasty" left) in opposition to an "izquierda de mongos" (a left of nerds) leads Leonor to write: "*El Cuy* portrays brilliantly the deliberations of a left which never succeeded in getting its leaders to rise above their ideological positions, interests, and personal initiatives in order to build a united front."[42] Orlando, meanwhile, remembers the physical fights that broke out between different factions of the left during the yearly pilgrimages to the Lima tomb of José Carlos Mariátegui, early twentieth-century Marxist writer and "father" of the Peruvian Left.[43] This factionalism, which in the strip is humorously represented in Cuy's political intransigence in his debates with Humberto (who rejects the factionalism), is perceived as an authoritarian streak in the left, as a form of *caudillismo*, by Elmer: "What a caudillo [Cuy is]! In social and political militancy, [*caudillismo*] was always a factor, and let's hope this type of attitude will weaken among those who think they are always right. . . . More citizenship, fewer caudillos."[44]

Such critiques of the left are evident particularly in reactions to a series of strips in which the panels are divided first in two, with a sanitized (and commercialized) version of *El Cuy* presented in the lower half, and then in three, with Videchet plotting to take over the comic strip becoming the narrative arc in the bottom third. These strips, and several others, are expressive of the fear in the Peruvian Left of the early 1980s that Peru could, at any moment, face a military coup of the sort that had befallen the Southern Cone countries. Faced with this takeover, Cuy decides to blow up the comic strip with a stick of dynamite. This leads to a discussion between Cuy and Humberto over the best strategy to pursue. Clearly this discussion reflects the struggles within the Peruvian Left in the early 1980s over whether, in light of the perceived threat of a military coup, a parliamentary and democratic path to socialism was possible or whether the only realistic strategy was armed struggle. As Orlando states: "Cuy and Humberto are part of the same left, one radicalized and the other moderate."[45] This was a debate that contributed to the division and atomization of the left at the very time that the armed struggle route had been adopted by Shining Path. Humberto eventually manages to convince Cuy that violence is not the best strategy. However, Cuy's son, Chutito, bombs the comic strip. After the bombing, Humberto is arrested and tortured, while Cuy goes underground. The upper third of the comic strip is taken over by soldiers.

The discussion that this sequence elicits among posters to the blog focuses on the error of the view represented by Cuy. Humberto's position, by contrast, is seen as having been the correct one. Rlajo, for example, writes: "Several sequences in *El Cuy*, such as this one, remind me how difficult it was for the left in the 1980s to distance itself from violence. And this makes me understand a little better those who will not forgive the left. Juan, as an artist, has been very honest in publishing these cartoons as they were originally conceived in that confusing time, but I think that [very few] politicians

FIGURE 5.1. Cuy attempts to blow up the comic strip in the top third of the panels, while puppets of Cuy and Humberto sing advertising jingles about commercial products in the middle section, and Videchet delivers a reactionary speech in the bottom third (final bubble: "Order, Fatherland, God, Freedom"). *El Cuy* 249. Reproduced with kind permission of Juan Acevedo.

FIGURE 5.2 Soldiers have taken over the top third of the panel, Humberto is tortured in jail in the middle, and Videchet laughs about having tricked the bourgeoisie in the bottom third. *El Cuy* 264. Reproduced with kind permission of Juan Acevedo.

and activists of the left are capable of opening up in this way."[46] A later strip, which shows Cuy imagining himself as José Carlos Mariátegui (Peru's great Marxist thinker), César Vallejo (an avant-garde Peruvian poet), and Che Guevara, elicits a commentary from leonorsuarezognio that locks on the megalomania of Cuy and, by extension, of the Peruvian Left of the early 1980s: "I studied in a state university in the 1980s and at that time people would discuss political matters furiously in a way that you no longer see. . . . I had the opportunity to get to know all types of guinea pigs at that time . . . the true ones (with their megalomaniac visions so well represented in our own Cuy), the rat-guinea pigs, the pig-guinea pigs, etc."[47]

Acevedo responds to this comment by remarking on Cuy's "unfortunate ego." Leonorsuarezognio, in turn, replies that egos, when they are not colossal, can be positive attributes in leaders. Cuy, she suggests, "helps us to understand the thoughts and motivations of many who had positions of leadership in our history." However, she notes regretfully, that the desire to lead, when it is exaggerated, sometimes results in division, "as happened to our 'united' left and [it] becomes a step that links *caudillismo* with tyranny."[48] These comments illustrate the current widespread disillusion and frustration with the Peruvian Left and the few figures of the left that remain. They express starkly how many Peruvians find it increasingly difficult to connect to a left that they see as having failed to evolve and adapt to changing times and address the problems that plagued it in the 1980s, including sectarianism and the grandstanding of its leaders as well as its ambiguous position in relation to representative democracy and armed insurrection.

This disillusion, not least among people who grew up on the left, such as those who have commented on the blog, is reflected in the left's dismal performance in most national and regional elections since the mid-1980s, which have contributed to making the "Old" New Left a political irrelevance and have made it extremely difficult for a "New" New Left to emerge. At the time of writing this chapter, a new force on the left, the Frente Amplio led by Verónika Mendoza, has done well at the 2016 national elections, capturing 20 percent of the vote. Whether it can sustain this support, or evolve into a permanent political movement that channels political mobilization on the left, remains to be seen. At the same time, Alfonso Barrantes and his tenure as mayor of Lima (1984–1986) is remembered positively. Although Barrantes's United Left did not unify the whole of the left and soon unraveled, for many of the blog commenters, this experience of the left in power is mobilized as a memory that arguably expresses a nostalgia not so much for Barrantes's mayorship but more generally for a left that could have been.

As the historian Pierre Nora (1989: 19) has suggested, a site of memory is material, symbolic, and functional. As the previous discussion shows, in its cyber-reincarnation as a blog (an immaterial materiality), *El Cuy* operates as a website of memory that mobilizes (and helps constitute) symbolic representations of the Peruvian Left. But it also serves as a platform from which to assess the left and to, implicitly or explicitly, draw lessons about the left for the present and the future. The online nature of the blog enables a particular type of interactive memory work that is in effect deterritorialized (with some commenters identifying their locations within and outside Peru) but at the same time clearly rooted in a specific national experience. It is also constitutive of the group that mobilizes such memories, since it is through the memory work that the blog (and through the blog, *El Cuy* as comic strip) enables the establishment of collective identity among those individuals who post to the blog. In other words, the blog—a particular technology of memory (Sturken 2008)—mobilizes collective memories of the Peruvian Left in ways specific to its deterritorialized nature as a digital artifact. At the same time, the blog allows the performance of specific practices of memorialization that emulate the practices of memory more often associated with more conventional memory sites, such as memorials like El ojo que llora in Lima or trauma sites like the ESMA in Buenos Aires or Villa Grimaldi in Santiago de Chile (Drinot 2009; Jelin and Langland 2003). Through their comments, the commenters act as memory cyber-entrepreneurs (Jelin 2002), linking the past and the present.

REMEMBERING SHINING PATH

Similar memory work occurs in the blog comments in relation to the rise of Shining Path. I want to start by discussing the comments attached to the torture scenes, involving Humberto, in the sequence of strips mentioned previously. These torture scenes are coupled with a sequence in the upper part of the comic strip in which the soldiers taunt a dove and eventually kill it. In the recollection of several commenters, this is the most traumatic sequence in *El Cuy*, although it is interesting to note that several find the killing of the dove, and what this symbolizes, more shocking than the torture of Humberto. The order of exchanges is in itself interesting. Leonorsuarezognio starts off the discussion: "Wow, how contemporary! . . . our leaders, our history, our methods are still the same (when I say 'ours' I am not referring exclusively to Peru but rather to 'the human') . . . some of the strips in *El Cuy*, as reflections of the period, should be in the 'Lugar de la Memoria' [the Place of Memory]."[49] The Lugar de la Memoria, la Tolerancia y la Inclusión Social, is a museum that has been a source of controversy since its creation was first proposed in the final report of the Peruvian Truth and Reconciliation Commission. Although now built thanks to a donation from the German government, the museum has largely been ignored by the Humala government and attacked by the right-wing press. Its fate is expressive of the broader politics of memory in Peru.[50]

Bruno Ysla Heredia responds to Leonorsuarezognio's suggestion by pointing to the fact that the strip, and in particular the torture scene, reflects not Peruvian history but the history of other Latin American countries:

FIGURE 5.3. A soldier kills a dove in the third panel. *El Cuy* 274. Reproduced with kind permission of Juan Acevedo.

"Regarding the 'Lugar de la Memoria,' I believe that the next story line in *El Cuy* is more appropriate because it is more realistic and personal (which is where I believe this memory [of Peru's internal armed conflict] originates); this section is based more on the Argentine and Chilean cases of the time . . . it is linked to a Latin American memory more properly speaking." Ysla Heredia is referring to the narrative arc followed by *El Cuy* later when Acevedo himself addressed directly the Shining Path insurgency. It is particularly interesting that Ysla Heredia adds: "However, and I point to this separately in order to make the distinction clear, in general *El Cuy* is a valuable testimony on the Peruvian Left (this becomes clear in the next section [of the comic])." He is thus framing, albeit cautiously, a consideration of Shining Path firmly within a broader consideration of the left; something that many on the left are, understandably, reluctant to do.[51] Although Acevedo intervenes in the discussion at this point, he responds to a comment by Carlos Wertheman about the soldier pig being representative of a sector of the armed forces, and on how each section of the comic strip reflects a different narrative line, but Acevedo does not comment on what the torture scenes represent.

Whether the torture depicted applies to Peru or not is a question that the commenters are clearly asking themselves but find difficult to answer. In response to a later sequence, Leonorsuarezognio writes: "The sequence in the middle represents so well the horror that passes just in front of our noses without us seeing it. . . . I don't know when these comic strips were made and published, but they reflect events that took place in our countries, caused by different governments, following the 'same school,' which, to this day, is not revealed, denounced and judged as it should be. . . . Without a doubt it will be known as a dark era in the history of humanity . . . like the

Inquisition."[52] But another contributor, Orlando, grounds the torture in a specifically Peruvian context with this intervention: "Máximo arrived in the neighbourhood in the 1980s and sometimes he would hang out with us. He came from Ayacucho, where he lived and studied at Huamanga University. We talked about everything that young people talk about, except the time he spent in Los Cabitos military base, we suspected or knew he had been tortured, that he was of the left, a university student, from Ayacucho and that his long silences and his reluctance to go out were not a product of a provincial timidity."[53] Acevedo clarifies: "Los Cabitos, the sinister military base in Ayacucho, where so many, involved or not, were disappeared in the 1980s."[54]

These comments illustrate the complex memories (and forgettings) that the references to the early 1980s in *El Cuy* mobilize. On the one hand, the comments largely elide the question of the threat of a Southern Cone–like military dictatorship, which was very much at the forefront of how the Peruvian Left understood the situation it faced in the early 1980s. But memories of this threat are weak; perhaps not surprisingly, since they are memories of something that did not occur—there was no Southern Cone–like military coup in Peru in the early 1980s. More important, memories of this nonevent have been pushed into the background by, or transformed into, memories of the internal armed conflict: a vague Latin American *cultural* memory (Assmann 1995) of the dirty wars of the Southern Cone alluded to in the comic strip is displaced by a more real and local memory of Peru's internal armed conflict. This is why the torture scenes in the strip, which represent a hypothetical situation of a military take-over leading to the repression of the left, which did not occur, mobilize memories of state repression and the torture of the innocent and the noninnocent in the context of Peru's internal armed struggle. This is clear from Leonorsuarezognio's suggestion that the torture scenes be included in the Lugar de la Memoria or from Orlando's reference to the Cabitos military base, where, as the Truth and Reconciliation Commission showed, some of the worst human rights abuses perpetrated by the armed forces took place. In some ways Cabitos was the one episode of Peru's internal armed conflict that most closely echoes the dirty wars of the Southern Cone.[55]

Starting around 1982, the specter of Shining Path appears increasingly clearly in *El Cuy*. The tense moment that the country experienced is first reflected in a series of strips that depict increasing acts of rebellion by Cuy's children, who are shown in several panels demanding, "The little guinea pigs to power! [Los cuysitos al poder!]."[56] Another sequence depicts war games played between Cuy's sons and Videchet's son, in which Cuy's daughter,

Anita, is drawn wearing a Che Guevara beret, armed with stones, and refuting the claim of Videchet's son, whom she has pelted with the stones, that she is a terrorist: "Terrorist, no. Guerrilla." This strip leads Carlos el baterillero to comment: "This was a game for the little guinea pigs, but it was beginning to take on violent nuances. It's the country, it's the city, in which a climate of anxiety and fear is beginning to appear. It's the 1980s."[57] This is followed by a series of strips in which one or more of the panels represent an explosion with an onomatopeic "¡PUM!" At the time it was still unclear, to Acevedo and one assumes to many Peruvians, who were responsible for these bombs. Humberto asks: "Are they of the Left or of the Right?"[58] The sequence of strips dominated by these explosions show Cuy and Humberto squabbling over what the bombings mean, over who or what is behind them, and what they should do about them. The uncertainty over who is behind the bombs is reflected in the shift in onomatopeia from the Spanish "¡PUM!" to the English-sounding "BOOM!" and the Chinese-sounding "CHING!" This leads both Cuy and Humberto to speculate about whether the Americans or the Chinese are behind the bombs.[59]

Sendero Luminoso is introduced through the character Senderito, who is represented as a nonidentified animal wearing a balaclava and carrying a submachine gun.[60] Senderito is portrayed along the lines that have come to characterize how Shining Path itself is portrayed: as dogmatic and ruthless.[61] In one strip Senderito reacts angrily to a discussion between two cuys on what is happening in Peru in which one cuy suggests that Peru is a contradictory country and the other responds that it is "magical." Senderito shouts: "Nothing magical about it! REVOLUTIONARY, POPULAR AND SCIENTIFIC!"[62] The left's, and indeed the country's, reaction to the appearance of Senderito is represented in one strip where Humberto is depicted staring into the void while a dialogue develops between two guinea pigs: "Is this the disconcerted Left?" asks one, to which the other answers: "I think it's Peru."[63] These strips capture very well the tensions, anxieties, and confusion that the rise of Shining Path in the early 1980s created within the Peruvian left.

The narrative arc that develops focuses first on Anita, Cuy's daughter, who falls in love with Senderito. The following panels depict the tensions within the left. Humberto claims that it is normal that Anita is attracted to Senderito. Senderito represents action, and the young find action attractive. Cuy wants to stop Anita from leaving with Senderito, but a discussion ensues with Humberto over whether he should engage Senderito as a father or politically. This is followed by a series of strips where the Andes are represented by the appearance of mountains in the distance and by discussions between

FIGURE 5.4. Representation of Sendero Luminoso in the strip. Final panel: "[Peru is] not magical! [It is] REVOLUTIONARY, POPULAR AND SCIENTIFIC!" *El Cuy* 599. Reproduced with kind permission of Juan Acevedo.

FIGURE 5.5. The Andes appear in the comic strip. *El Cuy* 646. Reproduced with kind permission of Juan Acevedo.

FIGURE 5.5. A river of blood flows down from the Andes. Cuy asks Humberto: "Is that Senderito's blood?" Humberto answers in panels two and three: "Yes, in part. It is also the blood of young police officers, in part. But above all it is the blood of innocent people whose impotence leads them to desperation." After Humberto is shot at in panel three, Cuy tells him in panel four: "Be careful Humberto! It looks like several people thought you were referring to them." *El Cuy* 652. Reproduced with kind permission of Juan Acevedo.

Cuy and Humberto that express their (and by implication, Lima's) lack of understanding of the highlands. Eventually, a river of blood descends from the mountains.

These and later strips that represent the developing internal armed conflict provoke a number of comments among posters to the blog. One strip shows a discussion between Cuy and Humberto in which Cuy tells Humberto that Senderito is committing atrocities, killing innocent people and destroying valuable infrastructure that benefits the poor. Cuy concludes that Senderito is irrational. Humberto answers that perhaps the reality that creates the rise of Sendero is even more irrational. "Do you support Senderito?" asks Cuy? "I try to understand what is happening," answers Humberto. This sequence provokes a single comment from Gonzalo Alva Novoa: "Just like Humberto, the Peruvian Left spent all of the 1980s making these arguments."[64] This poster expresses a critique often made of the Peruvian Left by many on the right: in trying to understand Shining Path, not only did the left fail to understand it (for example, in a later panel Humberto alludes to the idea that Shining Path is an expression of the oppression of the indigenous, which dates back hundreds of years) but more seriously failed to oppose it or to take a position against Shining Path. To be sure, other commenters who suggest that people on the left did reject Shining Path refute this idea.[65] However, as this suggests, *El Cuy*, and the way in which it recorded how the left debated the rise of Shining Path in the early 1980s, mobilizes memories of the internal armed conflict that are problematic for the left, which the right can use politically against it.[66]

The strips on Shining Path mobilize memories that are consonant with the narrative of the internal armed conflict that was constructed in the context of the Truth and Reconciliation Commission. In discussing the mountains that have appeared in the strip's background, Humberto remarks that "perhaps they were always there and we did not see them." Carlos el baterillero assents: "Humberto points to . . . the tragedy of our country: the invisibility of the other . . . the denial of the other's existence . . . the failure to discover the other . . . the failure to recognize him as equal in opportunities."[67] In response to the following sequence, Acevedo writes: "When I drew these panels, I was very taken by what Peru was experiencing: The war . . . unleashed by Shining Path and the armed forces, and also another war, everyday, secular, between discriminators and the discriminated, owners and the dispossessed, exploiters and the exploited."[68] These and other comments reflect closely the argument put forward in the final report of the Truth and Reconciliation Commission that while a number of armed actors, and primarily Shining Path, were responsible for the violence, the violence was also expressive of the myriad and historically rooted inequalities and exclusions that shape Peruvian society. As the president of the commission stated in his speech the day the final report was published: "[Peru] is a country where exclusion is so absolute that tens of thousands of citizens can disappear without anyone in integrated society, in the society of the nonexcluded, noticing a thing."[69]

However, not all posters share this interpretation. In one strip, which depicts one of the many blackouts provoked by Shining Path when they blew up electricity pylons or transmission towers outside Lima, Cuy and Humberto are shown discussing the impact that Shining Path's actions are having on the political fortunes of the left and, specifically, on Cuy's intention to run for mayor. Cuy laments that "Senderito appears and unbalances everything." Humberto retorts: "I didn't know that things were all that balanced before." This exchange is clearly read as an expression of the ambiguous position of the left toward Shining Path by Consultor, who comments ironically: "Senderito did not unbalance anything . . . 'structural violence' is to blame."[70] Consultor's comment is a reaction to the dialogue in the comic strip, but it is interpellating more broadly the interpretation of the Truth and Reconciliation Commission of the causes and nature of the violence that Peru experienced. As this suggests, the comment function on the *El Cuy* blog establishes itself as a cyberspace in which conflicting memories of Peru's internal armed conflict are mobilized. In a comment to a strip that represents the murder of eight journalists in Ucchuraccay, Ayacucho, one of the defining events in Peru's internal armed struggle, Carlos el baterillero writes: "A friend told me: *El Cuy* is the recent memory of our country. How true. Especially in a country like ours, where memory is so often a succession of forgettings."[71] But as Consultor's comment shows, *El Cuy*, like other sites (or websites) of memory in Peru, mobilizes not one but several memories of the nation.

The comments attached to the blog of *El Cuy* show how this cyber-reincarnation of the original comic strip mobilizes collective memories of the early 1980s, specifically of the Peruvian Left, in the context of the transition to democracy and the emergence of Shining Path. In remembering the Peruvian Left through *El Cuy*, many Peruvians find little to rejoice about. With the exception of the nostalgia that Alfonso Barrantes elicits, the memories of the left of the early 1980s reflect the ways in which most Peruvians, even those who are sympathetic to the left or whose political coming of age occurred in the ranks of the left, even of the extreme left, view the left today: as unable to find unity and riven by sectarianism, as dominated by self-absorbed caudillos, and as having failed to take a clear position in relation to Shining Path. These memories of the left, whether fair or unfair, whether mobilized for political purposes by the right or not, illustrate the difficulty the left, to the extent that it exists today in Peru, faces to construct a credible political project. Although in the early 1980s *El Cuy* the comic strip operated for many as a way to acquire a left-wing perspective on the world, and more specifically on Peru, today *El Cuy* the blog serves as a conduit for Peruvians to articulate the problems that are at the center of the recurring failure of the Peruvian Left to reemerge as a political force.

Like Proust's madeleine, the *El Cuy* blog elicits memories of one's personal experience of the *El Cuy* comic strip, through personal recollections of how the comic was acquired, how it was read, and what emotions reading the comic book produced. But it also elicits, more generally, individual memories of the whole period of history with which the comic strip is associated; a period that for most Peruvians remains subject to conflicting interpretations, regardless of whether they experienced it directly, experienced it as an inherited postmemory (Hirsch 1997), or through prosthetic memories (Landsberg 2004) of specific events, such as the Ucchuraccay massacre, that circulate in the cultural sphere. Because of the way in which the blog functions, these individual memories are confronted with, and (re-)constructed through, an interactive process that involves the memories of other commenters on the blog (and indeed Juan Acevedo's own recollections).

In this sense the *El Cuy* blog is a technology of memory that operates in ways that are different to, say, how *El Cuy tira*, the collection of *El Cuy* strips that Acevedo published in 2011, operates. *El Cuy* the website of memory functions as, and allows us and others to observe, the ongoing formation of collective memories. It offers a compelling window onto the memory practices that *El Cuy* the comic strip elicits and illustrates clearly how memories are not simply consumed but actively produced and negotiated. It reveals the singular importance of *El Cuy*, as comic strip and blog, as a cultural artifact through which Peruvians engage, both individually and collectively, the past, and in so doing, make sense of the present.

NOTES

1. Despite its importance in the context of Peru's small comics industry, *El Cuy* has not attracted systematic attention from scholars. For *El Cuy*'s place in the broader history of Peruvian comics, see Lucioni (2002) and Sagástegui (2009).
2. On *El Cuy* in *El diario de Marka*, see Agüero (2010).
3. See Acevedo's *El diaro del Cuy*, online at http://elcuy.wordpress.com/.
4. Acevedo also uploads *El Cuy* to a Facebook page, where comments are allowed. However, I have decided to focus here primarily on the blog comments.
5. See Nora (1989). On websites of memory, see Drinot (2011). On approaching comics as a conduit for accessing collective memories, see Hirsch (1992–1993).
6. Juan Acevedo, May 29, 2012, online at https://elcuy.wordpress.com/2012/05/, accessed on August 30, 2013.
7. As Acevedo explained on his Facebook page (www.facebook.com/juan.acevedo.peru, July 17, 2013), *El Cuy* appeared in *El diario de Marka* from May 13, 1980, through July 25, 1983. It reappeared, briefly (for a month), a year later in *El Observador*. *El Cuy* would later reappear in 1986 in *La Razón*.
8. Juan Acevedo, September 8, 2011, online at https://elcuy.wordpress.com/2011/09/05/el-cuy-por-juan-140/, accessed on August 30, 2013.
9. "Internal armed conflict" is the term used by Peru's Truth and Reconciliation Commission in its final report of 2003 to describe the violence the country experienced in the 1980s and 1990s, available online at www.cverdad.org.pe/, accessed on August 30, 2013.
10. On Peru's transition, see Mauceri (1997).
11. The literature on the Velasco regime is vast. Examples include Lowenthal (1975); McClintock and Lowenthal (1983); Chaplin (1976); Stepan (1978); Booth and Sorj (1983); Kruijt (1991); and Sánchez (2002). A more recent study, which focuses on the agrarian reform, is Mayer (2009).
12. On popular movements and democratization during this period, see Ballon (1986) and Stokes (1995).
13. On the left in the transition phase in Peru, see, among others, Stephens (1983); Rochabrun (1988); Sanborn (1991); Haworth (1993); Roberts (1998); and Adriánzen (2011). See also Feinstein (2013).
14. On the MIR and ELN guerrillas, see Béjar (1970) and Rénique (2004).
15. On *El diario de Marka*, see Uceda (1982) and Agüero (2010).
16. On becoming bourgeois, see June 16, 2011, online at https://elcuy.wordpress.com/2011/06/16/el-cuy-por-juan-124/, accessed on August 30, 2013.
17. Acevedo recalls the tensions between the different left-wing groups within *Diario de Marka* with some irritation on his blog: "I would arrive at the newspaper with

my *El Cuy* strip and I would feel the need to wear a bullet-proof vest." The different factions were constantly at loggerheads, but Acevedo did not belong to any of the parties: "I always wanted my work to serve the front, the popular movement as a whole, I was sick of those rivalries and absurd hatreds." Juan Acevedo, June 12, 2013, online at https://elcuy.wordpress.com/2013/06/12/el-cuy-por-juan-785/, accessed on August 30, 2013.

18. A sense of Acevedo's comics "philosophy" at the time when he was drawing and writing *El Cuy* can be gleaned from *Para hacer historietas*, a series of eight booklets published in the early 1980s that reflected a "popular education" experience he had been involved in in Villa El Salvador, a shantytown south of Lima. These booklets, printed on cheap paper, were intended to teach anyone to draw *historietas*. The short introduction to the first booklet, signed by Acevedo, and dated January 1980, noted that in the past comics had been thought of as "kids stuff." However, that had changed. Comics were no longer simply about entertainment. They had become an important means of mass communication and had a role in "influencing how the majority of people think and act." Acevedo added that "we believe that the working classes [*clases mayoritarias*] must not be divorced from the control of the means of communication, but, on the contrary, must dominate them. This is why this booklet is aimed at the teacher, the community organizer [*promotor*], the worker, and the shantytown dweller [*poblador de base*]." See Acevedo (1980).
19. In the blog Acevedo recalls that he was surprised when children started showing up at *El diario de Marka* in the early 1980s with cuttings of the strips, asking for his autograph. He had conceived of the comic strip for an adult readership, but it reached across generations. See Juan Acevedo, June 25, 2013, online at https://elcuy.wordpress.com/2013/06/24/el-cuy-por-juan-792/, accessed on August 30, 2013.
20. Alvaro, May 3, 2009, online at https://elcuy.wordpress.com/album/origenes-del-cuy-i/, accessed on August 30, 2013. The United Left (Izquierda Unida, IU) was an alliance of left-wing parties formed in 1980 and led by Alfonso Barrantes, who became mayor of Lima in 1984 and was IU's presidential candidate in the national elections of 1985. He lost the election to Alan García. On the history of IU see, among others, Roberts (1998) and Feinstein (2013).
21. Ivonne, September 25, 2008, online at https://elcuy.wordpress.com/2008/09/24/del-block-al-blog/, accessed on August 30, 2013.
22. Akane, September 25, 2008, online at https://elcuy.wordpress.com/album/origenes-del-cuy-i/, accessed on x August 30, 2013.
23. Edgar Vilca Figueredo, September 18, 2011, online at https://elcuy.wordpress.com/2011/09/18/el-cuy-por-juan-153/. accessed on August 30, 2013.
24. Lukysh, September 22, 2008, online at https://elcuy.wordpress.com/2008/09/21/regreso-del-cuy/. accessed on August 30, 2013.

25. Jairo, September 22, 2008, online at https://elcuy.wordpress.com/2008/09/21/regreso-del-cuy/, accessed on August 30, 2013.
26. Maykolt, October 2, 2011, online at https://elcuy.wordpress.com/2011/10/02/el-cuy-por-juan-167/, accessed on August 30, 2013.
27. Emilio Salcedo, September 22, 2008, online at https://elcuy.wordpress.com/2008/09/21/regreso-del-cuy/, accessed on August 30, 2013.
28. MiguelPlà, December 15, 2008, online at https://elcuy.wordpress.com/album/origenes-del-cuy-i/, accessed on August 30, 2013.
29. Javier, May 20, 2011, online at https://elcuy.wordpress.com/album/origenes-del-cuy-i/, accessed on August 30, 2013.
30. Emilio, May 17, 2011, online at https://elcuy.wordpress.com/2011/05/17/el-cuy-por-juan-97/, accessed on August 30, 2013.
31. Emilio, May 24, 2011, online at https://elcuy.wordpress.com/2011/05/24/el-cuy-por-juan-103/, accessed on August 30, 2013.
32. Patricia Temple Arciniega, December 14, 2011, online at https://elcuy.wordpress.com/album/origenes-del-cuy-i/, accessed on August 30, 2013.
33. José, November 13, 2008, online at https://elcuy.wordpress.com/album/, accessed on August 30, 2013.
34. José, March 17, 2011, online at https://elcuy.wordpress.com/2011/03/17/el-cuy-por-juan-46/, accessed on August 30, 2013.
35. Carlos el baterillero, September 15, 2011, online at https://elcuy.wordpress.com/2011/09/15/el-cuy-por-juan-150/, accessed on August 30, 2013.
36. César Flores Huallpa, September 19, 2011, online at https://elcuy.wordpress.com/2011/09/15/el-cuy-por-juan-150/, accessed on August 30, 2013.
37. César Flores Huallpa, September 29, 2011, online at https://elcuy.wordpress.com/2011/09/27/el-cuy-por-juan-162/, accessed on August 30, 2013.
38. Rafael Vega Llallapasca, September 20, 2011, online at https://elcuy.wordpress.com/2011/09/20/el-cuy-por-juan-155/, accessed on August 30, 2013.
39. Luis A. Ramírez, September 20, 2011, online at https://elcuy.wordpress.com/2011/09/20/el-cuy-por-juan-155/, accessed on August 30, 2013.
40. Juan Acevedo, September 20, 2011, online at https://elcuy.wordpress.com/2011/09/20/el-cuy-por-juan-155/, accessed on August 30, 2013.
41. José, September 22, 2011, online at https://elcuy.wordpress.com/2011/09/22/el-cuy-por-juan-157/, accessed on August 30, 2013.
42. Leonor, April 9, 2012, online at https://elcuy.wordpress.com/2012/04/09/el-cuy-por-juan-357/, accessed on August 30, 2013.
43. Orlando, April 5, 2012, online at https://elcuy.wordpress.com/2012/04/09/el-cuy-por-juan-357/, accessed on August 30, 2013.

44. Elmer, March 28, 2012, online at https://elcuy.wordpress.com/2012/03/28/el-cuy-por-juan-345/, accessed on August 30, 2013.
45. Orlando, January 24, 2012, online at https://elcuy.wordpress.com/2012/01/24/el-cuy-por-juan-281/, accessed on August 30, 2013.
46. Rlajo, January 2, 2012, online at https://elcuy.wordpress.com/2011/12/27/el-cuy-por-juan-253/, accessed on August 30, 2013.
47. Leonorsuarezognio, February 8, 2012, online at https://elcuy.wordpress.com/2012/02/08/el-cuy-por-juan-296/, accessed on August 30, 2013.
48. Leonorsuarezognio, February 9, 2012, online at https://elcuy.wordpress.com/2012/02/08/el-cuy-por-juan-296/, accessed on August 30, 2013.
49. Leonorsuarezognio, January 14, 2012, online at https://elcuy.wordpress.com/2012/01/14/el-cuy-por-juan-271/, accessed on August 30, 2013.
50. "Lugar de la memoria, la tolerancia y la inclusión social," online at http://lum.cultura.pe, accessed on August 23, 2013.
51. Bruno Ysla Heredia, January 14, 2012, online at https://elcuy.wordpress.com/2012/01/14/el-cuy-por-juan-271/, accessed on August 30, 2013.
52. Leonorsuarezognio, January 23, 2012, online at https://elcuy.wordpress.com/2012/01/23/el-cuy-por-juan-280/, accessed on August 30, 2013.
53. Orlando, February 7, 2012, online at https://elcuy.wordpress.com/2012/02/07/el-cuy-por-juan-295/, accessed on August 30, 2013.
54. Juan Acevedo, February 7, 2012, online at https://elcuy.wordpress.com/2012/02/07/el-cuy-por-juan-295/, accessed on August 30, 2013.
55. See the Truth and Reconciliation Commission's report, online at www.cverdad.org.pe/ifinal/pdf/TOMO%20VII/Casos%20Ilustrativos-UIE/2.9.%20CABITOS.pdf, accessed on April 23, 2016. See also APRODEH 2014.
56. See https://elcuy.wordpress.com/2012/06/27/el-cuy-por-juan-436/ and https://elcuy.wordpress.com/2012/06/28/el-cuy-por-juan-437/, both accessed on August 30, 2013.
57. Carlos el baterillero, August 23, 2012, online at https://elcuy.wordpress.com/2012/08/23/el-cuy-por-juan-493/, accessed on August 30, 2013.
58. See November 23, 2012, online at https://elcuy.wordpress.com/2012/11/26/el-cuy-por-juan-588/, accessed on August 30, 2013.
59. See the sequence of comic strips numbered 587–92, uploaded in late November 2012, accessed on August 30, 2013.
60. See https://elcuy.wordpress.com/2012/12/01/el-cuy-por-juan-593/, accessed on August 30, 2013.
61. See, among others, Manrique (2002); Degregori (2012); and Portocarrero (2012).
62. See https://elcuy.wordpress.com/2012/12/07/el-cuy-por-juan-599/, accessed on August 30, 2013.

63. See https://elcuy.wordpress.com/2012/12/05/el-cuy-por-juan-597/, accessed on August 30, 2013.
64. Gonzalo Alva Novoa, January 16, 2013, online at https://elcuy.wordpress.com/2013/01/16/el-cuy-por-juan-638/, accessed on August 30, 2013.
65. See, for example, Elmer, January 17, 2013, online at https://elcuy.wordpress.com/2013/01/17/el-cuy-por-juan-639/, accessed on August 30, 2013.
66. For a detailed study of the left's position as it relates to Shining Path, see Feinstein (2013).
67. Carlos el baterillero, January 25, 2013, online at https://elcuy.wordpress.com/2013/01/24/el-cuy-por-juan-646/, accessed on August 30, 2013.
68. Juan Acevedo, January 25, 2013, online at https://elcuy.wordpress.com/2013/01/25/el-cuy-por-juan-647/, accessed on August 30, 2013.
69. The speech, "Discurso de Presentación del Informe Final de la Comisión de la Verdad y Reconciliación," is online at www.cverdad.org.pe/informacion/discursos/en_ceremonias05.php, accessed on August 30, 2013.
70. Consultor, May 12, 2013, online at https://elcuy.wordpress.com/2013/05/11/el-cuy-por-juan-753/, accessed on August 30, 2013.
71. Carlos el baterillero, February 17, 2013, online at https://elcuy.wordpress.com/2013/02/17/el-cuy-por-juan-670/, accessed on August 30, 2013. On the Uchuraccay massacre, see Mayer (1991) and del Pino (2003).

REFERENCES

Acevedo, Juan. 2011. *El Cuy tira*. Lima: Ediciones Contracultura.

Acevedo, Juan. 1981. *¡Hola Cuy!* Lima: Ital-Perú.

Acevedo, Juan. 1980. *Para hacer historietas: Método basado en experiencias de educación popular*. Fasciculo 1. Lima: TAREA (Asociación de Publicaciones Educativas).

Adrianzén, Alberto, ed. 2011. *Apogeo y crisis de la izquierda peruana*. Lima: IDEA/Antonio Ruiz de Montoya.

Agüero, José Carlos. 2010. "La historieta en Marka, 1980–1990." *Artificios: Sociedad, reflexión, Arte* 2: 10–19. Online at www.scribd.com/doc/31617115/ARTIFIC-02. Accessed on August 30, 2013.

APRODEH. 2014. *Cuartel Los Cabitos: Lugar de horror y muerte*. Lima: APRODEH (Asociación Pro Derechos Humanos).

Assmann, Jan. 1995. "Collective Memory and Cultural Identity." *New German Critique* 65: 125–33.

Ballon, Eduardo, ed. 1986. *Movimientos sociales y democracia: La fundación de un nuevo orden*. Lima: DESCO (Centro de Estudios y Promoción del Desarrollo).

Béjar, Héctor. 1970. *Peru 1965: Notes on a Guerrilla Experience*. New York: Monthly Review Press.

Booth, David, and Bernardo Sorj, eds. 1983. *Military Reformism and Social Classes: The Peruvian Experience*. London: Macmillan.

Chaplin, David, ed. 1976. *Peruvian Nationalism: A Corporatist Revolution*. New Brunswick, NJ: Transaction.

Degregori, Carlos Iván. 2012. *How Difficult It Is to Be God: Shining Path's Politics of War in Peru, 1980–1999*. Madison: University of Wisconsin Press.

del Pino, Ponciano. 2003. "Uchuraccay: Memoria y representación de la violencia política en los Andes." In *Jamás tan cerca arremetió lo lejos: Memoria y violencia política en el Perú*. Edited by Carlos Ivan Degregori, 48–93. Lima: Instituto de Estudios Peruanos–Social Science Research Council.

Drinot, Paulo. 2011. "Web-Site of Memory: The War of the Pacific (1879–1884) in the Global Age of Youtube." *Memory Studies* 4, no. 4: 370–85.

Drinot, Paulo. 2009. "For Whom the Eye Cries: Memory, Monumentality, and the Ontologies of Violence in Peru." *Journal of Latin American Cultural Studies* 18, no. 1: 15–32.

Feinstein, Tamara. 2013. "How the Left Was Lost: Remembering Izquierda Unidad and the Legacies of Political Violence in Peru." PhD dissertation, University of Wisconsin–Madison.

Foster, David William. 1989. "Acevedo and De-Disneyfication." In *From Mafalda to Los Supermachos: Latin American Graphic Humor as Popular Culture*. Edited by David William Foster, 103–8. Boulder, CO: Lynne Rienner Publishers.

Haworth, Nigel. 1993. "Radicalization and the Left in Peru, 1976–1991." In *The Latin American Left: From the Fall of Allende to Perestroika*. Edited by Barry Carr and Steve Ellner, 41–60. Boulder, CO: Westview Press/Latin American Bureau.

Hirsch, Marianne. 1997. *Family Frames: Photography, Narrative, and Postmemory*. Cambridge: Harvard University Press.

Hirsch, Marianne. 1992–1993. "Family Pictures: Maus, Mourning, and Post-Memory." *Discourse* 15, no. 2: 3–29. Special Issue: The Emotions, Gender, and the Politics of Subjectivity.

Jelin, Elizabeth. 2002. *Los trabajos de la memoria*. Buenos Aires: Siglo XXI.

Jelin, Elizabeth, and Victoria Langland, eds. 2003. *Monumentos, memoriales y marcas territoriales*. Buenos Aires: Siglo XXI.

Kruijt, Dirk. 1991. *La revolución por decreto: Perú durante el gobierno militar*. Lima: Mosca Azul Editores.

Landsberg, Alison. 2004. *Prosthetic Memory: The Transformation of American Remembrance in the Age of Mass Culture*. New York: Columbia University Press.

La Serna, Miguel. 2012. *In the Corner of the Dead: Ayacucho on the Eve of the Shining Path Insurgency*. Chapel Hill: University of North Carolina Press.

Lowenthal, Abraham F., ed. 1975. *The Peruvian Experiment: Continuity and Change under Military Rule*. Princeton, NJ: Princeton University Press.

Lucioni, Mario. 2005. "Peruvian Comics: The Early Years." In *Cartooning in Latin America*. Edited by John A. Lent, 311–19. Cresskill, NJ: Hampton Press.

Lucioni, Mario. 2002. "La historieta peruana." *Revista Latinoamericana de Estudios sobre la Historieta* 2, no. 8: 203–18.

Manrique, Nelson. 2002. *El tiempo del miedo: La violencia política en el Perú, 1980–1996*. Lima: Fondo Editorial del Congreso.

Mauceri, Philip. 1997. "The Transition to 'Democracy' and the Failures of Institution Building." In *The Peruvian Labyrinth: Polity, Economy, and Society*. Edited by Maxwell A. Cameron and Philip Mauceri, 13–36. University Park: Pennsylvania State University Press.

Mayer, Enrique. 2009. *Ugly Stories of the Peruvian Agrarian Reform*. Durham, NC: Duke University Press.

Mayer, Enrique. 1991. "Peru in Deep Trouble: Mario Vargas Llosa's 'Inquest in the Andes' Reexamined." *Cultural Anthropology* 6, no. 4: 466–505.

McClintock, Cynthia, and Abraham F. Lowenthal, eds. 1983. *The Peruvian Experiment Reconsidered*. Princeton, NJ: Princeton University Press.

Nora, Pierre. 1989. "Between Memory and History: Les Lieux de Mémoire." *Representations* 26: 7–24.

Poole, Deborah, and Gerardo Rénique. 1992. *Peru: Time of Fear*. London: Latin American Bureau.

Portocarrero, Gonzalo. 2012. *Profetas del odio: Raíces culturales y líderes de Sendero Luminoso*. Lima: Fondo Editorial de la Pontificia Universidad Católica del Perú.

Rénique, José Luis. 2004. "De la 'traicion aprista' al 'gesto heroico': Luis de la Puente Uceda y la guerrilla del MIR." *Estudios Internacionales de America Latina* 15, no. 1: 89–114.

Roberts, Kenneth. 1998. *Deepening Democracy? The Modern Left and Social Movements in Chile and Peru*. Stanford, CA: Stanford University Press.

Rochabrun, Guillermo. 1988. "Crisis, Democracy, and the Left in Peru." *Latin American Perspectives* 15, no. 3: 77–96.

Sagástegui, Carla. 2009. "Acevedo and His Predecessors." In *Redrawing the Nation: National Identity in Latin/o American Comics*. Edited by Héctor Fernández L'Hoeste and Juan Poblete, 131–50. New York: Palgrave.

Sanborn, Cynthia. 1991. "The Democratic Left and the Persistence of Populism in Peru: 1975–1990." PhD dissertation, Harvard University.

Sánchez, Juan Martín. 2002. *La revolución peruana: Ideología y práctica política de un gobierno militar, 1968–1975*. Seville: Consejo Superior de Investigaciones Científicas.

Spiegelman, Art. 1991. *Maus*. Volume 2. New York: Pantheon.

Spiegelman, Art. 1986. *Maus*. Volume 1. New York: Pantheon.

Stepan, Alfred. 1978. *The State and Society: Peru in Comparative Perspective*. Princeton, NJ: Princeton University Press.

Stephens, Evelyne Huber. 1983. "The Peruvian Military Government, Labor Mobilization, and the Political Strength of the Left." *Latin American Research Review* 18, no. 2: 57–93.

Stern, Steve, ed. 1998. *Shining and Other Paths: War and Society in Peru, 1980–1995*. Durham, NC: Duke University Press.

Stokes, Susan C. 1995. *Cultures in Conflict: Social Movements and the State in Peru*. Berkeley: University of California Press, 1995.

Sturken, Marita. 2008. "Memory, Consumerism, and Media: Reflections on the Emergence of the Field." *Memory Studies* 1, no. 1: 73–78.

Uceda, Ricardo. 1982. "Como se hizo el diario de Marka." *Revista Latinoamericana de Comunicación Chasqui* 3: 72–77.

SIX

DEATH IN THE ANDES

COMICS AS MEANS TO BROACH STORIES OF POLITICAL VIOLENCE IN PERU

Cynthia E. Milton

From 1980 to the mid-1990s, Peru underwent an internal conflict that pitted principally the Maoist-inspired Shining Path (Sendero Luminoso) and state agents against each other, inflaming inter- and intra-community tensions. Nearly a decade after the capture of the Shining Path's leader, Abimael Guzmán, and only months after the sudden collapse of President Alberto Fujimori's government, a commission was erected to investigate the years of conflict from 1980 through 2000. In 2003 the Truth and Reconciliation Commission (Comisión de la Verdad y Reconciliación, or CVR) published its *Final Report* (*Informe final*) after two years of investigation. The commission's findings were staggering: more than sixty-nine thousand people dead and disappeared. Tellingly, their demographics replicated the geographical and ethnic divides of Peruvian society: two-thirds of these victims did not speak Spanish as their first language, and most of them had resided in remote regions.[1]

In the organization of their investigation and in the structuring of their *Final Report*, the CVR focused on what they considered the cases that illustrated best the general tendencies of the conflict. One of those cases was that of Uchuraccay: the death of eight journalists and their guide in 1983 in an isolated hamlet in the north of the department of Ayacucho. This massacre, the media coverage in the months following, the appointment of a government-mandated commission, and the eventual trial brought to the nation's attention the until then irregularly discussed violence in the highlands. Despite the scrutiny of this massacre, however, little consensual understanding emerged about what had happened, why it had happened, and by whom. The CVR attempted to give a fuller account of this case two decades later by examining not only the murders but also the subsequent reprisal deaths and the ultimate desertion of the hamlet. As an emblematic case—indeed perhaps the most well known among Peruvians and abroad—Uchuraccay may be representative not just of the violence that occurred but also of the fractured public memories and continued difficulties to broach publicly Peru's war years.

Much of the difficulty in writing a widely accepted version of what happened in Uchuraccay is mirrored in the numerous challenges that the truth commission faced in general: How to explain to Peruvians what had happened after the events when many were not aware of them as the violence was unfolding? And how to explain why this tragedy occurred? These challenges were made all the more difficult since entrenched elites—namely the beneficiaries of Alberto Fujimori's neoliberal politics, the armed forces, and sectors within Peru's churches—did not accept in full the commission's findings and continue to contest them into the present day. How to reach a public not openly willing to entertain a version of the conflict years that points responsibility to Shining Path as well as to the Peruvian state and conservative sectors?

Aware of these challenges, a collective of artists and researchers—Luis Rossell, Alfredo Villar, and Jesús Cossio—published the first graphic novel on the subject after the truth commission, *Rupay: Historias de la violencia política en Perú, 1980–1984* (Rupay: Stories of political violence in Peru, 1980–1984). By way of visual and textual narration, the authors attempted to reach readers more likely to pick up a comic book rather than the CVR's *Final Report*. The authors hoped that the combination of visual images with narration would allow them to enter into the debates over this recent past and hence participate in the formation of public memory.

The potential to reach the Peruvian public through an array of means raises the question of what kinds of truth claims and narratives are advanced through different modes and to which audiences. In this chapter I focus on the case of the murder of journalists and their guide in Uchuraccay in 1983 as a means to consider how the comic book form allows for distinct narratives of the past to come to light that would otherwise remain in the realm of rumor alone or as isolated memories. Comics are just one of the many alternative modes to recount a society's difficult past outside of more formal mechanisms of truth commissions and trials, such as cinema, monuments, stories, song, and poetry (Bell 2014; Bilbija et al. 2005; Jelin and Longoni 2005). In the decade since the CVR published their *Final Report*, there has been a boom of creative engagements with the CVR's finding and with memories of Peru's conflict, including the staging of art contests and performances, erection of memory sites and museums, films, commemorative events, novels, and Internet blogs, among other efforts (Lambright 2015; Milton 2014a; Saona 2014; Vich 2015). The diversity and richness of these creative engagements has led some scholars to note that it is perhaps in the realm of culture, and the arts more specifically, where truth commissions may have their greatest influence (Atencio 2014; Drinot 2009; Milton 2014b).

During my own research into these alternative modes of recounting past violence in Peru as part of the process of historical clarification, a colleague gave me a copy of *Rupay*, first printed in Lima in 2008 and the year after in Madrid.[2] Upon reading it, I was struck by how the authors were able to present many different accounts of this convoluted conflict in an accessible and fairly coherent way, and in so few pages (ninety-seven pages for the Peruvian edition). *Rupay*—a Quechua word meaning "ardor, heat, fire"—is a swift-moving, heart-wrenching textual and visual account of the early years of Peru's internal war that brings together the CVR's *Final Report*, academic studies, artworks, media, and testimonials. What is it that makes *Rupay*, for me at least (a North American researcher), an engaging and informative account of the years of internal conflict, and what explains the varying reaction by readers in Peru? Why and how do comics seem to serve so well the recounting of Peru's complex stories of violence?

In my quest to learn about the history of comics (*historietas*) in Peru, I turned to an unpublished manuscript by Mario Lucioni.[3] Although the study ends in the 1940s, Lucioni details the long history of comics (that laid the groundwork for their later offshoot, graphic novels) as a creative literary form in Peru that cuts across social, economic, and potentially ethnic barriers. While much of the comics studied in Lucioni's manuscript were aimed at the middle class and elite (presumably Lima-based) readers, as in other regions of Latin America the form was also picked up by the more "popular classes" (see also L'Hoeste and Poblete 2009; Rubenstein 1998; Sagástegui 2009). Indeed, the importance of visual imagery in reaching a wide readership extends beyond comics: a cursory look at the many newsstands in the streets of Lima indicates that the Peruvian press relies heavily on images to transmit the content's meaning.

In his history of comics after the Second World War, Lucioni (2001) sees *historietas* as taking up the challenge of describing the fractured Peruvian nation long before higher literary forms. Indeed, *historietas* not only became a way to reach weakly literate readers, but they also became a way to get more marginalized individuals and groups to express their reality. In the mid-1970s socially minded organizations promoted literacy and self-expression through workshops on *historietas* designed for recent highland migrants in the newly founded Villa El Salvador. According to one of the key participants, cartoonist Juan Acevedo (1984: 11n1), the success of these workshops led to the erection of similar workshops elsewhere in Latin America and Spain. More recently, Jesús Cossio gives talks on the making of comics and has held workshops for young people who want to create comics themselves.[4] The owner of the publishing house Ediciones Contracultura, which specializes in comics and graphic novels, has seen the market for graphic novels expand significantly.[5]

Rupay was not the first comic to address Peru's internal conflict. During the 1980s, in the absence of photographs, newspapers printed short serial drawings that depicted for their readership the violent acts of Shining Path (figures 6.1 and 6.2) and the "barbarism" of highland peoples (figure 6.3).[6] Juan Acevedo's *El Cuy* ("Guinea Pig") and Hugo Janco's *Gonzalito* ("Little Gonzalo") also drew the conflict. Carlos Tovar, whose pen name is Carlín, depicted in 1982 highland communities as trapped between Shining Path and state forces, among other references to the growing violence. The cartoonist Luís Baldoceda was contracted by the armed forces in the mid-1980s to produce *Confidencias de un Senderista: Juicio popular* (Confidences of a Senderista: Popular justice), a thirty-seven-page comic written from the perspective of a Shining Path militant that circulated principally in highland towns (figure 6.4).[7] Shining Path also employed political art, posters, and serial drawings as means to garner support—for instance, the black-and-white pamphlet presently housed in the DINCOTE museum in Lima (figure 6.5).

Rupay is distinct among Peruvian comics that draw the conflict in that it is a graphic novel based on extant published and digitalized sources that are cited in the book's bibliography. There is a combination of aesthetic elements and historical records. Most influential among these sources is the CVR's *Final Report*.[8] *Rupay*'s authors take several of the CVR's case studies as the focus of their representation of the early years of the violence. The influence of the CVR on the authors is especially evident in the 2009 Madrid-published version of *Rupay* that reproduces on its cover the worn hands of a highland woman cupping the black and white passport-sized photograph of a missing

Dramáticos momentos vivió la niña Epifania Chacchi Pérez, quien presenció el ataque terrorista contra el puesto policial de Tambo. "Disparaban como locos", declaró con voz balbuceante. El dibujo muestra cómo se produjeron los hechos.

El puesto policial de Minas Canarias soportó ayer el cruento asalto de medio centenar de terroristas que trataron de ingresar a ese local a sangre y fuego.

FIGURES 6.1 AND 6.2. Drawings from *Expreso*, October 16, 1981 (top) and March 19, 1982 (bottom). Translation of the bottom text (top image): "The young Epifania Chacchi Pérez experienced dramatic moments during the terrorist attack against the police station in Tambo. 'They fired like crazy [people],' she declared with a trembling voice. The drawing shows the attack." Translation of the bottom text (bottom image): "Yesterday, the police station Minas Canarias survived a bloody attack by some fifty terrorists who tried to get in by blood and fire."

FIGURE 6.3 Drawing about the murder of the journalists from *Expreso*, January 30, 1983. Translation of the bottom text: "In the drawing, the location of the small village in the Department of Ayacucho is indicated, where the tragic incident occurred that has plunged the national press into mourning."

loved one. It is a direct imitation of the cover of the CVR's own visual account of the conflict, the photography exhibit *Yuyanapaq: Para recordar* (In order to remember). Indeed, because of their close proximity to the work of the CVR, *Rupay*'s authors see themselves as picking up where the CVR left off, in disseminating the CVR's findings. Yet they are also somewhat critical of the CVR's *Final Report* and complement it with other sources taken from elsewhere.

When asked if the CVR was the "detonator" or inspiration for *Rupay*, Jesús Cossio, who made the drawings with Luis Rossell, answered in the affirmative, stating that it "was [a reaction to the] reaction to the *Final Report*, [a reaction to] all these people from the [political] right and the media who

FIGURE 6.4. Luís Baldoceda 1989, published in 1989
Confidencias de un Senderista: Juicio popular.

FIGURE 6.5. Serial drawing (ten panels, double-sided) portraying then president Alan García as a Nazi in his ordering of the attack on Lima's prisons and extrajudicial killing of prisoners. On display in the DINCOTE museum, October 26, 2012. Photo by author.

ranted against the CVR and dismissed its testimonies and conclusions. We believed that we could do something to combat these reactionary voices through our means [*desde nuestra escala*]" (*Love Lima* 2012). Thus, in their own way, the authors of *Rupay* employ comics as a potentially effective weapon in Peru's ongoing discursive battle over the past. The authors place themselves as participants in national debates over the past, offering a corrective both to the CVR and to the reactionary response that the CVR received from political elites.

COMICS AS ALTERNATIVE TRUTH-TELLING

Rupay is one of many works and public actions that engaged Peru's "truth" debates after the publication of the CVR's *Final Report*. Here, I focus on the comic-book form as a means to truth-telling compared with the CVR's report. Such a juxtaposition of *Rupay* and the CVR might seem ill-matched, considering their very different forms of presentation of a public account over the recent past—one a graphic novel, the other the findings of a truth commission. Yet both are important sources for disseminating "truths" of what happened during Peru's internal conflict. I am specifically interested in what it is that comics/*historietas* can accomplish when recounting the past that other modes, in particular the truth commission's publication of its findings, find more difficult to achieve.

To consider the potential of comics as a means to spread and produce knowledge about the past, I focus on the case of Uchuraccay because much has been written and said about Uchuraccay, yet still little seems to be agreed upon. Many versions and rumors circulate. Indeed, the plethora of versions and partial "truths" is probably rooted in the silences imposed by Uchuraccay members themselves on the events. In a profoundly nuanced study of what Uchuraccayans have chosen to disclose and not, historian Ponciano del Pino highlights the importance of such public secrets in community cohesion and how these silences and secrets may change at key junctures, thus altering our partial understandings of events (del Pino 2008, 2013). As historian Miguel La Serna's work on Huaychao (not far from Uchuraccay) has indicated, the insurgency and counterinsurgency efforts waged by Shining Path and the armed forces in the region dovetailed with and aggravated intra- and inter-community conflicts, a dynamic that makes the parsing out of events all the more complex (La Serna 2012).

I offer a rough outline of the event based on my reading of the CVR's chapter on Uchuraccay, *Rupay*, the 1983 government-mandated investigation led by author Mario Vargas Llosa (Vargas Llosa 1990), Vargas Llosa's subsequent piece published shortly after in the *New York Times Magazine* (Vargas Llosa 1983), and some academic works (Mayer 1991; del Pino 2003, 2008, 2013; La Serna 2012). By the end of 1982, the Belaúnde Terry government had ceded control of the department of Ayacucho to the military general Clemente Noel, having placed the military in charge of addressing the threat of Shining Path. Shortly after the military's arrival in the region, community members (*comuneros*) of Huaychao killed seven supposed Shining Path militants. Different possible explanations for this act of vigilante justice spread: the military advanced the theory of a reprisal killing by Huaychao residents; some intellectuals, journalists, and members of leftist organizations questioned whether the military itself had been involved. Not wanting to rely upon the military's account alone, eight journalists from various newspapers and magazines decided to go to the region to investigate: Félix Gavilán, Amador García, Octavio Infante, Jorge Luis Mendívil, Eduardo de la Piniella, Pedro Sánchez, Jorge Sedano, and Willy Retto. Along the way, they engaged the services of a guide, Juan Argumedo. The nine men never reached Huaychao. They were killed in Uchuraccay on January 26, 1983.

Who killed the journalists and their guide Argumedo, and why, were the questions that drove the investigation of a three-member commission appointed by Belaúnde Terry. It was the first government-mandated commission of this sort that gathered information from and involved the participation of members of government, the armed forces, civil society, and the general public to shed light on "a truth that the national consciousness and the rest of the world's public opinion urgently demands" (Vargas Llosa 1990: 88–89). The commission's findings, informally called the Vargas Llosa report, found some Uchuraccay community members responsible for the deaths. The Uchuraccayans' reasons for killing the journalists were explained as the consequence of cultural, linguistic, and temporal barriers. According to the Vargas Llosa report, responsibility for the journalists' deaths lay in the difficult-to-traverse distance between the Peru of centuries past in which the highland communities such as Uchuraccay still presided—traditional and archaic—and contemporary Peru.[9] In a trial in Lima, from 1983 through 1986, three Uchuraccayan men were sentenced to prison for the deaths of the journalists. Questions remained, however, as to the possible involvement of the military, whether directly or indirectly.

The theory of Uchuraccay as frozen in time soon lay exposed as a convenient myth: months after the Vargas Llosa commission's investigation into the massacre, the journalist Willy Retto's camera was discovered, containing photographs taken during the confrontation that put in question this idea of an insurmountable linguistic and cultural gap. These pictures showed attempts at dialogue and that some *comuneros* were wearing city clothes and items (such as watches), which contradicted the concept of their hermetic isolation and dispelled the idea that the peasants might have confused the cameras for weapons (a claim made to the press by the then military general supervising the region, Clemente Noel). Regardless of these unresolved contradictions, Uchuraccay remained firmly stigmatized. The effects of this massacre, the investigation, trial, and media portrayal were devastating for Uchuraccay's residents: Uchuraccay became synonymous with "horror," the residents viewed at the national level as "savages." By mid-1984, in the context of escalating violence, the residents had fled Uchuraccay, and the community remained abandoned until the return of some families in the early 1990s to resettle on grounds nearby their old hamlet.

Both the CVR and *Rupay* revisit the case of Uchuraccay and offer an account of the journalists' and their guide's death. The CVR's study into Uchuraccay stresses the injustices committed by the government against the community members by not having conducted a fuller investigation into what happened (a critique of the few hours the Vargas Llosa committee spent in Uchuraccay and the superficial trial—both further limited by the absence of Quechua translators), the government's abandonment of the community to certain death despite the *comuneros*' pleas for assistance, and the silence that fell upon the deaths of 135 residents following the fatal expedition. The CVR recounts the death on the same day of Severino Huáscar Morales Ccente, accused by some *comuneros* of having had ties with Shining Path. The CVR's study describes the context of escalating fear and violence in the region and the role of the armed forces in intensifying this fear and in provoking further violence. The CVR's version rejects the Vargas Llosa report's insistence on the inability to communicate as one of a problem of language, for at least three of the journalists could speak Quechua (one of the journalists was from Ayacucho and had kin in the area), and some Uchuraccayans could speak Spanish. The CVR describes the aftermath of the journalists' deaths and the tragedies that occurred after the Vargas Llosa investigation: a series of massacres against the community, their flight, and the sensationalization by the media of the events that further racialized and demonized the residents of Uchuraccay.

BOXES AND BUBBLES: THE MANY REGISTERS OF *RUPAY*'S "UCHURACCAY"

Although both the CVR's report and *Rupay* present an account of the journalists' death in Uchuraccay, they differ in content and form. In his essay "Historical Emplotment and the Problem of Truth" (1992), scholar Hayden White draws our attention to the potential problem that the narrative structure or mode of emplotment that we choose—comic, heroic, tragic, parodic, and redemptive, among the various possibilities—imbues different meanings to "real facts"—that is, we can use the same "facts" and end up with vastly distinct stories, depending on the narrative structure employed. Reading the sixty-two pages of the CVR's *Final Report* on the Uchuraccay case is a very different experience from reading the ten pages of *Rupay* (composed of sixty-one scenes). In part, this is because the information—the "facts" presented—differs but also because of the way the information is conveyed.

The CVR's report—like other truth commission reports—is an attempt to document what happened during the conflict. Yet it does not rely simply on listing a series of facts, as a chronicle might, but strings them together in the form of a narrative. By placing these facts into a narrative, the CVR presents a linear rendition of what happened (based on accounts of events, testimonies, forensic evidence, and other documentation) and does so employing the plot of a tragedy (the tragedy of what happened to Peruvians, to the nation). This presentation of a narrative may explain, in part, why the CVR's *Final Report* is open to criticism. White (1992: 40) writes: "For unless a historical story is presented as a literal representation of real events, we cannot criticize it as being either true or untrue to the facts of the matter. If it were presented as a figurative representation of real events then the question of its truthfulness would fall under the principles governing our assessment of the truth of fictions." The *Final Report* is not a "figurative representation"; it is the findings of a government-mandated investigation. Nor is it a simple chronology. If the truth commission had produced a list of facts and dates alone—such as the chronology at a chapter's end—then it would have perhaps provoked less controversy. Yet without a narrative structure how would we make meaningful sense of these facts, how would we understand them? Hence the importance of narrative: to provide meaning to scattered experiences.

But the problem is not one of narrative alone; there is also the challenge of what kind of plot in which to place the facts. Can we compare critically versions of the past whose facts are emploted differently, as Hayden White suggests? The CVR's *Final Report* presents the findings in the written narrative of a tragedy, a "high" genre, while *Rupay* uses the comic-panel form traditionally used for "low" genres of entertainment. Both present the past as a shameful national calamity, but the means by which they do so differ: one a written narrative with some graphs, tables, and timelines; the other a bricolage of written and visual texts with stylization, figuration, and allegorization. While the content may be similar, the specific forms differ; the former risks impenetrability because of its density and length, the latter perhaps risks the aestheticization of violence.

Take, for instance, the main protagonists in the two accounts. Both the *Final Report* and *Rupay* aspire to have the victims' memories drive the narrative. Indeed, the CVR's objective is to give voice to the *comuneros*, as they had been silenced or remained mute in all previous official accounts of events. Despite having interviewed Uchuraccayans, the Vargas Llosa report only provided three unattributed words and one partial quote, and in the trial of the Uchuraccayan *comuneros* only unidirectional translation was provided (from Quechua to Spanish); this means that the accused could not understand the proceedings and that they never came to speak in their own defense. As anthropologist Enrique Mayer (1991: 490) has noted: "In all the debate, publicity, opinions, and counter arguments, the voice of the *comuneros* of Uchuraccay was never once heard. Their point of view was always mediated by translators, interpreters, and experts." By contrast, the CVR's analysis of the events is interspersed by supporting direct citations from Uchuraccayans taken from the unpublished transcripts of the Vargas Llosa commission, gathered during the trial, and from later interviews conducted by members of the CVR research team (some of the latter are included in the CVR's *Final Report* in the original Quechua with Spanish translations).

Rupay similarly wants to privilege the voice of the victims but not only are their voices reproduced. In *Rupay* we "hear" directly from General Clemente Noel, Mario Vargas Llosa, the murdered journalists, and others who remain silent in the CVR's chapter. *Rupay* pieces together a layered, multivocal account of what happened. How *Rupay* is able to do this lies in the ability of comics to mix image with text and in this literary form's potential to fictionalize the past. For the same reason that White appreciates Art Spiegelman's *Maus*, we might appreciate *Rupay:* "It makes the difficulty of discovering and telling the whole truth about even a small part of it [the Holocaust] as much a part of the story as the events whose meaning it is seeking to discover" (White 1992: 41). White is referring to the often tense and interrupted conversations of an intergenerational testimony between the author and his father, a Holocaust survivor, that is closely depicted in

Maus. *Rupay* does not offer this proximity to experience, yet the difficulty of telling and the tensions produced by the layering of versions of the past are also "part of the story." *Rupay* presents many separate accounts of what happened, from various perspectives and from different registers, thus giving us insight into the complexity of trying to extract a single "truth" or to weave a national narrative out of many versions. The authors of *Rupay* do not attempt to write a single narrative as the CVR had when it offered its report as a national account of events; nevertheless, the authors of *Rupay* make their tale follow a readable narrative thread by employing various tools available to graphic artists.

Comics present a narrative through a mixture of media, of words and pictures, making the reader a participant-reader and a passive spectator. Scholar James Young finds the comic's strength (not just in *Maus*) in the in-between space between the text and the image, in the creation of a "mental language" that is "conjured in the mind's movement between itself and the page" (Young 1993: 18). As Spiegelman has explained: "[The story] operates somewhere between the words and the idea that's in the pictures and in the movement between the pictures, which is the essence of what happens in a comic. So by not focusing you too hard on these people you're forced back into your role as reader rather than looker" (as quoted in Huyssen 2003: 131).

Because of the sensationalistic quality of the way events about the massacre in Uchuraccay unfolded in the media, Peruvians were always positioned as spectators. *Rupay* seeks to change their role to that of engaged readers who have to consider the various possible scenarios and relationships. To do so, *Rupay* presents a series of black-and-white drawings set in boxes placed in sequential order; interspersed among the drawings are archiveable materials ("evidence" for the reader to consider) such as photographs taken by the journalists themselves of their murder, photographs and front pages from national papers, and local, traditional art forms. In the version published in Madrid (the 2009 edition), each chapter is followed by a two-page written text in which the authors reflect on the escalating violence in the highlands.

Rupay is able to present a distinct narrative and to layer many possible accounts precisely because it is a different literary form than the CVR's report. The authors of *Rupay* are not bound to "truth" in the same way. They can blur the boundaries of fiction and fact. Perhaps most important for conveying a historical past in a fictionalized way is the possibility to play with different texts, the boxes and bubbles, what Spiegelman has called the "comix-ture." The bricolage of mixed media and the two levels of communication—the square texts that provide factual information and the bubbles

FIGURE 6.6. *Rupay*, 50 (please note original is in Spanish, all translations by Jane Remick). Reproduced with kind permission of Rossell, Villar, and Cossío.

that present us with possible conversations—structure the various registers of *Rupay*. These registers capture the fluidity of memory, and how unclear it might be, and how memory and perceptions alter especially when juxtaposed to archiveable materials from the time, such as newspapers. The font in the boxes seems more authoritative than the looser script chosen for the dialogue. The boxes attempt to educate the readers about the conflict and the bubbles invite us to pretend. We cannot know these fictionalized conversations, but in comics we can imagine with the authors what *could* have taken place, what the protagonists *might* have said, such as what the journalists might have said on their long walk to Huaychao (figure 6.6).

We cannot, for instance, know for certain that the journalists had a conversation about Jorge Sedano being out of shape for this difficult trek. It appears in the CVR account—not as a dialogue but as a description (CVR 2003: 133). Yet actual recorded testimonies might have informed the bubbled conversations in *Rupay*. For instance, the relatives of the murdered journalist, Octavio Infante, gave testimony before the courts and the Vargas Llosa commission. Testimonies gathered recount that Infante's relatives received the journalists, offered lemonade (sweetened with the journalists' own supply of sugar), and spoke about their plans to carry on to Huaychao. The mother and sister of Juan Argumedo did not want him to guide the journalists "since they had heard on the radio of massacres occurring in Uchuraccay and Huaychao" (133). Like possible conversations, individual figures slip in and out of the narrative recounted. Folded into *Rupay*'s account of Uchuraccay is the inquiry headed by Mario Vargas Llosa. Shortly after the discovery of the journalists' deaths, Mario Vargas Llosa and two other commission members (jurist Abraham Guzmán Figueroa and journalist Mario Castro Arenas) set out to Uchuraccay to investigate what had taken place. In *Rupay*, we witness Mario Vargas Llosa conducting interviews, making pronouncements about what had happened, and we see a reproduction of the cover of *Caretas* magazine dedicated to the commission in Uchuraccay. *Rupay*'s portrayal of the Vargas Llosa commission reinforces perceptions of this commission as superficial, one that fell easily into racialized stereotypes.

One of the central protagonists in the Uchuraccay tragedy was the local authority Fortunato Gavilán. In the CVR's account, Gavilán's presence is noted at key moments as events unraveled. In *Rupay*, however, Gavilán is given a more prominent role: nearly a whole page is dedicated to wondering about him, including his life before becoming a community leader (figure 6.7). In this section the reader may be startled by Gavilán's quick recourse

FIGURE 6.7 *Rupay*, 56.

to violence yet also sympathetic to his own victimization. By providing a possible reconstruction of the life of the local leader Gavilán and his training with the military in Lima, the authors of *Rupay* further lay indirect blame on the military for having formed Gavilán into the man who would later incite the murder of the journalists.

The CVR's account and *Rupay* give different weight to various explanations of what took place by their choice of sequential ordering of how Uchuraccayans came to discover the journalists and the context in which they responded to the strangers' arrival. Take, for instance, the dialogue in the home of the local authority Fortunato Gavilán between community members and the journalists who were trying to explain who they were (figure 6.8). According to the CVR, the gathering of community authorities took place in Gavilán's home at three or four in the afternoon, while the journalists were en route and still unknown to the community. In Gavilán's house those gathered discussed the possibility of a revenge attack by Shining Path in response to a previous lynching of Shining Path militants, and what to do about Shining Path members still within their community, such as Severino Huáscar Morales Ccente, the representative of the Popular Committee of Uchuraccay.[10] It was during this already convened meeting that those present heard the warning shouts, "the terrorists are coming" (CVR 2003: 134).

Growing fear of an imminent Shining Path attack (combined with alcohol that they had confiscated earlier from a youth with possible links to Shining Path) gives context to the community members' quick decision to murder the intruders. In the CVR's account, witnesses describe how the remaining *comuneros* were gathered to take part in the murder of the journalists. But

FIGURE 6.8. *Rupay*, 55.

there does not appear to have been a subsequent discussion inside Gavilán's home after the journalists had arrived. This is an important difference, for in *Rupay* the scene in Gavilán's home takes place *after* the journalists had arrived, thus allowing for more communication and time to consider who these journalists were and how to respond to their presence. Also, in clearly displaying a decision taken at the community level, *Rupay* moves the readers away from the still largely held view that the highland communities were passively trapped between Shining Path and the armed forces, with little room to maneuver and a tendency to knee-jerk reactions. In *Rupay*'s account, the *comuneros* made their own decision, in this murky context of heightened fear, to participate directly in the conflict.

It is interesting to note that while the CVR asks about Severino Huáscar Morales Ccente, who was killed with the guide later the same day as the journalists, and *Rupay* asks about Fortunato Gavilán, neither addresses in detail the presence of the guide Juan Argumedo, even though the first section of the Vargas Llosa report, "what happened," was an important source both for the CVR and *Rupay*. In the Vargas Llosa report, a separate section is dedicated to answering the question, "What was the fate of the guide Juan Argumedo?" (Vargas Llosa 1990: 110–12). According to the Vargas Llosa report, "a diffuse and unverifiable rumor, but persistent," reached the Vargas Llosa commission from various sources, indicating Juan Argumedo as "a supposed harborer or accomplice of the Senderistas." And though his family members strongly rejected this rumor "perhaps with complete reason" ("tal vez con toda justicia"), the commission nonetheless cast doubt on the family's assertion of Juan Argumedo's innocence, as the family had also denied having seen or heard or known of Shining Path in their community of Chacabamba. After nearly a page documenting the presence of Shining Path in Chacabamba, the commission proposed the hypothesis that "for the highland peoples, Juan Argumedo could have very well represented—with or without reason—the tangible proof that this expedition was the terrorist [Shining Path] revenge attack that the people of Uchuraccay had been expecting." Thus, the commissioners asked, "was the individual Juan Argumedo a factor that contributed to the misunderstanding, or even that began it? This is a hypothesis that should not be discarded." Neither *Rupay* nor the CVR directly offers this hypothesis, although the latter makes a subtle connection (CVR 2003: 136).

In its explanation of why the journalists were murdered, the Vargas Llosa report offered various possible factors, concluding that the tragedy was the result of cultural differences and misunderstandings, heightened in a context of fear of a reprisal by Shining Path and inflamed by the armed forces' exhortations to kill *senderistas*. Many Peruvians found the report unsatisfactory, an extension of Mario Vargas Llosa's literary skills as opposed to a report based on factual research.[11] Rumors and contradicting versions of events continued to circulate despite this high-profile investigation and the subsequent trial. Anthropologist Enrique Mayer noted that in the three years following the deaths of journalists and their guide, newspaper reporters and talk show hosts worked to undermine the Vargas Llosa report's version. Regardless of their efforts, prior to the CVR no significant changes were made to the Vargas Llosa report's original explanations, notwithstanding the emergence of Willy Retto's photographs, the death and disappearance of key witnesses, and the reluctance of the police to speak openly—a stance that hinted they may have been suppressing information (Mayer 1991: 468–69).

Because of its narrative form as a graphic novel, with its various interpretive mechanisms, *Rupay* is able to fill in gaps left in the reports by both the Vargas Llosa commission and the CVR. *Rupay* recounts simultaneously contrasting versions of what took place and attributes agency and responsibility for the violence more widely. The authors of *Rupay* present three versions of what happened and a possible combination of these versions: (1) the armed forces were directly responsible for the killings; (2) the campesinos (peasants) were reacting to the threat of a Shining Path attack (and the armed forces warning that "the enemy comes by land"); (3) the journalists were walking into and got caught up in ongoing conflicts between campesinos, as "peasants have their conflicts [*líos*] too." By having the journalists reflect upon what had happened to the senderistas in Huaychao, they speculate about the reasons for their own impending deaths (figure 6.9).[12]

By offering many possible versions of events, the authors of *Rupay* shift attention away from individuals and the community to that of the quagmire in which Uchuraccayans, and Peru as a whole, were engulfed. Yet they do not fall back upon the stereotypical portrayal of "assaulted communities," whereby civilians were trapped in a crossfire; rather, by interweaving various viewpoints and scenarios, the authors illustrate the complexity of various actors' positions during the conflict. As historian Steve Stern (2014, 266) has noted: "The alternation of comic-book panels with occasional documentary photograph panels not only drives home the reality of the Limeño victims [the journalists] as (once) living human beings but also subtly reinforces empathy by avoiding the stereotyping of Indians." By sparingly using the color red for emblems of the nation (the flag and coat of arms) and in other chapters red for Shining Path (their flag and graffiti of hammer and sickle) as well as for

FIGURE 6.9. *Rupay*, 51.

the blood of victims, the authors of *Rupay* equate the violence of the armed forces with that of Shining Path. In so doing, they place the blame for the death of Peruvians on both the state and Shining Path.

The Vargas Llosa account, the CVR's report, and the *Rupay* version greatly differ in their descriptions of the possible military involvement in the Uchuraccay massacre. The hypothesis of military involvement was adamantly rejected by Vargas Llosa, for the military could not be present in all parts of the region at the same time and thus not likely present on the day of the journalists' arrival and death (Vargas Llosa 1990: 87–88). The CVR states that there were such rumors, but the commission does not give any further explanation than the presence of the military in the region exacerbating local fears and that the residents of Uchuraccay might have been following the military warning that friends come by air, not by land (i.e., the military traveled by helicopter and Shining Path by foot). *Rupay* seems to put heavier weight on the military's responsibility for the death of the journalists by providing visual representations of these rumors and by presenting repeatedly this suspicion as voiced subsequently by journalists, *comuneros*, and family members of the deceased journalists (figures 6.10 and 6.11). Undocumented rumors are allowed to circulate openly and on equal footing to documented accounts in *Rupay* and not in the CVR's account.[13]

FIGURES 6.10 AND 6.11. *Rupay*, 54.

The ability of comics to tell both facts and fiction allows for the presentation of many versions at the same time and still have a "truth effect." According to Alfredo Villar, who worked on gathering information for the text, "*Rupay* is fictionalized, but people take it as if it were the truth. It is not the CVR, but they take it as if it were. We are giving one possibility among various possibilities."[14] The authors do not claim that *Rupay* is anything but fiction; it is fiction based on research (hence the bibliography at the book's end). They do not claim to be objective: they have their own beliefs and position. For instance, they think that the violence committed by the state is underacknowledged in the CVR's *Final Report*.[15] Jesús Cossio, who made the drawings for *Rupay*, published a sequel comic, *Barbarie: Cómics sobre la violencia política en el Perú, 1985–1990* (Barbarity: Comics about the political violence in Peru, 1985–1990). In *Barbarie* he explains, "my book does not try to be 'objective.' It takes a stance against both powers, State power (represented by the armed forces) and Shining Path power. My documentary work tries to show the abuse and lies of these [two] authoritarianisms. The difference is that the State version (one that exonerates [armed forces' abuses]) presents itself and its representatives as 'official,' and for this reason, we need to combat against this version with more force" (as quoted in *La Nuez* 2012c).

Perhaps because of the unresolved nature of what took place in Uchuraccay this case lends itself to comics. Other versions of contentious past events that cannot be documented or agreed upon—that remain "loose" or marginalized memories (to borrow from Steve Stern [2006])—can find expression in the form of comics. Other media have been employed to explain Uchuraccay, such as the unfinished documentary on Uchuraccay by Carmen Valdivieso Hulbert, which seems to be based on similar sources to that of *Rupay* with the addition of interviews nearly thirty years after the events.[16] The trailer for *Uchuraccay* suggests that the film is narrated like a crime thriller: various witnesses advance theories of who killed the journalists, that the journalists were killed by state actors so that they might not discover something, and a subsequent coverup of the events. The soundtrack reinforces the perception of this film as one of suspense.

As well, a memorial has been erected in the former location of Uchuraccay, dedicated to the eight journalists. The memorial is shaped like a star, with eight points each holding the name of a slain journalist (no point is dedicated to the guide), and a dove of peace sits upon a central pillar. There does not seem to be an explanation for the memorial, although there may have been a commemorative plaque on the central pillar at one point, as suggested by the outline of a now empty spot.[17] Most recently, the story of the community of Uchuraccay is one of the three cases featured in the museum opened in Lima in December 2015 called the Place of Memory, Tolerance, and Social Inclusion (Lugar de Memoria, la Tolerancia y la Inclusión Social), along with armed state actors' killings of community members of Putis and Shining Path violence and enslavement of the Asháninka people.

BLOCKS, BLURBS, AND BLOGS: THE COMICS DEBATED

Rupay has enjoyed relative success in reaching readers in the comic world, in the blogosphere, and among those participating in Peru's human rights network.[18] The first print run sold out (*Rupay* and *Barbarie* each had a thousand copies printed). Yet not all reactions within Peru are positive. Initially, some members of human rights NGOs did not feel that the use of comics was an appropriate medium for depicting the internal conflict. This concern may be similar in part to views initially expressed over Spiegelman's *Maus* that led one academic to claim that he would not touch it "with a ten-foot pole" (Rothberg 2000: 2), a debate that asked whether the use of comics somehow undermined the seriousness of the subject. *Maus* is now required reading for many in memory and literature studies, despite this earlier critique. In Peru another concern seems to be that the use of drawings depicts the violence too graphically and thus may be voyeuristic. However, *Rupay*, like *Maus*, is "a picture comic driven by word" (Spiegelman as quoted in Huyssen 2003: 131)—that is, the text is necessary to understand the images. The difference is striking between *Rupay* and *Barbarie*, where the latter has more images that stand alone without text and thus may turn the reader more into a spectator. Yet Cossio avoids this pitfall in his later project: through his close-up panels, some with a single face in the frame, he may promote empathy for the victim, and in other frames, such as that of the mass burial pit, he places the spectator in the same viewpoint of that of perpetrators, thus raising the possibility of the complicity of the silent bystander.[19]

In Peru, where recent memory still sparks heated debate, the authors of *Rupay*, in particular Jesús Cossio, have been the object of criticism, accused of taking too negative a stance against the armed forces (and implicitly too positive a stance on Shining Path). Most of this debate has taken place on the Internet, the anonymous format of which allows for tremendous mudslinging.[20] Although some commend Cossio and the authors of *Rupay* for using the comic form as a means to "reveal the truth" about what happened in Uchuraccay, others accuse Cossio of being biased, or worse—a Shining Path sympathizer (*La Nuez* 2012a). This blogger analyzes Cossio's work, coming to the conclusion that a disproportionate amount of his comics display state violence and are "a simplified, partial and biased testimony of the war against terrorism" (*La Nuez* 2012c). Furthermore, this blogger's use of highlighted text and italics draws visual parallels between them; for instance, in one paragraph only the words *Rupay, Barbarie, Sendero Luminoso*, MRTA (the Revolutionary Movement of Túpac Amaru), and *terroristas* appear in red italics. Cossio was reminded again of the seriousness with which his work is read in October 2012, when one of his comics, along with eleven others, was censored by the justice minister in an exhibition held in Villa El Salvador.[21] His comic showed Abimael Guzmán in various stages of transformation from a defiant leader of a subversive group, to a submissive prisoner seeking a peace accord, to an old man requesting pardon from the Peruvian state.[22]

The portrayal of the past in comics is a hot topic in Peru for two other concurrent debates about Peruvian youth: one on education and the other on political mobilization. Former members of the CVR have pushed for the CVR's findings to be included in the school curriculum (*La Mula* 2012). While this has been a goal for human rights groups since the publication of the CVR's recommendations, more recent concerns have been aired by members of a broader political spectrum that today's youth are too young to remember the conflict and thus are dangerously uninformed. The political wing of Shining Path (Movimiento por Amnístía y Derechos Fundamentales, or MOVADEF), which gained greater notoriety around 2011, seeks status as an official political party. Its main support base seems to be young people.[23] The lack of awareness by Peru's youth about the violence committed by Shining Path led one political humorist to suggest that youth are more likely to recognize the body parts of a famous supermodel than the whole of Abimael Guzmán, the leader of Shining Path.[24]

Despite earlier concerns about using the comic form to depict a national tragedy, some view comics as having the potential to teach and explain this past to Peruvian youth, especially Lima-based youth.[25] One of the few areas where the established political left and right seem to agree upon is in the fear that Peruvian youth (as a homogenous group) do not remember the past.[26] Thus CVR supporters seek diffusion of a human rights narrative through the teaching of the CVR's findings in school. As well, those who feel Peruvians need to remember the threat that Shining Path posed and the heroic acts of the armed forces to eradicate this threat have also turned to comics, such as the resurfaced *Confidencias* as a "graphic novel" that "came at the right time" when groups (such as MOVADEF) "wish to hide behind the fragile memory of some" (see figure 6.4) (*La Nuez* 2012b). As Carlos Iván Degregori, a former CVR commissioner, wrote in the preface to Cossio's *Barbarie* (2010), "the language of comics is easier for the younger generation to assimilate, for whom, moreover, these times of horror are behind," a reference to Peru's postmemory generation (Hirsch 2012). Degregori was most likely reflecting on the imposing size and language of the truth commission's *Final Report* and even their 477-page abbreviated version, although he might have also had in mind other visually rich creative means to reach this audience, such as television or film.[27] However, the resources needed to produce television and film limit this possibility, even if some highland filmmakers, most notably Palito Ortega, have addressed the conflict through the medium of film (del Pino 2014).

BROACHING DIFFICULT PASTS THROUGH COMICS

In the absence of a sense of collective responsibility to remember, comics—along with other cultural expressions and public actions—bring to light experiences that otherwise would remain in the realm of rumor or isolated memories. Stories of Uchuraccay circulate—among individuals, within groups, within national forums—in part because they are unresolved and remain contested. Comics allow the communication of alternative versions. Not all comics, of course, support a human rights narrative nor use historically grounded research to portray the years of violence. The posting on the Internet of *Confidencias*, a comic that portrays as senseless Shining Path violence, is rumored to be republished by the Naval Academy, thus suggesting that comics is a media used by competing memory camps, among other cultural interventions (Milton, 2017).

Rupay contributes to these memories of the war years by recounting different versions or registers of what happened. *Rupay* brings together the many stories of Uchuraccay into one narrative account. This was perhaps something the CVR had hoped to do, by collecting various testimonies of Uchuraccay. Yet the commission was limited in its dissemination of these findings in part because of the many volumes of the *Final Report* but also because the commission was circumscribed by the rules of truth-telling for a truth commission. They could not fabricate dialogues or juxtapose accounts or present possible explanations without specific proof, all linking strategies that facilitate the recounting of a fluid story. The authors of *Rupay* were not limited by such constraints and thus could present a more multilayered (and perhaps coherent) narrative of the death of the journalists and their guide. They could write fiction, but let the reader take his or her own account "como si fuera la verdad" ("as though it were the truth"). Indeed, the CVR's *Final Report* and *Rupay* are the only two sources listed on the Spanish-language Wikipedia website's bibliography under the heading of

"Sendero Luminoso."[28] Yet *Rupay* is fiction. While the CVR laid claims to truth, *Rupay*'s authors have not.

These observations into the successful engagement of *Rupay* with public memory is not intended to downplay the impact of the CVR but rather to point to the importance of creative interventions in present-day battles over what and how to remember. The CVR's report was one exercise to build a public forum for discussion of the past and to establish a complex national narrative, and *Rupay* another. Spheres of representation are prominent in memory negotiation precisely because of the little political weight of the CVR and the official history that the CVR wished to pass as Peru's collective memory. *Rupay*, like other cultural forms that speak to the past, is an attempt to transform these loose memories, rumors, and marginalized experiences into units of the national, collective discourse. Alone, however, this myriad of cultural engagements may not be enough to promote human rights as the norm nor sufficient enough to teach today's youth about the perils of the past.

NOTES

1. See Comisión de la Verdad y Reconciliación online at www.cverdad.org.pe.
2. I thank Eduardo González Cueva for introducing me to *Rupay*. Subsequent to this writing, Markus Klaus Schäffauer (2014) published a conference presentation on documentaries, films, and *historietas*, including *Rupay* as an example of *violentografía* (the writing about violence).
3. I thank Benjamín Corzo for lending me this manuscript, which he intends to publish with Ediciones Contracultura. Parts of this manuscript are available on the Internet.
4. Author interview with Jesús Cossio, Lima, June 22, 2011.
5. Interview with Benjamín Corzo, "La novela gráfica es el género con mayor proyección en la historietas peruana," May 18, 2011, online at http://contracultura.pe/, accessed on September 12, 2012.
6. Louis Otis (2011) has argued that these images contributed to the Peruvian press's sensationalistic representation of the conflict. Marco Antonio Sotelo Melgarejo (2012) has described the portrayal of the "perpetrators of terrorist acts" (meaning Shining Path) by *Diario Expreso* as "sociopaths or common criminals, looking to avoid legitimizing the politics and ideology of their acts."
7. It is difficult to gather information on this graphic novel. The publication date seems to be 1989. According to a conversation with Jesús Cossio (author interview, Lima,

October 23, 2012), the armed forces (the Cultural Commission of the Navy) commissioned Luís Baldoceda to produce this comic. They supplied Baldoceda with tape recordings of an imprisoned *senderista* (Jorge Cañari Vásquez, Comarada Javier) and with an already completed script which he was to place into the *historieta* format. The comic was not distributed in Lima but rather was meant as part of the efforts to win the hearts and minds of highland peoples.

8. The authors of *Rupay* prefer the term "comic" rather than "graphic novel" to describe their work. Author interviews with Cossio and Villar, Lima, June 2011.
9. The expression "Perú profundo" does not appear in Vargas Llosa's report, but is alluded to in his description of the cultural divides of Peru, where he juxtaposes "official Peru" against "a culture—perhaps archaic but rich and profound, that is connected with all of our pre-hispanic past" (Vargas Llosa 1990: 125). In a subsequent interview for the magazine *Oiga*, Vargas Llosa refers to "lo que Basadre llamaba el Perú profundo" ("what Basadre called deep Peru") (Vargas Llosa 1990: 134). Vargas Llosa's emphasis on the cultural and temporal divide between the Iquicha ethnic group (to which Uchuraccay belongs) and "official Peru" reifies the former as "archaic" and "primitive" and effaces Uchuraccayan engagement within contemporary Peruvian society (see, for instance, Mayer 1991: 476–85).
10. For the actual murder of the journalists, an event that lasted some thirty minutes to an hour on January 26, the CVR relies on a core testimony, No. 203432, the son of Severino Huáscar Morales Ccente, who was killed later that same night.
11. Mayer (1991: 468–75) analyzes the various critiques against the Vargas Llosa report. See also del Pino 2008 (especially chapter 2).
12. *Rupay* is not the only comic-panel format to address the murder of the journalists in Uchuraccay. In the art contest held during the CVR titled "Rescate por la memoria" ("Recovery of Memory"), a resident of the province of Huanta, Albino Jahuín Soto, submitted a five-page *historieta* titled "Uchuraccay, the massacre of the journalists." The comic strip won a prize of honorable mention (Colectivo Yuyarisun 2004: 80–84). It is interesting to compare this short comic produced by someone from the region with that of *Rupay*. Albino Jahuín Soto presents the journalists as much more naïve (thus partially blaming them for walking into something of which they had no clue); he also clearly implicates the armed forces as the perpetrators of the murders.
13. On the importance of rumor in the CVR processes in Ayacucho, see Yezer 2008. There are a few observations in the CVR's report that we cannot know for certain took place—for instance, that the journalists "did not imagine that they would never return" (CVR 2003: 132) or that the trek was "extremely exhausting for some" (133), perhaps described by Argumedo's family but not cited in the CVR's report.
14. Author interview with Alfredo Villar, Lima, June 22, 2011.
15. Author interview with Jesús Cossio and Alfredo Villar, Lima, June 24, 2011.

16. A synopsis and trailer for the film *Uchuraccay* are online at www.uchuraccay.com/index_en.htm, accessed on September 17, 2013. The events of Uchuraccay is also described in the manuscript "Plumas y montañas" by a Shining Path member, "Suni Puni," written in 1985 and that the CVR cites.
17. I have not been to this memorial. This information is from photographs taken by Ing. Rubén de la Torre Toscano and posted on the Internet in 2011, online at www.panoramio.com/user/4102086?with_photo_id=50519268, accessed on September 17, 2013.
18. Original funding for the project came from outside Peru, from the Ford Foundation. Author interview with Jesús Cossio, Lima, October 23, 2012.
19. I thank Matthew Penney—a historian and comics veteran, especially of the Japanese tradition—for his close reading of *Rupay* and *Barbarie*, and for sharing these insights.
20. See, for example, the Internet conversation about the War of the Pacific (discussed in Drinot 2011). A particularly virulent attack on the Internet against Cossio was in response to a photograph of Cossio taken in jest that he had posted on his Facebook page. While he saw himself as mocking Shining Path, some online viewers interpreted the photograph otherwise (Comicapol 2012).
21. See "Acusan a Ministerio de Justicia de censurar muestra fotográfica en Villa El Salvador," October 22, 2012, online at www.peru.com/actualidad/mi-ciudad/acusan-ministerio-justicia-censurar-muestra-fotografica-villa-salvador-noticia-93245, accessed on September 23, 2013.
22. See also the video of Jesús Cossio in which he reflects upon the role of comics in Peru's present memory battles, on the CVR, and the response to his works. Online at www.youtube.com/watch?v=rpU-x-XeTfw, accessed on September 23, 2013.
23. On MOVADEF, see Muñoz-Najar (2012) and Tanaka (2012).
24. Comments posted on January 24, 2012, online at http://carloslavida.blogspot.com/2012/01/cultura-general.html, accessed on February 16, 2011.
25. Conversation with Salomón Lerner, Lima, August 17, 2008. Indeed, Cossio's comics adorn the cover of the Legal Defence Institute's publication on the ten-year anniversary of the CVR's *Informe final,* online at www.revistaideele.com/ideele/content/número-233, accessed on October 21, 2013. The incorporation of Cossio's drawings suggests an acceptance by previously skeptical members of human rights NGOs to use comics as a means to depict Peru's internal conflict.
26. Yet we have to be careful not to make "youth" a homogenous group, as one that is generally unaware of the past, or poorly instructed. There are Peruvian youth who affirm a lack of knowledge about the past—the students who might write in the visitor books in a memory museum or photography exhibit of the violence such phrases

as "Thank you for opening my eyes" (Milton and Ulfe 2011: 323). Yet there are also young people who are aware of this history or are already politicized because of their own experiences as descendants of these conflict years, whether the children of harm committed by Shining Path or the armed forces, or both.

27. The CVR employed many visual means to engage a wider public: street theater by the troupe Yuyachkani, the Lima-based photography exhibition *Yuyanapaq: Para recordar,* a traveling version of this exhibition, and the circulation of booklets of postcard-sized photographs.
28. "Sendero Luminoso," at http://es.wikipedia.org/wiki/Sendero_Luminoso, accessed on May 2, 2016. *Rupay* is not cited in the English version.

REFERENCES

Acevedo, J. 1984. *Para hacer historietas*. Madrid: Editorial Popular.

Atencio, R. 2014. *Memory's Turns: Reckoning with Dictatorship in Brazil.* Madison: University of Wisconsin Press.

Baldoceda, L. 1989. *Confidencias de un Senderista: Juicio popular.* Online at http://lanuez.blogspot.it/search?q=confidencias+de+un+senderista. Accessed on February 14, 2012.

Bell, V. 2014. *The Art of Post-Dictatorship: Ethics and Aesthetics in Transitional Argentina*. Abingdon, UK: Routledge.

Bilbija, K., J. E. Fair, C. E. Milton, and L. A. Payne, eds. 2005. *The Art of Truth-Telling about Authoritarian Rule*. Madison: University of Wisconsin Press.

Colectivo Yuyarisun. 2004. *Rescate por la memoria*. Ayacucho: Colectivo Yuyarisun, Ministerio Británico para el Desarrollo International, Organización Holandesa para la Cooperación International al Desarrollo.

Comicapol. 2012. "Palabras finales: Respuesta a la tendenciosa editorial y a la complaciente entrevista realizada a Jesús Cossío publicadas en el blog 'La Nuez.'" Online at http://comicapocalipsis.blogspot.it/search/label/Jesús Cossio. Accessed on February 14, 2012.

Comisión de la Verdad y Reconciliación (CVR). 2003. "Anexo 2." In *El informe final 1980–2000: Una compilación del informe final de la Comisión de la Verdad y Reconciliación*. Lima: Oxfam-DFID and SER. Online at www.cverdad.org.pe. Accessed on February 14, 2012.

Cossio, J. 2010. *Barbarie: Comics sobre violencia política en el Perú, 1985–1990*. Lima: Contracultura.

del Pino, P. 2014. "Ayacuchano Cinema and the Filming of Violence: Interview with Palito Ortega Matute." In *Art from a Fractured Past: Memory and Truth-Telling in*

Post–Shining Path Peru. Edited by Cynthia E. Milton, 153–75. Durham, NC: Duke University Press.

del Pino, P. 2013. "En el nombre del gobierno: Políticas locales, memoria y violencia en el Perú del siglo XX." In *Las formas del recuerdo: Etnografía de la violencia política en el Perú*. Edited by Ponciano del Pino and Carolina Yezer, 27–70. Lima: Instituto de Estudios Peruanos, Instituto Francés de Estudios Andinos.

del Pino, P. 2008. "En busca del gobierno: Comunidad, política y la producción de la memoria y de silencios en el Perú del siglo XXI." PhD dissertation, University of Wisconsin–Madison.

del Pino, P. 2003. "Uchuraccay: Memoria y representación de la violencia política en los Andes." In *Jamás tan cerca arremetió tan lejos: Memoria y violencia política en el Perú*. Edited by Carlos Iván Degregori, 49–93. Lima: Instituto de Estudios Peruanos.

Drinot, P. 2011. "Website of Memory: The War of the Pacific (1879–84) in the Global Age of YouTube." *Memory Studies* 4, no. 4: 370–85.

Drinot, P. 2009. "For Whom the Eye Cries: Memory, Monumentality, and the Ontologies of Violence in Peru." *Journal of Latin American Cultural Studies* 18, no. 1: 15–32.

Hirsch, M. 2012. *The Generation of Post-Memory: Writing and Visual Culture after the Holocaust*. New York: Columbia University Press.

Huyssen, A. 2003. *Present Pasts: Urban Palimpsests and the Politics of Memory*. Stanford, CA: Stanford University Press.

Jelin, E., and A. Longoni, eds.. 2005. *Escrituras, imágenes y escenarios ante la repression*. Madrid: Siglo Veintiuno de España Editores.

Lambright, A. 2015. *Andean Truths: Transitional Justice, Ethnicity, and Cultural Production in Post-Shining Path Peru*. Liverpool: Liverpool University Press.

La Mula. 2012. "Los caviares y el informe final de la CVR." Online at http://elmulonario.lamula.pe/2012/02/04/los-caviares-y-el-informe-final-de-la-cvr/xileone. Accessed on February 16, 2012.

La Nuez. 2012a. "Comunicado al respaldo al creador local Jesús Cossio." Online at http://lanuez.blogspot.com/2012/02/comunicado-de-respaldo-al-creador-local.html?showComment=1328999010195#comment-c8894119165915099516. Posted February 9, 2012. Accessed on February 14, 2012.

La Nuez. 2012b. "Confidencias de un Senderista, cuando la memoria puede salvar el futuro." Online at http://lanuez.blogspot.it/search?q=confidencias+de+un+senderista. Posted on January 28, 2012. Accessed on February 14, 2012.

La Nuez. 2012c. "Se acaba el mundo: El juego de las etiquetas." Online at http://lanuez.blogspot.com/2012/01/se-acaba-el-mundo-el-juego-de-las.html. Posted January 23, 2012. Accessed on February 14, 2012.

La Serna, M. 2012. *The Corner of the Living: Ayacucho on the Eve of the Shining Path Insurgency*. Chapel Hill: University of North Carolina Press.

L'Hoeste, H. F., and J. Poblete. 2009. *Redrawing the Nation: National Identity in Latin/o American Comics*. New York: Palgrave MacMillan.

Love Lima. 2012. Interview with Tilsa Otta. Online at http://lovelima.pe/arte-diseno/una-invitacion-a-quebrar-la-enajenacion-del-olvido/. Accessed on February 14, 2012.

Lucioni, M. N.d. "Histoira de la historieta en el Perú, 1873-1944." Unpublished manuscript.

Lucioni, M. 2001. "La Historieta peruana, 1." *Revista Latinoamericana de Estudios sobre la Historieta* 1, no. 4: 257–64. Online at www.rlesh.110mb.com/04/04_lucioni.html. Accessed on February 14, 2012.

Mayer, E. 1991. "Peru in Deep Trouble: Mario Vargas Llosa's 'Inquest in the Andes' Reexamined." *Cultural Anthropology* 6, no. 4: 466–504.

Milton, C. E. 2014a. *Art from a Fractured Past: Memory and Truth-Telling in Post–Shining Path Peru*. Durham, NC: Duke University Press.

Milton, C. E. 2014b. "Art from Peru's Fractured Past." In *Art from a Fractured Past: Memory and Truth-Telling in Post–Shining Path Peru*. Edited by Cynthia E. Milton, 1–34. Durham, NC: Duke University Press.

Milton, C. E. 2017. *Counter Memories: Military Cultural Interventions and the Human Rights Era in Peru*. Madison: University of Wisconsin Press.

Milton, C. E., and M. E. Ulfe. 2011. "Promoting Peru: Tourism and Post-Conflict Memory." In *Accounting for Violence: The Memory Market in Latin America*. Edited by Ksenija Bilbija and Leigh Payne, 304–43. Durham, NC: Duke University Press.

Muñoz-Najar, S. 2012. "Otra vuelta de tuerca." Online at www.noticiasser.pe/15/02/2012/grupo-memoria/otra-vuelta-de-tuerca. Accessed on February 16, 2012.

Otis, L. 2011. "Chronique, enquête et silence: Autopsie de la présentation du conflit interne par la presse de Lima jusqu'au massacre d'Uchuraccay, 1960–1983." MA thesis, Université de Montréal.

Rossell, L., A. Villar, and J. Cossio. 2009. *Rupay: Historias de la violencia política en Perú, 1980–1984*. Madrid: La Oveja Roja.

Rossell, L., A. Villar, and J. Cossio. 2008. *Rupay: Historias gráficas de la violencia en el Perú, 1980–1984*. Lima: Contracultura.

Rothberg, M. 2000. *Trauma Realism: The Demands of Holocaust Representation*. Minneapolis: University of Minnesota Press.

Rubenstein, A. 1998. *Bad Language, Naked Ladies, and Other Threats to the Nation: A Political History of Comic Books in Mexico*. Durham, NC: Duke University Press.

Sagástegui, C. 2009. "Acevedo and His Predecessors." In *Redrawing the Nation: National Identity in Latin/o American Comics*. Edited by H. F. L'Hoeste and J. Poblete, 131–50. London: Palgrave Macmillan.

Saona, M. 2014. *Memory Matters in Transitional Peru*. London: Palgrave Macmillan.

Schäffauer, M. K. 2014. "Trabajo de violencia en los medios peruanos tomando como ejemplo historietas, documentales y el cine." In *Perú: Medios, memoria y violencia. Conferencias en Hamburgo*. Edited by M. K. Schäffauer et al., 93–102. Lima: Universidad Antonio Ruiz de Montoya.

Sotelo Melgarejo, M. A. 2012. "Representación gráfica de la violencia política en el Perú 1980–2012: Una aproximación a las historietas durante tiempo de violencia interna." *Pacarina del Sur* 4:14. Online at www.pacarinadelsur.com/home/pielago-de-imagenes/626-representacion-grafica-de-la-violencia-politica-en-el-peru-1980–2012-una-aproximacion-a-las-historietas-durante-tiempo-de-violencia-interna. Accessed on February 16, 2012.

Stern, S. J. 2014. "The Artist's Truth: The Post-Auschwitz Predicament after Latin America's Age of Dirty Wars." In *Art from a Fractured Past: Memory and Truth-Telling in Post–Shining Path Peru*. Edited by Cynthia E. Milton, 255–76. Durham, NC: Duke University Press.

Stern, S. J. 2006. *Remembering Pinochet's Chile: On the Eve of London 1998*. Durham, NC: Duke University Press.

Tanaka, M. 2012. "Memoria y MOVADEF." *La República*. 29 January. Accessed on February 16, 2012.

Vargas Llosa, M. 2013. "Contrapunteo peruano: Entre el humor y la violencia." In *Memorias en tinta: Ensayos sobre la representación de la violencia política en Argentina, Chile y Perú*. Edited by Lucero de Vivanco Roca Rey, 379–99. Santiago: Ediciones Universidad Alberto Hurtado.

Vargas Llosa, M. 1990. "Informe sobre Uchuraccay." In *Contra viento y marea, III (1964–1988)*. By M. Vargas Llosa, 87–128. Barcelona: Editorial Seix Barral.

Vargas Llosa, M. 1983. "Inquest in the Andes." *New York Times Magazine*, 31.

Vich, V. 2015. *Poéticas del duelo: Ensayos sobre arte, memoria y violencia política en el Perú*. Lima: Instituto de Estudios Peruanos.

White, H. 1992. "Historical Emplotment and the Problem of Truth." In *Probing the Limits of Representation: Nazism and the "Final Solution."* Edited by Saul Friedlander, 37–53. Cambridge: Harvard University Press.

Yezer, C. 2008. "Who Wants to Know? Rumours, Suspicions, and Opposition to Truth-Telling in Ayacucho." *Latin American and Caribbean Ethnic Studies* 3, no. 3: 271–89.

Young, J. E. 1993. *The Texture of Memory: Holocaust Memorials and Meaning*. New Haven, CT: Yale University Press.

SEVEN

MEMORY ON THE ROAD

AMERICAN HIGHWAYS AND PROSTHETIC PASTS IN GONZALO MARTÍNEZ AND ALBERTO FUGUET'S *ROAD STORY*

James Scorer

I used to be somebody else, but I traded him in.
THE PASSENGER

In his 1998 autobiographical work, *Heading South, Looking North*, Ariel Dorfman (1998: 30) admitted: "If it had not been for Susana la Semilla, a cartoon character I invented, I would not have survived the coup against Allende." He created Susana in 1973 for a Ministry of Agriculture television advertising campaign designed to criticize those participating in a crippling transport strike. With a meeting to discuss the advertisements scheduled elsewhere, Dorfman did not attend his usual place of work, the Palacio de La Moneda, where he worked as cultural adviser to the Allende government. Instead, on that fateful September 11, he learned of the military coup against the president via radio. Dorfman went into hiding and some days later, while watching television, he saw copies of a book being thrown into a bonfire (139). The book was *Para leer al Pato Donald* (How to read Donald Duck), a stringent critique of U.S. cultural imperialism that Dorfman had coauthored with the Belgian Armand Mattelart in 1971. For the Chilean right, the work symbolized the misguided, ridiculous, and indeed dangerous path of socialism. If before the coup they cried "Long live Donald Duck!" after General

Augusto Pinochet came to power, they were able to brazenly ditch copies of a later edition of the book into the harbor at Valparaíso (253).

Some twenty years after Dorfman went into exile in the United States, the young Alberto Fuguet caused a stir in Latin American literature with the publication of a collection of short stories titled *McOndo* (1996), edited with compatriot Sergio Gómez. Fuguet's contribution to the collection was "La verdad o las consecuencias," a story about a Chilean taking a road trip in the United States, which he later rewrote under the title "Road Story" for his 2004 collection *Cortos*. A few years later, Fuguet wrote the introduction to Gonzalo Martínez's graphic adaptation of *Road Story* (Fuguet and Martínez 2007). *Road Story* then, the graphic novel that provides the focus for this chapter, has its origins in Fuguet's contribution to *McOndo*, the story that he felt encapsulated the salient characteristics of the body of literary work he and Gómez had described in their introduction to the collection. Playing on the name Macondo, Gabriel García Márquez's famous fictional town, *McOndo* (1996) represented a symbolic shift in the region's literary production above all because it offered a way "to challenge a Latin American narrative imaginary dominated by regionalist narratives in the first half of the century, and magical realism in the second" (Paz-Soldán and Castillo 2001: 16). Instead, writers like Fuguet, who had spent the first decade of his life in California despite being born in Santiago, were far more attuned to the globalized nature of their world, offering gritty, often urban portraits of a transnational Latin America full of references to technology, global brands, and popular culture.[1]

When encapsulated in comic book form, Fuguet's cultural sensibility might be seen as the exact opposite to Dorfman's understanding of culture as expressed in *Para leer al Pato Donald* and the cartoon character Susana la Semilla. Whereas Susana was an exaggeratedly Chilean character, defying the neocolonial activities of the United States and implicitly providing a graphic counterpoint to Donald Duck, *Road Story* embraces U.S. cultural influences, drawing heavily on the geography of the American West and the genre of the road movie. In the early 1970s at least, Dorfman used comics as part of his expressed rejection of the United States, the country where, like Fuguet, he had grown up. But *Road Story* offers no such cultural rebuke. Instead, it incorporates references to a borderless, global Latin American existence—a vision encapsulated in Fuguet's (2001: 68) declaration that *McOndo* writers believe "your roots are packed in your hard drive."[2] Finally, if we agree with Idelber Avelar, who follows John Beverley in claiming that September 11, 1973, marks the allegorical end of the Latin American Boom (Avelar 1999:

35), then *Para leer al Pato Donald* and Susana la Semilla would be the last vestiges of a cultural, as well as political, era. *Road Story*, as a comic book adaptation of "La verdad o las consecuencias," Fuguet's first intervention under the banner of *McOndo*, is symptomatic of a literary movement that has always been expressly post-Boom.

Given the political, moral, and existential significance of memory politics in contemporary Chilean history (Stern 2010: xxii), this comparison between Dorfman's and Fuguet's understanding of culture via comics makes a work like *Road Story* heavily loaded in terms of its use of the past. Replacing national sympathies with a sense of global belonging via references to U.S. cultural products and multinational companies, not to critique neocolonialism but to express a transnational Chilean reality, Fuguet taps into the contemporary tendency described by Andreas Huyssen (2003: 4), by which "national traditions and historical pasts are increasingly deprived of their geographic and political groundings, which are reorganized in the processes of cultural globalization." Indeed, much of the economic success of Chile during the 1990s and the new millennium can be ascribed to a repackaging of national history as a means of stimulating economic growth, an approach that reconfigured the trauma of the dictatorship into specious forms of memory consensus in what Jon Beasley-Murray (2010: 277) called the "interminable interregnum" of the Concertación. The origins of this eternal present of neoliberalism lie not in the return to democracy in 1990 but with the military coup of 1973. The dictatorship simultaneously ushered in neoliberal market reforms and state restructuring at the same time as it institutionalized disappearance and the eradication of the archive.

Failing to recognize the extent of those practices of disremembering is precisely what makes the transition to democracy one that framed "the neoliberal present as an intransitive and stationary reality" (Fornazzari 2013: 74). As a result, uncritical engagements with global products and celebrations of U.S. popular culture such as those undertaken by Fuguet not only reverse the global political standpoint of works like *Para leer al Pato Donald* but also implicitly celebrate a country tainted (via Richard Nixon, Henry Kissinger, and the CIA) with connections to the Pinochet dictatorship. Moreover, as part of a wider generational shift, *Road Story* places its emphasis on individual suffering and memory rather than on collective trauma. While on a business trip for the family company in the United States, the Chilean protagonist Simón decides to neglect his responsibilities and take a road trip through the American West. Though partly motivated by dissatisfaction with his work, Simón has decided, following the collapse of his marriage and the fact that his wife has left him for his best friend, to embark on the road trip. As such, the story is intently focused on Simón's individual crisis and his inability to overcome this personal trauma. For all these reasons, *Road Story* might readily be construed as encapsulating a kind of memory that undermines the very necessary postdictatorship practices in Chile that seek out justice and the restoration of the archive.

I suggest, however, that remembering in *Road Story*, particularly because of its graphic form, does offer a productive and significant contribution to postdictatorship memory politics in Chile. After Simón meets the Bolivian-American Adriana on the road, journeying with her from Arizona to New Mexico via Ciudad Juárez, he is able to transcend his self-centered individualism, developing a broader, more productive form of memory—one that enables him, literally and metaphorically, to finally move on. In particular, Simón's embrace of the road trip and, crucially, the road trip genre (one tied up with cultural heritage and memory) means that *Road Story* locates a transnational Chilean within the cultural past of the United States, an encounter that probes relations of culture and memory in the Americas.[3] The use of the road trip genre here, combined with the way that Simón begins to construct fictional memories as his journey progresses, indicates that a kind of "prosthetic cultural memory" is at play in Fuguet and Martínez's work. This term is a fusion of Jan Assmann's (2006: 9) theory that memories are culturally determined and Alison Landsberg's (2004) term "prosthetic memory."

Landsberg (2004: 14) has argued that the expansion of mass cultural forms, particularly cinema, has created a form of memory in which individuals take on a past they did not actually experience. Prosthetic memory, she explains, "emerges at the interface between a person and a historical narrative about the past" (2), creating, as a result of the destabilizing effects of globalization, "shared social frameworks for people who inhabit, literally and figuratively, different social spaces, practices, and beliefs" (8). Rather than critiquing mass media productions, Landsberg argues, we should live with them and be attune to how the prosthetic memories they create can help reformulate an individual's "subjectivity and politics" (2) and bring together people from diverse backgrounds by providing them with "a shared archive of experience" (14). Simón embodies Landsberg's approach to memory, drawing on the cultural memory of road trips, particularly Michelangelo Antonioni's film *The Passenger*, as part of his metaphysical journey. Far from undoing other forms of memory practices or suggesting that the past has no place in contemporary Chile, *Road Story* encourages us to think about how contemporary memory politics might be informed by prosthetic cultural memories.

FRAGMENTS, COMICS, AND MEMORY

The transformation of Fuguet's literary short story into comic form exaggerates *Road Story*'s suitability for thinking about postdictatorship imaginaries and memory politics in Latin America. To begin with, comics tap into the way that *McOndo* literature symbolizes the end of the Latin American Boom by taking up cultural forms that highlight the demise of "the aura of the literary" (Avelar 1999: 13). By drawing on the historical trajectory of the road trip, a genre that lies at the heart of the cultural imaginary of the United States, *Road Story* becomes a visual engagement with the American past and the eternal present of being on the road. As a graphic adaptation of a story that has itself gone through several versions (Fuguet 2007: 7), the "creative past" of the work mirrors the rewritings, reproductions, and displacements that are themselves part of the visual, textual, and cultural narrative of the work, just as the coauthored nature of the written/drawn text highlights the social nature of both the creative process and cultural memory itself. The comic form is well-suited to engage with Nelly Richard's (2004: 16) argument that postdictatorship democracy in Chile attempted to create consensus as a means of "exorcis[ing] the ghost of multiple fissures and dislocations of signs produced during the dictatorship," thereby confronting what she earlier (2000: 274, emphasis in the original) called the "*break in signification* [that] subjects thought, categories and languages to a broken, wounded, incomplete, disintegrated, convulsed condition." Rather than seek consensus, she argues, cultural practices need to turn such fragmentations into "an expressive multiplicity of connotations of meaning that displace lack into a surplus of images" (274). The comic book is symbolically apt in this regard because it is a medium built on the expressive multiplicity of fragments and the synchronicity of possible times.

As a form of "sequential art," the term Will Eisner (2008 [1985]) used to describe the medium, comics and graphic novels are tied up with time and memory. As Scott McCloud (1994) has put it, when reading comics, "both past and future are real and visible and all around us" (104), a simultaneity that links the image to "the composition of memory" (115). Built around the empty space of the gutter, the comic's temporal fracture is patched back together by the reader, whose imaginative labor fills in these visual

FIGURE 7.1. Page 14 from *Road Story* (Fuguet and Martínez 2007). Reproduced by kind permission of Gonzalo Martínez and Alfaguara.

FIGURE 7.2. Page 18 from *Road Story* (Fuguet and Martínez 2007). Reproduced by kind permission of Gonzalo Martínez and Alfaguara.

gaps, an act of visual investment that resembles the patchwork nature of remembering. With readers moving temporally back and forth, chronology sits alongside synchronicity. As well as being instances in time, each individual panel can itself incorporate a stretch of time or even several moments in time (Duncan and Smith 2009: 137). More commonly, a sense of time passing (or not) is built between panels. Though panels sometimes suggest a sequence of moments passing, they can also, following McCloud's (1994: 79) analysis of frame sequences, shift on the basis of an "aspect to aspect" change, in which action is less important than the varying elements or sensations of one instance, such that "rather than acting as a bridge between separate moments, the reader here must assemble a single moment using scattered fragments."

Though Martínez's visual adaptation of Fuguet's story largely follows the plot and written text of the original very closely, the graphic form gives him the scope to intensify and exaggerate in visual terms the key themes and tropes of the written text, particularly those of time and memory. The opening panel, for example, in which Simón sits at the wheel of his car, runs off the edges of the page, a bleed that suggests a timeless, eternal present (Fuguet and Martínez 2007: 13).[4] The following page, however, uses the classic technique of superimposing a photograph (drawn, in this case) over another image, a montage technique that highlights the layered nature of memory. If the long, thin layout of the top panels suggests time passing, then the images themselves depict Simón's stationary car. The contrast between a present animated by memory is exaggerated in the panel depicting Simón, his wife, and her future partner changing from being a superimposed photo into an image box incorporated into the narrative (18).

As Simón remembers the photograph, we are presented with two close-ups broken by an extreme close-up of Simón's eyes, a sort of shot–reserve-shot that highlights the graphic and filmic nature of the memory on display. In the rest of the work, Martínez uses a variety of other techniques to construct graphic memory and the juxtaposition of diachronic and synchronous time. In the image of Simón visiting the laundrette and dumping his clothes—an act suggestive of leaving behind the past—several moments are layered into one image; on other pages images seep beyond the rigid structure of the panels and speech boxes are located between images; some pages are filled entirely, such as the images of Simón's wedding, in which different images, including photographs, come together in a confusing mix of pictures; and others include images of one moment in time split into different boxes to

FIGURE 7.3. Page 63 from *Road Story* (Fuguet and Martínez 2007). Reproduced by kind permission of Gonzalo Martínez and Alfaguara.

exaggerate the passing of fragments of time (Fuguet and Martínez 2007: 65). All these techniques emphasize how the comic book form exaggerates the fluctuating nature of memory and time in the work.

THE DESERT OF THE PRESENT

The first half of *Road Story* fashions Simón as a representative figure of neoliberalism, mirroring Stern's (2010: 9) descriptions of the social and political transformations of the postdictatorship era in Chile: "The privatization of culture grew more powerful and tipped the balance toward the individual as self-actualizing agent and consumer, away from the individual as citizen whose actualization occurs *through* relationships of mutual claims with state, society, and community." In one of the few direct references to Chile, for example, we discover that the family firm Simón is escaping trades in salmon farming, a business that became successful on an industrial scale only in the 1990s, during which time it became one of Chile's leading exports (United Nations 2006: 6–7). That *Road Story* opens with so many images of cars and includes frequent references to road movies heightens the sense of Simón as an isolated neoliberal figure since, as David Laderman (2002: 3) has observed, "both cars and movies promised to express the idealized uniqueness of the individual consumer." Under neoliberalism it is the acts, spaces, and objects of consumption that become the driving force behind configurations of citizenship and identity formation.

In the case of this particular work, however, it is the comic book form itself that encourages the reader to see Simón as symbolic of a particular postdictatorship Chilean subject—namely, an introspective private consumer little concerned for either past or future, uninterested in a national past, and lost in the fragmented reality of neoliberal Chile. Simón's inability to escape his present situation is evident right from the start, where he is apparently unable to move. In one panel, for example, Simón's hand is shown turning the keys of his rental car, indicating that the car is being set in motion, a point reinforced by the exhaust fumes in the following panel (Fuguet and Martínez 2007: 15). But those fumes disappear in the following panels, and the lack of other motion lines around the car gives the impression that the car is in fact stationary. A later sequence of panels constructs "aspect to aspect" transitions, shifts that exaggerate an ongoing instant rather than the passing of time (25). Earlier, with the way the top and bottom panels bleed, exaggerating the sense of infinite time, the image of the stationary car mirrors Simón's realization that he has been driving in circles (19). *Road Story* thus begins with a journey in which Simón cannot budge: the road prevents him from *moving on.*

The second way that the comic form highlights Simón's postdictatorship subjectivity is through the fragment, not just in the panel form itself but also because of the specific arrangement of those panels. In one image, for example, Simón's traveling car and surroundings are split over three panels, indicative of his fractured identity (Fuguet and Martínez 2007: 21). Later, four separate panels make up a fragmented image of Simón lying on his bed (63). The panels, which themselves give the impression of looking at him through a window, are superimposed on two other images of Simón reclining on his bed but from a side-on perspective. Emphasizing Simón's divided self, these images are not just a reminder that "the cartoonist . . . works in a medium the very syntax of which demands that the subject always be split and frequently be multiple" (Rifkind 2008: 403); they also mirror Richard's (2004: 49) description of postdictatorship Chilean identity as "a ruined fragment of discarded totality."

The final way that Martínez ties Simón to postdictatorship Chilean identity is by constantly directing our gaze at the protagonist and his isolation. Martínez captures Simón's loneliness on several occasions, such as the frames that depict him in his car, where he has taken refuge after a conversation during which he realizes he has no friends (Fuguet and Martínez 2007: 41). The entire page is taken up with four panels that exaggerate his inward-looking self-obsession, private introspection that is also evident earlier in the work, where the panels alternate between the interior and exterior of the car, with Simón looking out on the emptiness of the surrounding desert. Such interiority indicates how *Road Story* appears to reflect Fuguet's statement that although *McOndo* writers "went global," their narratives "went private, introspective" (Fuguet 2001: 71). Martínez thus uses the comic form to express static time, fragmentation, and a focus on the individual—all of which establishes an oblique but persistent visual link to the everlasting present of neoliberal consensus.

It is no surprise, then, that Simón's eternal present begins in the desert of the American West, portrayed as a space dominated by a depthless present. The empty desert, depicted by the swathes of white in Martínez's images, exaggerates Simón's private—and somewhat self-indulgent—metaphysical and geographical journey. The apparent depthlessness of the landscape is heightened by the divided image in which we learn that Simón studied cartography (Fuguet and Martínez 2007: 21), a choice that, according to Rory O'Bryen (2011: 164) in his comments on Fuguet's original story, "reinforces his [Simón's] disdain for (con)sequential thought and his subjection to the depthless, two-dimensional abstractions of the image." Such two-dimensionality would seem to make the desert an especially apt setting for the story, a landscape described by Jack Sargeant and Stephanie Watson (1999: 14) in their study of the road movie as a zone "in which recognizable signifying practices collapse and identity loses its previous boundaries," and which "exists outside of quantifiable time."

In this sense the landscape of *Road Story* harks back to Jean Baudrillard's descriptions of the desert in his 1988 book *America*. Whether Fuguet was directly influenced by *America* is unclear, but it certainly haunts both his attempt to express the timelessness of the postmodern via the desert and Martínez's images of the cultural geography of the American West, complete with interstate highways, roadside diners, the strip, and the expanses of mountain ranges and desert. Of particular relevance is the way Baudrillard (1988: 9) engages with the relationship between travel, the desert, and time, referring to "the extensive banality of deserts" and describing driving as "a spectacular form of amnesia," part of his celebration of the United States as a kind of utopian nonplace: "America ducks the question of origins; it cultivates no origin or mythical authenticity; it has no past and no founding truth. Having known no primitive accumulation of time, it lives in a perpetual present. Having seen no slow, centuries-long accumulation of a principle of truth, it lives in perpetual simulation, in a perpetual present of signs. It has no ancestral territory" (76). As Devin Orgeron (2008: 1) has argued, Baudrillard sees road travel as unveiling "a landscape of constantly evolving, barely sustainable 'newness.'" Baudrillard's statements about the desert, which he further calls "an ecstatic form of disappearance" (Baudrillard 1988: 5) and a "triumph of forgetting over memory, an uncultivated, amnesic intoxication" (6–7), resonate with the belief that travel enables leaving the past behind, symbolized in *Road Story* by Simón's uncle, Gaspar, who we learn went to a conference in Portland and never returned to Chile (Fuguet and Martínez 2007: 16).[5] As a result, the United States becomes a space to erase yourself, leaving your (Chilean) past behind by writing yourself off the map.

But Baudrillard takes a very partial reading of the desert, the road, and the American past—one that fails to appreciate the complexities of nomad history and memory, which (like Martínez's image) reads the desert all too quickly as a space of emptiness. This is one reason why, though it has become a key reference point in studies of the road, *America* is frequently critiqued. Certainly, as studies of U.S. road movies are at pains to point out, the United

States is a land with a long tradition of movement and travel. Brian Ireland (2003: 474), for example, has stated that "Americans are a restless people," and Ron Eyerman and Orvar Löfgren (1995: 55) have written that "the freedom to move upward and outward is one of the most central persistent images America has of itself." But as Richard Grant (2003: 12) has illustrated, those who enact what he calls the "nomad's creed"—from hobos to the Comanche—are hardly bereft of memory: American wanderlust itself has a well-established history. And, as Santiago Vaquera, a transnational writer of Fuguet's generation, put it: "The Chicano communities of California are characterized by movement and migration, which does not mean that they have no historical memory but rather that their memory, like their history and roots, are constructed in movement and being uprooted" (cited in Navarro-Albaladejo 2006: 237). Therefore, neither being on the road nor driving through the desert necessarily denote an inability to develop, recognize, or assemble a past.

ROAD STORIES AND FICTIONAL MEMORIES

At one point in *Road Story*, Simón admits that "the U.S. has colonized his unconscious" (Fuguet and Martínez 2007: 21), an observation evident in the way that the United States provides Simón with his frame of reference. For example, he calls the man who runs off with his wife "Luke Skywalker." Martínez's drawings of Gallup, New Mexico, are strikingly similar to those of Pichlemu in Chile. When Simón watches television in the Hotel Congress, he sees the itinerant Chilean TV presenter Don Francisco hosting his U.S. show, suggestive of a Latin culture being marketed for the United States. That *Road Story* draws on the road trip might further suggest that the work is, like Simón, "colonized" by cultural forms that originate north of the border, creating an imaginative space in which places seem familiar because they are all the same, whether you have a lived memory of them or not. And yet all genre exchanges construct dialogues between each specific cultural production and its predecessors. As Laderman (1996: 43) has argued, the road movie in particular is inherently "an amalgam of genres," one that, often via genre itself, can set up a struggle "between the dominant cultural ideology and rebellion against that ideology" (55). When Latin Americans take up genres "imported" from Hollywood, they are therefore not being "colonized" but are constructing a cultural dialogue. Whether these appropriations reflect on "the hybridizing potential of cultural texts at the periphery" (Page 2009: 108), explore "the way capitalist globalisation is experienced from a particular location" (Andermann 2011: 154), or provide a means of cultural resistance, they all revisit the very nature of the genre in question.

It is precisely *Road Story*'s engagement with the road genre that emphasizes the wider significance of Simón's journey and his treatment of memory. *Road Story* is full of references to the road genre, including quotations from Jack Kerouac's *On the Road*, visual allusions to Route 66, and narrative citations of such road films as *The Passenger* (1975) or *Gerry* (2002), the latter directed by Gus Van Sant, who also directed the seminal road trip film *My Own Private Idaho* (1991). Not only a means of leaving the past behind, a characteristic that would make the genre symbolic of the neoliberal present, road trips are rather inherently infused with questions of memory and the past.[6]

Just as they journey into the eternal present and the possibilities of the open highway, they also engage with a different era, symbolized by the classic segue from metropolitan city to small-town, premodern America.[7] As Orgeron (2008: 7) has suggested, although the genre ostensibly expresses a desire to rebel against tradition and move ever onward, road movies in fact "rebel against the corrosion of the substantial and buoying myths that once sustained [their protagonists] . . . , against a culture that, in the name of modernity, has buried its traditions, cinematic and otherwise." A similar point is made by Ron Eyerman and Orvar Löfgren (1995: 61), who write that the road genre moves "backwards in cultural time" as part of a nostalgic quest for an authentic, untouched-by-time America, meaning that "from its beginnings the road movie was constituted around nostalgia" (68).

Simón's engagement with the road movie, and the interactions between his empirical journey and the cultural past, enables him to rethink and reformulate his own past and construct relations with individuals and groups who are otherwise strangers to him. The development of Simón's character in *Road Story*, in fact, highlights how it is being on the road that makes the protagonist increasingly aware of the possibilities of the past. The point is exaggerated in an early line from Fuguet's (2004: 166) short-story version that is not included in the graphic adaptation: "Simón [. . .] is paying the cost of always living in the present. The problem is that his present is exactly the same as his past and, if something doesn't give, his future isn't particularly promising." A key moment in his recognition of the importance of the past is his stay in Tucson's Hotel Congress. For Simón the hotel captures something authentic and unblemished about U.S. traveler and immigrant culture and the way that they turn displacement into belonging: "The Congress dates back to the start of the century and is still more or less the same because Tucson isn't a tourist city . . . but one for students and Mexicans who stayed on this side of the border" (Fuguet and Martínez 2007: 58).[8]

In that sense Simón's degree in cartography, a profession he left behind to work in the family business but that is taken up (remembered) as part of his journey, may refer to the collapsing of space into two dimensions. As the image of the map highlights (Fuguet and Martínez 2007: 19), however, it also relates to a complex sense of time, functioning as a visual depiction of the past (where you've come from), the present (where you are), and the future (where you're going). Bennet Schaber (1997: 32) has called road trips an "aleatory sequence of images," a description that echoes the impact of the comic book layout, especially because, as he puts it, road trips "take on meaning because they always go in two directions at once: to go forward . . . is to go backwards" (26). Reading comics can have the same effect.

As a result, memory in *Road Story* is slightly different than the way that Patrick O'Connell (2005: 33) has described Fuguet's use of memory in his 1998 novel *Por favor, rebobinar*, in which "the harsh reality of past political events is metaphorically shrouded by references to mass consumerism, placing the characters' psyche in a state of amnesia and/or anamnesis that ultimately distorts their perceptions of reality and of themselves." In *Road Story*, by contrast, there is an allusion to a moment when even the Chilean state refashioned the past: the company name of the business owned by Simón's family is "Selkirk-Dafoe" (Fuguet and Martínez 2007: 26)—an allusion to Daniel Defoe's *Robinson Crusoe*, which is based on the story of Alexander Selkirk, castaway on the island now known as Robinson Crusoe. In 1966 the Chilean state renamed the islands formerly known as Más a tierra and Más afuera to Robinson Crusoe and Alejandro Selkirk, respectively, with the aim of emphasizing their (literary) history. Likewise, in *Road Story*, Simón is not suffering from amnesia, but rather his journey sets in motion a series of fictional memories that he starts to appropriate as real. It is those memories that allow him to escape the boomerang trajectory that he finds himself on at the start of the work, which would otherwise have taken him on an elliptical road trip back to where he started (Fuguet and Martínez 2007: 13).

During his journey Simón undergoes a series of identity reconfigurations and adopts various invented memories. He has his hair cut in a military style because he is in the military town of Twentynine Palms, a cut that later results in servicemen mistaking him for an officer. He likes the Hotel Congress so much that he thinks of becoming a permanent resident, symbolic of his ongoing transitory identity. Later, Simón shaves off his temporary goatee, saying to himself "welcome back, Simón" (Fuguet and Martínez 2007: 78), but on the very next page he introduces himself to Adriana as Roberto del Río, the name he has adopted for his road trip. Yet such inventions are not entirely lacking in truth. Roberto del Río is the name of the street on which he grew up, and when he tells Adriana that he is alone not because his wife left him but because she died, his fabrication cannot mask his real solitude. Adriana herself—a Bolivian but, as she says, "made in the USA" (80), symbolic of her split identity—also turns out to have been playing with her past by using one surname and not another. When she tells Simón that he is a great guy despite everything, his reaction reveals how invented stories can still speak the truth: "It had been a long time since Simón felt that someone was telling him the whole truth—even if everything she was saying was perhaps a lie" (113). The character's memory is not straightforward chronological recollection, but is based around a deictic series of visual images and narratives. Simón does not advocate forgetting but is prepared to select from and utilize his past, thus deploying a prosthetic memory to liberate himself from the eternal present.

It is no accident that the comic spends a page on *The Passenger*, Antonioni's 1975 road movie that provides a sort of template for *Road Story*. Indeed, the page on which Simón watches *The Passenger* in his hotel room is placed opposite the one about the family salmon business, a spatial distribution that highlights the narrative link between the two. The film's immediate influence on Simón's journey is that, after watching it, he decides not to return to Santiago and the family business. *The Passenger* has a deeper significance, however, since it also provides a template for Simón's decision to mold his past. In Antonioni's film the journalist David Locke, played by Jack Nicholson, is lost and out of place in an African town. When a man (Martin Knight) staying in the same hotel dies, Locke decides to assume Knight's identity, falsifying the dead man's passport and traveling to Barcelona. Once there he tries to escape from the inquisitive search of his "widow" and eventually falls foul of the enemies of the dead Knight, who turns out to have been involved in arms smuggling.

The Passenger expresses the possibilities and dangers of changing one's identity, a task that Locke admits is nearly impossible when Knight tells him before he dies that airports, taxis, and hotels are all the same: "I don't agree. It's us who remain the same. We translate every situation, every experience into the same old codes. We just condition ourselves. . . . I mean, however hard you try, it stays so difficult to get away from your own habits." Later,

Locke admits that he used "to be somebody else, but I traded him in," to which the Spanish woman he meets replies: "I'm talking to someone who might be someone else." The whole film is based on the protagonists' acceptance of the shifting performances of identity that both perform: they embrace the identity appropriation that Locke accomplishes. The desire to escape the past is encapsulated by the road trip that Locke and the woman undertake. In one telling scene, she asks what Locke is running away from as they drive down a tree-lined country road, to which he responds: "Turn your back to the front seat." The white lines painted on the trees draw the eye away to the nothingness behind them, a symbol of his desire to escape the past.

Antonioni's film is one road movie among many that forefronts the notion of being on the road as a means of leaving behind the past and transforming one's identity: Eyerman and Löfgren (1995: 57) suggest that being on the road draws on the frontiersman myth by emphasizing the dangers and possibilities of a new beginning. Laderman (1996: 44) writes that in 1945's *Detour* the road encourages "the dissolution of Tom's sense of who he is." But, as Sargeant and Watson (1999: 9) indicate, road movies offer constant reminders of how unfounded this belief is that being on the road allows the past to be left behind. In that sense the film's tragic finale, in which Knight's enemies catch up with Locke, indicates that though you can escape your past by appropriating other pasts, those new pasts are equally meaningful and significant. Pasts can be fictionalized or appropriated, but those new pasts have their own consequences and cannot be escaped. Antonioni's film thus emphasizes the potency of self-determination and of all memories, whether real or not. That idea is reworked in *Road Story*, since, like *The Passenger*'s Locke, Simón's invented memories and refashioned past are nonetheless still infused with the past—both Simón's own and the one he appropriates. Thus he does not erase memory but rather recognizes how its fictional qualities allow him to transcend rather than forget the past.

LATIN AMERICA ON THE ROAD

Choosing *The Passenger* as a narrative template reveals how the prosthetic cultural memory employed in *Road Story* is not simply a straightforward assimilation of a Hollywood form. Directed by an Italian with an American actor playing the protagonist, set in Africa, England, and Spain, and starring a Frenchwoman already famous for her role in 1972's *Last Tango in Paris* (itself a highly transnational film), Antonioni's film symbolizes the global nature of the road trip genre.[9] Road movie criticism often reflects on whether this archetypal Hollywood genre is truly North American or simply expresses universal human desires, as evidenced by the innumerable road movies created by foreign directors or made outside the United States (Eyerman and Löfgren 1995; Cohan and Hark 1997; Ireland 2003; Lindsay 2003; Mazierska and Rascaroli 2006; Everett 2009). In perhaps the most searching critique, in which Orgeron (2008: 3) argues that the road movie "is first and foremost about the cinema, about the culture of the image," he suggests that the road movie was in fact heavily influenced by postwar European cinema, particularly French New Wave.

Orgeron's argument is useful because it highlights how road trip criticism struggles with the genre's heritage, overlooking, for example, the importance of Latins and Latin America to the genre. Brian Ireland (2003) has highlighted how the genre engages with a series of long-standing geographical movements in the United States, depicting not just "the North" or "the West" but the transference of, say, "East to West" (to frontier freedom) or "South to North" (for escaped slaves). But his discussion fails to account for the frequent passage from "North to South," a surprising omission given that two of the founding texts of the road trip genre—Jack Kerouac's *On the Road* (1957) and Dennis Hopper's *Easy Rider* (1969)—both incorporate this particular trajectory. Indeed, *Easy Rider* ushers in the modern road movie not with Captain America and his Harley Davidson chopper emblazoned with the Stars and Stripes but with the words "buenos días" spoken outside "La Contenta Bar" in Mexico. This land—stereotypes aside—is the land that Kerouac (2011 [1957]: 241) refers to when he writes: "I couldn't imagine this trip. It was the most fabulous of all. It was no longer east-west, but magic *south*." The land to the south in *On the Road* is the promise of opportunity, sex, and drug-fueled adventure: "Do you know there's a road that goes down Mexico and all the way to Panama?—and maybe all the way to the bottom of South America where the Indians are seven feet tall and eat cocaine on the mountainside?" (209).

Certainly, Kerouac's frame of reference is still the United States—"The strange radio-station antenna of Ciudad Mante appeared ahead, as if we were in Nebraska" (2011 [1957]: 270)—and the vision is stereotypical and stylized, Mexico referred to as "this strange Arabian paradise" (265), "these vast and Biblical areas of the world" (275), and "one vast Bohemian camp" (275). But it is still Latin America that dominates the novel's conclusion. "We had no idea what Mexico would really be like" (249), Sal writes, only to add when they arrive, "to our amazement, it looked exactly like Mexico" (250).

Indeed, earlier in the novel, after he hooks up with a Mexican woman, Sal confesses that the whites living near where the couple are camped think that he is a Mexican, which, he adds, "in a way I am" (88).

The road movie is American in the true sense of the term—that is, it is formulated around a series of negotiations, transferences, and physical migrations between north and south. The importance of recognizing this Latin American influence is indicated in Kris Lackey's (1997: 21) reading of road narratives, in which he makes the point that the road trip genre is often dominated by "solvent white drivers" who are blind to the fact that they are, precisely, solvent and white. Expressing nostalgia for the "ancestral Plains Indian past" and celebrating "folk atavisms and other pockets of resistance to modern mass culture" (55), they drive their cars as if they were time machines, "figuratively set[ting] the traveler outside history and render[ing] history static and consumable" (125). Lackey highlights that, by contrast, black Americans offer a rather different take on the road trip, since, because of their skin color, they "cannot enjoy an illusion of disinterested liberty" (xi) nor "a vantage outside the forces and events they observe" (118). Latin Americans, much like African Americans, historicize the road trip and provide a caveat to Baudrillard's (1988: 80) suggestion that "Octavio Paz is right when he argues that America was created in the hope of escaping from history."

Latin America and Latin Americans in *Road Story* are decidedly not "romanticized as 'repositories of authenticity,' antidotes to white urban angst," as Laderman (1996: 43) suggests Blacks, Mexicans, and Native Americans tend to be in road movies. But they are reminders of how Latin America informs U.S. cultural memory. That influence is evident in the reference to the Alamo, a focal point for U.S.–Latin American relations, and symbolized by the figure of Adriana, the Bolivian-American who met her husband via an encounter with Raquel Welch (117), itself a significant reference as the Hollywood star had a Bolivian father. Here, as with all immigrant, peripatetic imaginaries, there is a constant, implied, albeit sometimes hidden, dialogue with the past. More particularly, the prosthetic cultural memory deployed by Simón allows him to build up a set of affinities and connections with traditions and peoples that go beyond his strictly Chilean past.

The references to *The Passenger*, in which Locke goes on a road trip with a Spanish woman with no name, draws attention to the way *Road Story* taps into the road trip's balance between the traveling loner and "the possibility of strange encounters" (Eyerman and Löfgren 1995: 65). In *Road Story* the arrival of Adriana transforms Simón's loneliness into a two-hander balanced between outsiders estranged both from each other and from themselves. Such personal estrangement is expressed in *Road Story*'s epigraph, which is taken from *On the Road*: "I looked at the cracked high ceiling and really didn't know who I was for about fifteen strange seconds. I wasn't scared; I was just somebody else, some stranger, and my whole life was a haunted life, the life of a ghost" (Kerouac 2011 [1957]: 15). The quotation reveals not just identity displacement but also the role of the past in that migration—"the life of a ghost." Sal reminds us that being on the road transforms his contemporaneity both into a living past and a past that is no longer familiar.

Simón, moreover, is by no means a stereotypical Latin. Not only is he out of the place in the United States, he also appears to be out of place in Latin America. Crossing over into Ciudad Juárez with Adriana, the difference between them could not be more marked: Adriana is the one who steers Simón away from the tourist bar, the one who explains the difference between tequila and mescal (Fuguet and Martínez 2007: 86–87). The significance of their encounter is magnified when Adriana persuades Simón to get off the train they are traveling on and cross over into Mexico and not, as he intends, to carry on and see the Alamo (82). Adriana thus lures him away from the foundational site of the American past and toward the contemporary Latin America that is so distant to him. Simón's palpable distance from Adriana creates not so much an encounter with difference as one with his own estranged Latin American other (not least, perhaps, because Chile [Simón] and Bolivia [Adriana] have a long history of antagonism). Their encounter gradually breaks down Simón's distance from Adriana and, as result, his internal schism.

BEYOND THE WILD ONES

In the final sequences of *Road Story,* Simón arrives in the town of Truth or Consequences and stops to fill the car. When the gas pump assistant sees Simón's reaction to learning that the motels are full because of a Hell's Angels meetup, the assistant offers him a mild rebuke: "Don't pull that face, those guys are good people" (Fuguet and Martínez 2007: 121). The Native American assistant—"an indigenous guy" (Fuguet 2004: 216) in the written version—highlights how it is precisely the internal outsider who is able to redress Simón's stereotypical view about another group of internal outsiders. In his 1966 study of the gang, Hunter S. Thompson (2009 [1966]: 272) suggested that the Hell's Angels, themselves frequently treated as pariahs,

FIGURE 7.4. Page 127 from *Road Story* (Fuguet and Martínez 2007). Reproduced by kind permission of Gonzalo Martínez and Alfaguara.

turn to the past because "they can't grasp the terms of the present, much less the future."[10]

Thus Simón's smile in the final panels of the work, partly directed at the passing Hell's Angels, simultaneously denotes that he has started to overcome his personal trauma (it is almost the only time he is seen smiling in the work), that he has been able to establish some kind of affinity with a group of previously threatening strangers (the Angels) and with another figure of difference (Adriana, who, amid the sequence of Simón watching the motorcycles, is seen in one panel sleeping peacefully in bed). Furthermore, it indicates that he has been able to engage with and critique the very prosthetic cultural memory that he otherwise deploys by overcoming his negative vision of the Hell's Angels, typified by László Benedek's 1953 film *The Wild One*.

Simón's ability to evaluate and overcome that prosthetic memory is further evident in the story's conclusion, which deviates slightly from the short story: in both short story and graphic novel, Adriana keeps her invented name and Simón has his restored. However, in the former it is Simón throwing his wedding ring into a puddle that symbolizes his reconciliation with the past, whereas in the latter he mails the piece of writing he had previously stolen from the typewriter of the eastern European woman who committed suicide in the Hotel Congress during his stay. The scene not only suggests that he has left his journey behind, returning what is not his; it also indicates how Simón does not become subsumed by the past that he appropriates, unlike Locke in *The Passenger*. Nevertheless, the sensation is hardly one of a return to his previous life. Simón is still out of place and involved in a relationship that allows a perpetual interruption to develop and take on a life of its own. He is still Simón but a different Simón to the one at the start of the work. He ends up, after all, in Truth or Consequences, a town that had its name changed from Hot Springs after a referendum. The new name, which highlights the tension between veracity and action, indicates how Simón has reconciled himself to the vitality of displacement by deploying invented truths.

Road Story goes against Andreas Huyssen's (2003: 27) argument that there is a "growing need for spatial and temporal anchoring in a world of increasing flux in ever denser networks of compressed time and space." Nor does it support Huyssen's (28) view that "imagined memories" are less "active, alive, embodied in the social" than "lived memories." On the contrary, Simón's use of prosthetic cultural memory, brought about by the road trip genre, provides him with the means to deploy an alternative set of memories and imagine an alternative future in which he is able to overcome the trauma of repetition and establish a relationship with a Latin American stranger and internal outsider. If, as Richard Grant (2003: 142) has written, the nomad "only feels stable when experiencing velocity," then by the end of *Road Story* Simón has reached that stability precisely through the instability of his memories. That he has finally been able to move on is evident in the images themselves. As the work draws to a conclusion, the number of panels representing fragmentation and static time decreases; by the end the panels restore a less disjointed, more progressive sense of time, movement intensified by the motion lines and dust around the motorcycles of the Hell's Angels. *Road Story* thus responds to Nelly Richard's (2000) vision of postdictatorship Chile by depicting how Simón ends up existing in positive fragmentation rather than languishing in the trauma of division.

NOTES

Epigraph: *Passenger* (1975).

1. Paz-Soldán and Castillo (2001: 12) make the point that at stake in criticisms of new literary forms such as those set out by *McOndo* is "not transnationalism per se . . . but an unstated disdain for a particular sort of transnational cultural effect."
2. Unless otherwise indicated, all translations from the original Spanish are the author's.
3. In the "road trip" genre I include all cultural forms that take a journey—usually by car—as their subject, whether that trip is portrayed in film, literature, travel writing, music, comics, and so on.
4. In comics terminology, "bleed" refers to a panel that has no border and that spreads to the edge of—and thus off—the page.
5. The use of the verb *borrarse* ("to erase oneself") to describe Gaspar's disappearance is highly charged in the wake of practices employed by recent Latin American military governments. Fuguet (2011) later wrote a book about his attempts to track down his uncle, Carlos Fuguet, years after he disappeared in the United States. Like *Road Story*, therefore, *Missing (una investigación)* also includes an act of disappearance that, at least on the face of it, has no connection to the politics and practices of the Chilean dictatorship.
6. In Kerouac's *On the Road* (2011 [1957]: 156), for example, Sal speaks of the "ecstasy" of taking "the complete step across chronological time into timeless shadows" and of the "innumerable lotus-lands falling open in the magic mothswarm of heaven" (157). The will to forget included in this reference to Homer's *Odyssey* is offset by Sal's acknowledgment that his trip will also form part of another set of memories when he looks at Dean's family photographs: "I realized these were all the snapshots which our children would look at someday with wonder, thinking their parents had lived smooth, well-ordered, stabilized-within-the-photo lives and got up in the morning

to walk proudly on the sidewalks of life, never dreaming the raggedy madness and riot of our actual lives" (231). In fact, roads and road trips can themselves become part of the past, as the books *Ghost Towns of Route 66* (Hinckley 2011) or *Route 66 Lost and Found* (Olsen 2011) demonstrate. In a rather different context, Ana Amado (2004: 66) has highlighted the links between topography and Argentine postmemory by suggesting that María Inés Roqué's film about her disappeared father is "a kind of road movie."

7. Claire Lindsay's (2003: 90) argument that the Mexican films *Sin dejar huella* and *Y tu mamá también* are Latin American road movies because they engage with the disparate chronologies of a postmodern Mexico balanced between the modern and the traditional is true only insofar as we recognize that such heterogeneous coexistences are also part and parcel of the Hollywood road movie canon.
8. The Congress, as its website makes clear, markets itself around its past, not just referencing the hotel's several ghosts but also participating in the annual reenactment of the capture of the infamous Depression-era bank robber John Dillinger at the hotel (Hotel Congress n.d.).
9. In *Road Story*, Simón also makes a stop at Zabriskie Point in Death Valley (Fuguet and Martínez 2007: 20), the key location for the eponymous 1970 film *Zabriskie Point*, also directed by Antonioni.
10. The Hell's Angels have close ties to U.S. cinematic history, both in terms of their name, traced by some to Howard Hughes's 1930 war film *Hell's Angels*, and also in terms of their negative reception, linked to Benedek's 1953 *The Wild One* (Thompson 2009 [1966]: 74–75). Indeed, Thompson's journalistic study of the gang is itself indebted to cinematic references such as this one: "The scene reeked of Hollywood: the showdown, *High Noon*, *Rio Bravo*" (148).

REFERENCES

Amado, Ana. 2004. "Ordenes de la memoria y desórdenes de la ficción." In *Lazos de familia: Herencias, cuerpos, ficciones*. Edited by Ana Amado and Nora Domínguez, 13–81. Buenos Aires: Paidós.

Andermann, Jens. 2011. *New Argentine Cinema*. London: I. B. Tauris.

Assmann, Jan. 2006. *Religion and Cultural Memory: Ten Studies*. Stanford, CA: Stanford University Press.

Avelar, Idelber. 1999. *The Untimely Present: Postdictatorial Latin American Fiction and the Task of Mourning*. Durham, NC: Duke University Press.

Baudrillard, Jean. 1988. *America*. London: Verso.

Beasley-Murray, Jon. 2010. *Posthegemony: Political Theory and Latin America*. Minneapolis: University of Minnesota Press.

Cohan, Steven, and Ina Rae Hark, eds. *The Road Movie Book*. London: Routledge.

Detour. 1945. Directed by Edgar G. Ulmer.

Dorfman, Ariel. 1998. *Heading South, Looking North*. London: Sceptre.

Dorfman, Ariel, and Armand Mattelart. 2002 [1971]. *Para leer al Pato Donald*. Buenos Aires: Siglo XXI.

Duncan, Randy, and Matthew J. Smith. 2009. *The Power of Comics: History, Form, and Culture*. New York: Continuum.

Easy Rider. 1969. Directed by Dennis Hopper.

Eisner, Will. 2008 [1985]. *Comics and Sequential Art: Principles and Practices from the Legendary Cartoonist*. New York: W. W. Norton & Co.

Everett, Wendy. 2009. "Lost in Transition? The European Road Movie, or A Genre 'Adrift in the Cosmos.'" *Literature-Film Quarterly* 37, no. 3: 165–75.

Eyerman, Ron, and Orvar Löfgren. 1995. "Romancing the Road: Road Movies and Images of Mobility." *Theory, Culture, and Society* 12: 53–79.

Fornazzari, Alessandro. 2013. *Speculative Fictions: Chilean Culture, Economics, and the Neoliberal Transition*. Pittsburgh: University of Pittsburgh Press.

Fuguet, Alberto. 2011. *Missing (una investigación)*. Santiago de Chile: Alfaguara.

Fuguet, Alberto. 2007. "En el camino." In *Road Story* by Alberto Fuguet and Gonzalo Martínez, 5–10. Santiago de Chile: Alfaguara.

Fuguet, Alberto. 2004. *Cortos*. Santiago de Chile: Alfaguara.

Fuguet, Alberto. 2001. "Magical Neoliberalism." *Foreign Policy* 125: 66–73.

Fuguet, Alberto. 1996. "La verdad o las consecuencias." In *McOndo*. Edited by Alberto Fuguet and Sergio Gómez, 109–32. Barcelona: Mondadori.

Fuguet, Alberto, and Sergio Gómez, eds. 1996. *McOndo*. Barcelona: Mondadori.

Fuguet, Alberto, and Gonzalo Martínez. 2007. *Road Story*. Santiago de Chile: Alfaguara.

Gerry. 2002. Directed by Gus Van Sant.

Grant, Richard. 2003. *Ghost Riders: Travels with American Nomads*. London: Little, Brown.

Hinckley, Jim. 2011. *Ghost Towns of Route 66*. Minneapolis: Voyager Press.

Hotel Congress. N.d. "Hotel History." Online at http://hotelcongress.com/history/. Accessed on April 27, 2015.

Huyssen, Andreas. 2003. *Present Pasts: Urban Palimpsests and the Politics of Memory*. Stanford, CA: Stanford University Press.

Ireland, Brian. 2003. "American Highways: Recurring Images and Themes of the Road Genre." *Journal of American Culture* 26, no. 4: 474–84.

Kerouac, Jack. 2011 [1957]. *On the Road*. London: Penguin.

Lackey, Kris. 1997. *RoadFrames: The American Highway Narrative*. Lincoln: University of Nebraska Press.

Laderman, David. 2002. *Driving Visions: Exploring the Road Movie*. Austin: University of Texas Press.

Laderman, David. 1996. "What a Trip: The Road Film and American Culture." *Journal of Film and Video* 48, nos. 1–2: 41–57.

Landsberg, Alison. 2004. *Prosthetic Memory: The Transformation of American Remembrance in the Age of Mass Culture*. New York: Columbia University Press.

Last Tango in Paris. 1972. Directed by Bernardo Bertolucci.

Lindsay, Claire. 2003. "Mobility and Modernity in María Novaro's *Sin dejar huella*." *Framework* 49, no. 2: 86–105.

Mazierska, Ewa, and Laura Rascaroli. 2006. *Crossing New Europe: Postmodern Travel and the European Road Movie*. London: Wallflower.

McCloud, Scott. 1994. *Understanding Comics: The Invisible Art*. New York: Kitchen Sink Press and HarperPerrenial.

My Own Private Idaho. 1991. Directed by Gus Van Sant.

Navarro-Albaladejo, Natalia. 2006. "Entrevista: Manifestaciones del nacionalismo y la globalización en la literatura contemporánea: En diálogo con Santiago Roncagliolo, Edmundo Paz Soldán y Santiago Vaquera." *Arizona Journal of Hispanic Cultural Studies* 10: 231–50.

O'Bryen, Rory. 2011. "McOndo, Magical Neoliberalism, and Latin American Identity." *Bulletin of Latin American Research* 30: 158–74.

O'Connell, Patrick L. 2005. "Santiago's Children of the Dictatorship: Anamnesis versus Amnesia in Alberto Fuguet's *Por Favor, Rebobinar*." *Chasqui* 34, no. 1: 32–41.

Olsen, Russell A. 2011. *Route 66 Lost and Found: Mother Road Ruins and Relics*. Minneapolis: Voyager Press.

Orgeron, Devin. 2008. *Road Movies: From Muybridge and Méliès to Lynch and Kiarostami*. New York: Palgrave Macmillan.

Page, Joanna. 2009. *Crisis and Capitalism in Contemporary Argentine Cinema*. Durham, NC: Duke University Press.

The Passenger. 1975. Directed by Michelangelo Antonioni.

Paz-Soldán, Edmundo, and Debra A. Castillo. 2001. "Introduction: Beyond the Lettered City." In *Latin American Literature and Mass Media*. Edited by Edmundo Paz-Soldán and Debra A. Castillo, 1–18. New York: Garland.

Richard, Nelly. 2004. *Cultural Residues: Chile in Transition*. Minneapolis: University of Minnesota Press.

Richard, Nelly. 2000. "The Reconfigurations of Post-Dictatorship Critical Thought." *Journal of Latin American Cultural Studies: Travesia* 9, no. 3: 273–82.

Rifkind, Candida. 2008. "Drawn from Memory: Comics Artists and Intergenerational Auto/biography." *Canadian Review of American Studies* 38, no. 3: 399–427.

Sargeant, Jack, and Stephanie Watson. 1999. "Looking for Maps: Notes on the Road Movie as Genre." In *Lost Highways: An Illustrated Guide to the Road Movie*. Edited by Jack Sargeant and Stephanie Watson, 6–20. London: Creation Books.

Schaber, Bennet. 1997. "'Hitler Can't Keep 'Em That Long': the Road, the People." In *The Road Movie Book*. Edited by Steven Cohan and Ina Rae Hark, 17–44. London: Routledge.

Stern, Steve J. 2010. *Reckoning with Pinochet: The Memory Question in Democratic Chile, 1989–2006*. Durham, NC: Duke University Press.

Thompson, Hunter S. 2009 [1966]. *Hell's Angels*. London: Penguin.

United Nations. 2006. "A Case Study of the Salmon Industry in Chile." Online at http://unctad.org/en/docs/iteiit200512_en.pdf. Accessed on September 22, 2012.

The Wild One. 1953. Directed by László Benedek.

Zabriskie Point. 1970. Directed by Michelangelo Antonioni.

EIGHT

PROSTHETIC MEMORY AND NETWORKED TEMPORALITIES IN *MORRO DA FAVELA* BY ANDRÉ DINIZ

Edward King

In recent years the graphic novel form in Brazil has opened up an important space of intervention into the circulation of memory discourses. The increasing health of the publishing industry, coupled with a mounting critical and popular interest in comics, has led to a boom in which seasoned cartoonists and comic book artists are being rediscovered and reedited while a new generation is being given the financial and creative freedom to produce book-length graphic narratives.[1] One of the dominant themes in this production is memory. Comics have become a platform for the reassertion of individual and national memories and the site of a critical engagement with the circulation of memories through information technologies. National narratives dating back to the beginning of the First Republic (1889–1930) have been reinvented in such books as *Estórias gerais* (2007) by Wellington Srbek and Flávio Colin and *Bando de dois* (2010) by Danilo Beyruth, both of which return to stories of banditry in the *sertão*, the backlands of the Northeast. Other books focus on characters immersed in globalized networks of information, from the teenage superheroes of Rafael Coutinho's *O beijo adolescente* (2011), who use their superpowers to build lucrative brand identities, to Lourenço Mutarelli's many crisis-hit amnesiacs (see, for example, *Mundo pet* [2004]).

Elsewhere, I have used Alison Landsberg's (2004) concept of "prosthetic memory" to explore how Mutarelli uses the comic form to stage the anxieties attendant on the processes through which the boundaries between individual and collective memories become blurred as more and more private information is circulated publicly (King 2013). Landsberg (2004) argues that this challenge to the barriers between individual and collective memory that has been exacerbated by developments in the mass media has become an opportunity to elaborate ethical relations beyond "traditional" community ties. A number of comic book artists in Brazil have used the form to explore this opportunity. The form is positioned at an intersection between techniques and discourses, between global conventions and national narratives, and between literature and image culture.[2] Rather than reassert the boundaries among individual, national, and globalized networks of memory, such artists as Coutinho and Mutarelli have used comic books and graphic novels to explore the possibilities opened up by the blurring of these categories to rearticulate individual and collective identities.

The tension between these two reactions to the "prostheticization" of memory, between "reterritorializing" and "deterritorializing" tendencies, are evident at the level of publication and marketing strategies. Comic book artists have taken advantage of the Internet to encourage a more affective connection between the texts and their readership, inviting readers to be witnesses to the process of creation. Comic creators Fábio Moon and Gabriel Bá use their Facebook pages to provide a constant commentary on the progress of their latest projects. Emphasis has also been placed on what Francophone critic Philippe Marion has called the "trace"—that is, the mark of the manual process of drawing and as such a direct connection between the body of the artist and the comic book page (Marion 1993). A 2012 edition of Mutarelli's trilogy of detective comics, *Diomedes: A trilogia do acidente*, included a section of half-rendered sketches of pages that were later discarded by the author.[3] The assertion of the individual "trace," and the connection with embodied memory to which it points, functions as a counterpoint to the vertiginous abandonment of the fantasies of individual subjectivity that is staged elsewhere in Mutarelli's work.

These tensions are not uniquely the property of graphic fiction produced in Brazil. Indeed, a number of critics have argued that they are inherent to the comic book form. Thierry Groensteen (2001), for instance, has argued that readers of comics are caught between two tendencies: between a chronological ordering, the process of restricting multiple temporalities into one spatiotemporal order, and a network logic that opens up and connects multiple temporalities. With its compartmentalized text and image boxes and its history of distributing texts in collectable and affordable editions, the comic book form appeals to the dream of ordering and categorization in a more compelling way than either literature or cinema. However, the dominant structure of commercial comics also demands an engagement between the reader and the text characterized by a network logic that undermines the linearity of traditional narrative forms.

Groensteen (2001: 117–29) uses the term "tressage" ("weaving") to describe the process through which the reader makes connections between and within panels that push against the forward flow of the narrative: "The network formed by the comic book panels is certainly a determined network, since it is traversed by the power of the narrative, but it also functions with an unchronological logic, that of the collection, of dispersion and coexistence, creating the possibility of translinear connections and plurivectoral narrative routes."[4] It is no accident, therefore, that comics and graphic novels have become the most visible platform on which to stage these tensions between reaffirming the individual and national ownership of memory and the dissolution of the individual in the ever-more visible global networks of memory discourses. The prominence of these tensions in the form makes it a useful tool for intervening in the wider processes of negotiating and reaffirming the boundaries between individual and collective memory that is sparked by the increasing "prostheticization" of memory discourses.

This chapter aims to explore how these tensions play out in the 2011 graphic novel *Morro da favela*. The book, a collaborative project between the photographer Maurício Hora and comic artist and scriptwriter André Diniz, is presented (and has been critically received as) an attempt to preserve the collective memory of Morro da Providência, the favela widely believed to have been the first to spring up on the hills in and around Rio de Janeiro. This process of preservation took place at a time when the favela came under threat from construction projects taking place in preparation for the Rio Olympics of 2016. With minimal consultation of the local residents, plans were drawn up for almost a third of the favela to be razed to widen roads and make way for a funicular railway. *Morro da favela* uses a visual style reminiscent of *xilogravura* (woodblock printing), most closely associated with the traditional *folheto* narratives originating in the Northeast known as *literatura de cordel,* to interweave a biographic narrative of the photographer Maurício Hora with the story of the favela itself. Diniz and Hora draw upon a number of conventions to intervene into the network of images and narratives used to represent Rio's favelas in the global mass media. The book focuses on the points of intersection between Maurício's own childhood memories and the now "prosthetic memories" of the mythical Rio favela circulating in mass media narratives. The threat presented to the favela by the building projects sparked by the Olympics draws attention to the fact that Diniz and Hora's preoccupation with the connections between individual and collective memories is a reaction to a moment of particularly pronounced temporal instability.

Andreas Huyssen (2000: 28) has argued that "the turn toward memory is subliminally energized by the desire to anchor ourselves in a world characterized by an increasing instability of time and the fracturing of living space." Drawing from Huyssen's treatment of the proliferation of memory discourses at the end of the twentieth century as a symptom of the current vertiginous stage of globalization and the consequent "transformation of temporality in our lives," this chapter explores how the book's insistence on the points of intersection between individual and collective memories (the phenomenon of "prosthetic memory") functions as a way of staging the overlapping and discontinuous temporalities constitutive of contemporary favela life.

My intention is not to argue that the network of temporalities staged here are in any way specific to Brazil's or even Latin America's experience of modernity. Rather, I want to explore how Diniz and Hora use the specificities of the comic medium as a critical tool for constructing identities at the intersections of these networks. In this way I hope to avoid restaging the set of debates about multiple temporalities and Latin American postmodern identities inaugurated by Néstor García Canclini's *Culturas híbridas*—a set of debates that is arguably constitutive of the field of Latin American cultural studies. Instead, I analyze *Morro da favela* to argue that the book-length graphic narrative has become an important medium for staging and intervening into these unstable and constantly changing temporal networks characteristic of the latest stage of modernity in Brazil. In an article on "palimpsestic aesthetics" in Brazilian culture, Robert Stam (1999: 64) has argued that cinema "is ideally equipped to express cultural and temporal hybridity." The audiovisual possibilities afforded by cinema and video technology, Stam explains, make it the perfect platform for staging what he calls "chronotopic multiplicity." According to Stam (64), "An electronic 'quilting' can weave together sounds and images in ways that break with linear single-line narrative, opening up utopias (and dystopias) of infinite multiplicity."[5]

This chapter demonstrates how the novel-length comic form is joining the cinema as a space for aesthetic strategies of "chronotopic multiplicity" in Brazilian culture. Jared Gardner (2006: 787) has explored the theme of cultural archives in contemporary graphic novels, "archives in the loosest, messiest sense of the word—archives of the forgotten artefacts and ephemera of American popular culture, items that were never meant to be collected." He argues that the form opens up a "space of reflection" on how the past is inscribed in the present, a space that is opened up by the constitutive tension between word and image. Whereas this tension or "rupture" is all too easily sutured by the process of "electronic quilting" Stam describes, it cannot be "neutralized" in comics. Instead, "it is the responsibility of the comics creators to put this tension to good use" (Gardner 2006: 789).[6] I therefore examine how *Morro da favela* "uses" the inherent tensions in the medium in relation to the processes through which memory becomes increasingly "prosthetic."

In interviews Diniz (2013) has described his project as a faithful document of the experience of living in the favela, insisting that "não há nada lá de ficcional" ("there is nothing fictional there"). But despite the author's insistence that he based his narrative exclusively on Hora's experiences as recounted to him in interviews, the book engages on a critical level with a number of modes of representing the Rio favelas that have exerted an increasingly strong presence in Brazilian culture. In her overview of the representations of urban experience in contemporary literature in Brazil, Flora Süssekind (2012: 5) identifies the emergence of a tendency for narratives that deal with favela life to be "marked by a kind of overlapping of the ethnographic and the fictional." She includes within this category such books as *Capão Pecado* and *Cidade de Deus* by Ferréz and Paulo Lins, respectively. Both of these authors were brought up in the favelas that provide the setting for the narratives—a fact that insisted upon both writers in the way the novels were marketed and in their critical reception. As Claire Williams (2008: 487) put it in her analysis of the "boom in neo-naturalist fictional narratives" about favela life since the 1990s: "Lins and Ferréz were received onto the market as legitimate, authentic voices with the necessary credentials for telling the truth about favela life."

Clearly, *Morro da favela* echoes this claim to authenticity and in the process presents itself as the product of individual memory. The book's final image is a photograph of Diniz and Hora standing in front of a crumbling wall on the *morro* with electricity wires crisscrossing the blue sky above them. Hora gazes straight at the camera with a look of weary defiance. A narration is provided throughout the book in the form of first-person text boxes, from the perspective of Hora himself. This emphasis on experience would fit with what Hora has said elsewhere in defense of the importance of the individual memories that are being torn down along with the streets and buildings of Providência. In a short documentary distributed through

FIGURE 8.1. A photograph of comic book artist André Diniz (left) and photographer Maurício Hora (right). *Source*: Diniz 2011b. Reproduced by kind permission of André Diniz.

the Globo website that explores the transformations in Providência through interviews with planners and local residents, Hora argues that "o legado mais interesante da favela são as pessoas" ("the most interesting legacy of the favela is the people"). And yet the critical effect of the book is not that of a truthful document about life in Providência, but as a complex engagement with how memories of favela life have circulated in the mass media, both in Brazil and internationally. Landsberg's notion of prosthetic memory is a useful tool for thinking about how the book plays on the borders between Hora's individual memory of his childhood and the proliferating narratives of favela life that have inserted themselves firmly into an increasingly globalized collective memory of the city.

The book repeatedly insists upon this blurring of the difference between individual and collective memory and the consequent overlapping of temporalities. One of the ways it achieves this is by framing the narrative within a national imaginary. The text is bookended by simplified *xilogravura* renderings of the Brazilian national flag. Meanwhile, in the aforementioned final photograph of the book, patches of the green and yellow belonging to a deteriorating national flag are visible on the wall behind the figures of Diniz and Hora. A brief text inserted before the narrative reaffirms this national framing of the book by contextualizing the narrative within a history of Providência that dates back to the end of the nineteenth century, when veterans of the bloody war in Canudos built makeshift homes on the hill after the housing they were promised by the federal government failed to materialize. The text, which imitates the format of a dictionary, ends by breaking this national frame open with a mention of how Rio's favelas are seen outside of Brazil: "Over time, the term favela took on a new meaning, and came to designate all the disordered aggregations in Rio de Janeiro, and later elsewhere in Brazil, and is now becoming known all over the world" (Diniz 2011b).[7]

This insistence on the intersection between national and global imaginaries inserts the text into a discursive tendency, dating back to the early years of the First Republic, to use representations of the favela to stage shifts in national identity. Beatriz Jaguaribe (2004) has explored how Rio's favelas have on the one hand been "cast as both the locus of the 'national imagined community' and . . . an emblem of Brazil's uneven modernization"; on the other hand, they have also been used as a site upon which hopes and anxieties about the possibilities and dangers of globalized belonging are projected. In her analysis of the 1999 documentary *Notícias de uma Guerra Particular* by João Moreira Salles, Jaguaribe argues that the film's effect is to show how the young drug dealers interviewed by Salles consciously insert themselves into globalized regimes of visibility: "What is telling in these interviews is not so much the social view that is being displayed in a favela world of brutal options, but the dramatization of such a self-fashioning in front of the camera. Their heavy posturing and the drawling accent become an acting out of the gangster role-playing that is overtly theatricalized and self-conscious" (Jaguaribe 2004: 337). Similarly, she argues that the use of clichés drawn from gangster films in Fernando Meirelles's 2002 film adaptation of *Cidade de Deus* is to perform the self-image of the young members of the drug cartels, mediated by a globalized set of representations of criminality. The final image of the crumbling Brazilian flag in *Morro da favela*, coupled with Diniz's very conscious appeal to an international audience, positions the book at a point of intersection between individual and collective narratives of memory as well as national and global discourses.

Morro da favela therefore does not restrict itself to an attempt to convey the authenticity of Hora's individual memory, as Diniz has argued in interviews. Rather, the book foregrounds the multiplicity of narratives that determine representations of Rio's favelas and the temporalities these set up. The most striking way in which the book foregrounds the tensions between memory discourses and temporalities is through the *xilogravura* style of illustration associated with *literatura de cordel*. The term refers, on the one hand, to a genre of writing characterized by rhymed verse with themes most frequently taken from local myth and folklore. But it also refers to a medium: cheaply produced pamphlets illustrated with a range of printing techniques. The use of *xilogravura* would seem to speak of a retrenchment into local cultural memory, a reaction against the disembedding of imagined communities from territorial roots. In this respect, it could be argued that Diniz's book echoes a tendency that has run through the *modernismo* of the 1920s and 1930s as well as the *folklorismo* of the 1950s and 1960s to see *cordel* literature and the *xilogravura* techniques that became associated with it as an authentic expression of the Northeast and, as such, a kind of reservoir of national identity to tap into. In fact, the imitation of *xilogravura* has almost become a convention in comic book illustrations of the space of the *sertão* in Brazil. The influential comic book artist Flávio Colin used the technique in *Estórias Gerais* (Srbek and Colin 2007). In that book the clean figural lines bring the starkness of the desert landscape, as well as the moral terrain it becomes a stage for, into sharp relief. Colin also used the technique when he collaborated with Diniz for the 2000 book *Fawcett*, a retelling of myths concerning the British explorer Percy Fawcett's disappearance in the Amazon jungle in 1925. Diniz has since developed his own version of the style in a series of publications, including a version of the Castro Alves poem *A cachoeira de Paulo Afonso* (Diniz 2011a), most of which base their narratives on Afro-Brazilian mythology. The style has become a visual shorthand for evoking a national-popular imaginary.

One of the effects of this use of *xilogravura*, at least for a readership familiar with popular visual conventions in Brazil, is to overlay the space of the favela with the space of the *sertão*. As such, the book evokes the work of the poet José João dos Santos (known as Axulão), who has used *cordel* and *xilogravura* to narrate the experiences of migrants from the Northeast in the big city of Rio de Janeiro. The clash between the rural associations of the medium and the urban content of the narrative and images conveys something of the overlapping of temporalities proper to the experience of migration. The visual style of *Morro da favela* also echoes a similar spatial elision that took place in the poet Ítalo Moriconi's collection about *carioca* life of *Quase sertão* (1996). In her analysis of the collection, Süssekind (2012: 20) argues that this overlap between city and *sertão* reinforces the notion of there being "dois Brasis" (two Brazils) that persist in the literary imagination, reaffirming "oppositions and mediations between cosmopolitanism and the local datum element, between universalization and themes of regional, coastal and interior character. A duality which is latent, in a somewhat ironic way, in the city that is read as rural."

It could be argued, therefore, that Diniz is feeding a discourse that emphasizes the Otherness of the favela in relation to the rest of the city, the separation between *morro* and *asfalto*, a nostalgic evocation of a mythical premodern temporality. Read from this perspective, the use of *xilogravura* takes on a somewhat sinister aspect, with the solidity of the figures and the clearness of the lines pointing to the rigidity of representational conventions that condemns *favelados* to exclusion from the benefits of modernity. After all, the reason why Diniz can evoke a scene using the bare minimum of incursions into a blank black page (an almost solid rectangle for a pistol; an abstract sun and palm tree to connote the tropical heat) resides in the familiarity of the scenes described. However, his use of *xilogravura* cannot be reduced to an assertion of an imagined national cultural memory. The book constantly draws the reader's attention to a mixture and overlap between visual styles and the regimes of temporality that they produce.

The technique that Diniz uses is a digitalized imitation of *xilogravura*. The figures were not carved from wood but configured using design software. In interviews Diniz has explained his technique as a digitalization of the manual "traço": "I persist with Photoshop, instead of moving on to vector programmes like Illustrator, for example, because it still conveys a sense of being drawn by hand. That perfection of lines and curves does not suit my style" (Diniz 2013).[8] Although Diniz does avoid the "perfection" that design software would allow him, the reader is never in doubt that the style is a computerized version of *xilogravura*. There is no imitation wood grain or blurring of ink. The visual presence of the computer is highly significant. The fact that *Morro da favela* is a digital appropriation of *xilogravura* evokes a whole range of studies of *cordel* literature that have approached the genre (and medium) as popular appropriations of the technologies of modernity. Sylvia Nemer (2008: 9–10) has explained that, rather than a kind of "manifestação a-histórica," "cordel literature is today seen as a medium that, already at its point of emergence at the end of the nineteenth century, was a part of technological modernity, with its poets using presses to print their pamphlets and the railways to distribute them."[9]

Encoded in Diniz's use of the form, therefore, is a long history of negotiations between local traditions and the technologies of modernity. Vilma Mota Quintela (2008: 120) has argued that the *cordel* form is symptomatic of the process of negotiation entailed by the discursive consolidation of the nation from the end of the nineteenth century through to the early part of the twentieth century: "This process is characterized by tensions deriving from the intersection of different historical perspectives, evidently resulting from the conflict, but also the dialogue between traditional and modernizing influences."[10] This connection between *cordel* and a vision of national identity rooted in the Northeast resurfaced in the celebration of *xilogravura* by folklorists such as Théo Brandão in the 1950s. Everardo Ramos (2005) has argued that the current association of *cordel* with the *xilogravura* style is down to the likes of Brandão and their vision of popular culture as the product of manual workmanship and a rejection of the technologies of modernity.[11] In fact, Ramos insists, the first *cordel* publishers were quick to use the latest printing techniques and actually more frequently used the *zincogravura* style (a printing process using zinc plates) that was more amenable to the demands of mass production. So, rather than a naïve defense of popular memory from the incursions of globalizing media, the book's use of *xilogravura* brings with it a reference to a complex history of negotiations, accommodations, and interactions between different modes of inscribing, presenting, and distributing popular memory. In fact, this quotation from Diniz denies the opposition between the manual craftsmanship and computer design that subtends the folkloric discourse typified by Brandão. This confusion of the opposition between handcraft and computer design is mirrored by the confusion of temporalities within the structure of the comic itself.

The overlapping of techniques and temporalities evoked by the digitalization of the *xilogravura* style is further emphasized by *Morro da favela*'s thematic focus on photography. One of the dominant narrative threads in the comic is Maurício's own apprenticeship and development as a photographer. The book recounts how Maurício was first exposed to the world of photography when he became fascinated with his uncle's darkroom. The transformation involved in the development process makes it seem to be "um lugar mágico." He is later able to indulge his interest in photography when he is given a camera by one of the clients of the goldsmith business he worked for from the age of thirteen. Much of the second half of the book

FIGURE 8.2. A detail of *Morro da favela* in which Hora practices the skill of photographic framing without a camera. *Source*: Diniz 2011b. Reproduced by kind permission of André Diniz.

recounts the challenges Hora faced in resisting a life of crime and becoming a photographer. Diniz uses the theme of photography to emphasize the highly mediated nature of the reader's knowledge of Rio's favelas as well as favela life itself. After his discovery of the "magical" world of his uncle's darkroom, Maurício starts practicing taking photographs of the city before he has had the chance to use a real camera. Four symmetrical panels show Maurício in different areas of the *morro* pretending to take photographs by using his two thumbs and forefingers as a frame and making a *click* ("clic") sound.

The coalescence of a symmetrical panel formation out of the slippery disorder of the borderless pages mirrors the emerging sense of control Maurício possesses now that he can impose a frame on the world around him. One panel shows Maurício pointing his imaginary camera at a neighbor, who herself is already framed by her kitchen window as she stands smoking and watching the world outside. Maurício's imaginary frame conforms to and repeats a frame previously existing in the world around him. By drawing attention to this overlap of material and imaginary frames, Diniz evokes how the young Maurício, before he has developed alternative modes of viewing the built environment, merely repeats internalized regimes of representation. When he finally manages to get hold of a Pentax camera, the first photographs he takes are model shots of his girlfriend, imitating the style of fashion magazines: "Faz uma pose de modelo!" ("Strike a model's pose!").

In another episode Diniz emphasizes how Maurício's experience of the world around him is mediated by mass media technologies. The first exposure Maurício has to the hard realities of prison life takes place through the television. In a two-page sequence Maurício's mother finds her son watching a TV prison drama. He is clearly horrified by the life of violence and hardship it depicts. In two consecutive panels the television screen fills the comic frame with images of men clinging to prison bars and blood dripping from knives. The following panel shows a close-up of the boy's wide eyes as he gazes at the screen with horrified absorption. The alternation of screen and eyes suggests Maurício's internalization of the experience of violence depicted in the television show. Later in the narrative, once Maurício has established himself as a well-known photographer, he starts to use his art as a tool to challenge the stereotypes circulating in the mass media about favela life.

One episode recounts a visit Maurício made to a school in Providência to show the children his archive of photographs of the *morro*. One child excitedly points to a photograph when he recognizes his own house: "É ali que eu moro, gente! Aquele ali na foto é a minha casa!" ["That's where I live, everybody! That's my house in the photo!"]. Maurício later learns the child in question had always been ashamed of where he lived and never allowed his teacher to visit him. But the sight of the house in the photograph confers on it a legitimacy that erases his sense of shame. A text written in the first person from Maurício's perspective comments: "But when he saw his house in that photo, his shame disappeared. It was his world transformed into art. [. . .] And that's when I discovered that photography transforms."[12] For the school boy, his house and the identity it confers only gain legitimacy when they are mediated by visual culture. In this sense the boy can be read as a stand-in for Maurício himself, whose memories of his own childhood are inextricably intertwined with mass media narratives. This observation allows Maurício to understand photography as a social tool through which to reconfigure identity and a communal sense of belonging. Rather than a rejection of the false representations and prosthetic memories of favela life distributed through communications technologies, Maurício's strategy is to intervene into these representations and to take advantage of the lines of communication opened up by them.

The powerful image of the internalized camera returns toward the end of the comic. Maurício is invited by one of the city's cultural centers to offer free photography lessons to his fellow inhabitants of Morro da Providência. When he discovers that only a few of his sixty students actually own cameras, he decides to teach them to develop their "olhar fotográfico" ("photographic gaze") as he did—that is to say, without a camera. He plays a CD of *O Trenzinho do Caipira* by Egberto Gismonti and asks them to create images of the urban landscape in their mind's eye. Over two pages the residents are shown walking around the *morro* imposing frames on the world around them with their thumbs and forefingers. The residents are converted into walking camera-eyes, their vision determined by the fantasies of popular culture. Their incursions into the world around them can happen only through layers of mediation. The moment is reminiscent of José Padilha's 2002 documentary *Ônibus 174*, a film that revisits a traumatic standoff between police and a would-be robber on a bus that took place in the Jardim Botânico area of Rio de Janeiro under the watchful eye of the national media. In her article on the film, Lorraine Leu (2008) analyzes how Sandro, the would-be robber and protagonist of the media spectacle, exploits the opportunity to achieve a kind of visibility that the national public sphere had previously denied him. Leu emphasizes how this visibility can take place only through the sedimented codes of mass culture. When Sandro performs for the cameras, he does so playing the clichéd role of the *bandido*-as-popular hero, an idealized "avenger of his class, confronting the forces of capitalism and private property" that was frequently evoked in images of revolt and resistance during the early years of the military dictatorship (Leu 2008: 182). In a similar way to how Sandro is represented in Padilha's documentary, the human cameras in *Morro da favela* are presented as nodes in the network of images of urban marginality in Brazil. They act as receptors and reproducers of these images but also retain a capacity to intervene into them.

Through these reflexive strategies the book functions as a critique of another prevalent tendency in the circulation of prosthetic memories of favela life—namely, the use of photography in fictional narratives about favela life that combine an ethnographic approach with fiction. In her analysis of *Capão Pecado*, which incorporates two sets of photographs into the body of its text,

Süssekind describes the book as being "marked by a double record, where photos and accounts are mirrored" and the images seem to "materialize" the fictional geography of the urban space. She writes: "It seems that the function of the photography is to supply evidence for the narrative, which, though lending it immediate visibility and recognition, also produces a relationship of discursive dependence evident in the narrative style [spare and unadorned] as regards its visual counterpart" (Süssekind 2012: 6). The result, Süssekind argues, is a type of neutralization of the plurivocal potential of the fiction which, because of the "documental imposition," tends to "reproduce already visible typologies and prevailing, standardized conceptions as far as these populations are concerned, and in so far as the fact that the perspective for observing . . . is frozen in a restrictive presentification, whose model is the collection rather than the historical experience" (6).

Morro da favela breaks with this documentary use of the photograph. The photographs inserted at the end of the book are not presented as a neutral visual register of the urban space described in the narrative. By foregrounding the transformative potential of photography throughout the narrative, as well as insisting on the power dynamics at stake in visual representations of marginal communities, the book conditions the reader to connect the photographs with the networks of images of which they form a part. Rather than a "restrictive presentification," the insertion forms part of the book's staging of "cronotopic multiplicity" of the favela. Their incorporation into the text inserts them into the comic book logic of *tressage* in which the reader is urged to connect them back to panels earlier in the book in a series of superimpositions and clashes with the *xilogravura*'s encoding of *sertão* and migration.

Another representational tendency that the book engages with is what Ivana Bentes (2007) has termed a "cosmética da fome" in an article on cinematic renderings of favela life such as 2002's *Cidade de Deus* and 1998's *Central do Brasil*. Bentes sets up a comparison between how these areas of urban marginality were represented during the 1960s in the movement known as *cinema novo*, and how they are generally being represented in these global blockbusters. *Cinema novo* employed what the filmmaker Glauber Rocha defined as an "estética da fome" and described as a mode of visual violence aimed to shock complacent viewers into confronting the brutal realities of poverty. These contemporary films, Bentes (2007: 244) claims, are characterized by a "cosmética da fome" and present poverty as beautiful and somehow natural: "If we leap abruptly from 1964 to 2001, we find the favela inserted into a different context and imaginary, where misery is consumed increasingly as something 'typical' or 'natural' about which we can do nothing."[13]

Maurício's frequent talk of finding beauty in Providência makes it tempting to accuse the book of the kind of aestheticization identified by Bentes. The last section of the book consists of nine panels of equal size, all of which are images of Dona Iracema (one of Maurício's neighbors), framed as if from the point of view of Maurício's camera lens. When Dona Iracema asks why Maurício wants to take a photograph of her, he replies: "To record what is beautiful about the favela. To show the world that there is life here."[14] The very last panel of *Morro da favela* is in color and as such stands out in sharp contrast with the rest of the book that conforms to the *xilogravura* oppositions of black and white. The shift from black and white to color, seen through Maurício's camera lens, seems to stage the transformative potential of photography to change the terms of entry into visual "registers" of the city. It is the reflexivity that structures *Morro da favela* that distances the book from the aestheticizing discourse that Bentes labels "cosmética da fome." By using the *xilogravura* technique, Diniz is inserting Hora's photography into this visual tradition of technological appropriation. The book incorporates the visual technologies that have driven the "cosmética da fome" approach to representing the favela into the visual style of the woodblock print. The comic repeatedly draws attention to this overlap. *Morro da favela* exploits its overlapping of visual techniques and the concepts of temporality encoded within them. The form itself speaks of different memories of the struggles and adaptations of urban modernity.

This overlapping of techniques is reproduced by the tension between the linear structure of the plot of *Morro da favela* and the process of readerly "tressage" that pushes against this structure. On the one hand, the book seems to reproduce the temporality of the nation according to the historicist conceptions of time as progress that were central to the nineteenth-century universalizing accounts of social Darwinism and Hegel. The first text panels start by recounting the foundation of the favela: "The favela was created on this hill. Everybody would call it favela hill."[15] The last panel, as previously mentioned, is in color and depicts a resident speaking to Maurício's camera. The transition from black and white to color seems to highlight the transition from technological backwardness to full insertion into global media networks and the latest regime of modernity of which these networks are both agents and emblems. However, the overlapping of visual techniques—the digital imitation of woodblock printing depicting (literally) handmade versions of digital photography—complicates this setup by overlaying it with a network of competing temporalities.

Another way in which it achieves this is by evoking parallels between the structure of the comic and the space of the favela that it takes as a setting. The page layout of *Morro da favela* captures the spatial configurations of the *morro*. The panels appear devoid of a grid and the frames seem to spring out of a common background. They are often set out in a jumbled formation and appear to bleed into one another. The sequence of panels is not always clear and at times the eye has to content itself with leaping back and forth across the page. With the lack of fixed borders, the eyes slide across the images, unrestricted by any rigid panel-to-panel rhythms. One sequence acknowledges

FIGURE 8.3. A detail of *Morro da favela* in which Hora meets a neighbor on the way to a meeting of the favela residents. *Source*: Diniz 2011b. Reproduced by kind permission of André Diniz.

this parallel between the comic page and the irregular space of the *morro* in a fairly explicit fashion when Hora picks up a friend from his house on the way to a meeting of community members. The friend expresses his delight with his new home wedged on top of another house, accessible only with a step ladder. The event is narrated on a page made up of six panels of roughly equal size. The harmonious spatial configuration of the page jars with the irregularity elsewhere in the book and seems to provide a visual corollary of the precarious sense of comfort Hora's friend has found in his house perched in the gaps between other houses. Such is the fluidity of the page layout that the same white spaces on the black page seem to reconfigure and rearrange themselves in a new pattern as the reader turns the page. The space of the favela itself defies the theories of urban development that sought to materialize the universalizing nineteenth-century narratives of modernity and that persist in the projects that sought to make the *morros* safe and accessible in time for the Olympics. As Jaguaribe put it, the Rio favela has become an emblem of Brazil's "uneven modernity," a space in which the conflicting temporalities that characterize the region's experience of modernity are at their most evident. By drawing parallels between the material structure of the *favela* and the page layout, *Morro da favela* reproduces these conflicting temporalities for the reader. This visual narrative strategy is an example of how the book positions itself at the intersection between national and global narratives and techniques. As evidenced by the recent essay collection *Comics and the City*, the connection between comic structure and urban structure has been a key feature of the history of comics from all over the world (Ahrens and Meteling 2010). *Morro da favela* strategically inserts itself into this tradition to reproduce the network of conflicting temporalities associated with the favela.

As is clear from this reading of *Morro da favela*, the graphic novel form has become an important critical medium through which national and individual narratives of memory are reconfigured in reaction to more global changes in the way we accrue experience and conceive of time. The book is part of a debate in Brazil about the politics of urban memory in its largest cities, a debate that is part of the continual questioning of the processes of modernity and a reminder of that which gets left behind by or excluded from these processes. But it is also symptomatic of the shifts in the conceptualization of memory that are taking place in the information age. The medium of the comic book, as a consequence of the tensions that are constitutive of its form, is uniquely placed to intervene into these processes. André

Diniz's book, by foregrounding the points of intersection between individual memory and the memory discourses circulated by the mass media, and by creating a palimpsest of the technologies and techniques that function as the material supports and vehicles for distributing these memories, exploits the form's potential to create a critical "space of reflection" on processes of prosthetic memory. As such, it is a powerful demonstration of how the medium can function to critically frame the processes of information and image culture.

NOTES

1. Paulo Ramos (2012) contextualizes these developments within a wider history of the comic form in Brazil.
2. Néstor García Canclini (1989: 314) has discussed the potential of the comic form in a similar manner, as creating a space of reflexivity at the point of intersection between national-popular and global imaginaries.
3. In 2013 the publishing house Quadrinhos na Companhia also published a book entirely of Mutarelli's sketches: *Os Sketchbooks de Lourenço Mutarelli*.
4. From the original French: "Le réseau que forment les vignettes d'une bande dessinée est certes un réseau orienté, puisqu'il est traversé par l'instance du récit, mais il existe aussi sur un mode déchronologisé, celui de la collection, de l'étalement et de la coexistence, ménageant la possibilité de relations translinéaires et de parcours plurivectoriels."
5. Stam's (1999) conviction about the connection between the medium of film and "chronotopic multiplicity" has been widely accepted by scholars of Latin American cinema, as Joanna Page and Ignacio M. Sánchez Prado (2012) have recently argued.
6. Benoît Peeters (1998: 48) has also explored this idea in *Lire la bande dessinée* in which he argues that the "double temporalité" of the comic form constitutes a significant difference from cinema, "art fondamentalement linéaire." This double temporality consists of a tension between "récit" (in which the individual panels are subordinated to the construction of the narrative) and "tableau" (in which the narrative is forgotten in contemplation of the individual panel).
7. From the original: "Com o passar dos anos, o termo favela ganhou um novo significado, passou a designar todos os agrupamentos desordenados do Rio de Janeiro, depois do Brasil, e já começa a ser conhecido em todo o mundo."

8. From the original: "Insisto no Photoshop, em vez de programas vectoriais como o Illustrador, por exemplo, porque ele me dá ainda um certo toque de manuel no traço. Aquela perfeição das retas e curvas vetoriais não se encaixariam no meu desenho."
9. From the original: "a literatura de cordel hoje é vista como uma manifestação que já em seu nascimento, no final do século XIX, estava inserida na modernidade técnica, com os poetas utilizando as tipografias para a impressão de folhetos e os transportes ferroviários para sua distribuição."
10. From the original: "Tal processo se caracteriza pelas tensões decorrentes da intersecção de diferentes perspectivas históricas, resultando evidentemente do conflito, mas também do diálogo, da negociação entre forças tradicionais e modernizadoras."
11. Ramos (2005: 143) explains that "dans le regard folklorique et dans les visions régionalistes, la gravure populaire et, à plus forte raison, la gravure populaire du Nordeste, ne peut exprimer que le souvenir d'une époque révolue, d'un âge mythique et rêvé, berceau d'une 'pureté originelle' qui se serait perdue par la suite, devant le progrès de la raison, du capital et de la machine." ["From the point of view of the folkloric tradition and in the regionalist vision, popular engraving and, more precisely, popular engraving from the Northeast, can express only the memory of a bygone age, an age shrouded in myth and dream, the cradle of an 'original purity' which would subsequently be lost in the face of the progress of reason, capital and the machine."]
12. From the original: "Mas quando viu sua casa na foto, a vergonha sumiu. Era o mundo dele transformado em arte. . . . Ali eu descobri: a fotografia transforma."
13. From the original: "Dando um salto abrupto de 1964 para 2001, encontramos [o sertão e] a favela inserido[s] em um outro contexto e imaginário, onde a miséria é cada vez mais consumida como um elemento de 'tipicidade' ou 'natureza' diante da qual não há nada a fazer."
14. From the original: "Pra registrar o que a favela tem de mais bonito. Vamos mostrar pra todo mundo que aqui também tem vida."
15. From the original: "A favela se criou nesse morro. As pessoas chamavam aqui de Morro da favela."

REFERENCES

Ahrens, Jörn, and Arno Meteling, eds. 2010. *Comics and the City: Urban Space in Print, Picture, and Sequence*. London: Continuum.

Bentes, Ivana. 2007. "Sertões e favelas no cinema brasileiro contemporâneo: Estética e consmética da fome." *Revista Alceu* 8, no. 15: 242–55.

Beyruth, Danilo. 2010. *Bando de dois*. São Paulo: Editora Zarabatana.

Coutinho, Rafael. 2011. *O beijo adolescente*. São Paulo: Narval Comix.

Diniz, André. 2013. "Cultura Negra em Quadrinhos." Interview with Bruno Dorigatti. Online at www.riocomicon.com.br/cultura-negra-em-quadrinhos. Accessed on February 10, 2013.

Diniz, André. 2011a. *A cachoeira Paulo Afonso*. Rio de Janeiro: Pallas.

Diniz, André. 2011b. *Morro da favela*. São Paulo: Barba Negra/Leya Editora.

Ferréz. 2005. *Capão Pecado*. Rio de Janeiro: Objetiva.

García Canclini, Néstor. 1989. *Culturas híbridas: Estrategias para entrar y salir de la modernidad*. México, D.F.: Editorial Grijalbo.

Gardner, Jared. 2006. "Archives, Collectors, and the New Media Work of Comics." *Modern Fiction Studies* 52, no. 4: 787–806.

Groensteen, Thierry. 2001. "Le réseau et le lieu: Pour une analyse des procédures de tressage iconique." In *Time, Narrative, and the Fixed Image*. Edited by Mireille Ribière and Jan Baetens, 117–29. Amsterdam: Rodopi.

Huyssen, Andreas. 2000. "Present Pasts: Media, Politics, Amnesia." *Public Culture* 12, no. 1: 21–38.

Jaguaribe, Beatriz. 2004. "Favelas and the Aesthetics of Realism: Representations in Film and Literature." *Journal of Latin American Cultural Studies* 13, no. 3: 327–42.

King, Edward. 2013. *Science Fiction and Digital Technologies in Argentine and Brazilian Culture*. New York: Palgrave Macmillan.

Landsberg, Alison. 2004. *Prosthetic Memory: The Transformation of American Remembrance in the Age of Mass Culture*. New York: Columbia University Press.

Leu, Lorraine. 2008. "Spaces of Remembrance and Representation in the City: José Padilha's Ônibus 174." *Luso-Brazilian Review* 45, no. 2: 177–89.

Lins, Paulo. 2005. *Cidade de Deus*. Rio de Janeiro: Companhia de Bolso.

Marion, Philippe. 1993. *Traces en cases: Travail graphique, figuration narrative et participation du lecteur*. Louvain: Academia.

Moriconi, Ítalo. 1996. *Quase Sertão*. Rio de Janeiro: Diadorim.

Mutarelli, Lourenço. 2013. *Os Sketchbooks de Lourenço Mutarelli*. São Paulo: Quadrinhos na Companhia.

Mutarelli, Lourenço. 2012. *Diomedes: A Trilogia do Acidente*. São Paulo: Quadrinhos na Companhia.

Mutarelli, Lourenço. 2004. *Mundo pet*. São Paulo: Devir Livraria.

Nemer, Sylvia. 2008. "Apresentação: O panorama atual das pesquisas em literatura de cordel no Brasil." In *Recortes contemporâneos sobre o cordel*. Edited by Sylvia Nemer, 7–11. Rio de Janeiro: Edições Casa de Rui Barbosa.

Page, Joanna, and Ignacio M. Sánchez Prado. 2012. "Temporalities in Latin American Film." *Arizona Journal of Hispanic Cultural Studies* 16: 203–10.

Peeters, Benoît. 1998. *Lire la bande dessinée*. Tournai: Casterman.

Quintela, Vilma Mota. 2008. "Cordel, mídias e mediações culturais." In *Recortes contemporâneos sobre o cordel*. Edited by Sylvia Nemer, 119–37. Rio de Janeiro: Edições Casa de Rui Barbosa.

Ramos, Everardo. 2005. *Du marché au marchand: La gravure populaire bresilienne*. Montreuil: Musée du dessin et de l'estampe originale, Gravelines.

Ramos, Paulo. 2012. *Revolução do gibi: A nova cara dos quadrinhos no Brasil*. São Paulo: Devir Livraria.

Srbek, Wellington, and Flávio Colin. 2007. *Estórias gerais*. São Paulo: Conrad Editora.

Stam, Robert. 1999. "Palimpsestic Aesthetics: A Meditation on Hybridity and Garbage." In *Performing Hybridity*. Edited by May Joseph and Jennifer Natalya Fink, 59–78. Minneapolis: University of Minnesota Press.

Süssekind, Flora. 2012. "Deterritorialization and Literary Form: Brazilian Contemporary Literature and Urban Experience." Working Paper Series, Centre for Brazilian Studies, University of Oxford.

Williams, Claire. 2008. "Ghettourism and Voyeurism, or Challenging Stereotypes and Raising Consciousness? Literary and Non-literary Forays into the Favelas of Rio de Janeiro." *Bulletin of Latin American Research* 27, no. 4: 483–500.

CONTRIBUTORS

EDOARDO BALLETTA (PhD) is a research fellow in Latin American studies at the University of Bologna (Italy). His research interests include twentieth-century poetry in the Southern Cone and representation of history and memory in Latin American culture.

CHRISTIANE BERTH is a Swiss National Science Foundation Ambizione fellow at the University of Bern. She holds a PhD in history from the University of Hamburg. Her research interests include the history of coffee trade, migration, and food policy and consumption, with a regional focus on Central America. Currently she is working on a research project about telecommunication, social change, and modernity in twentieth-century Mexico.

JORGE L. CATALÁ CARRASCO is a senior lecturer in Hispanic studies at Newcastle University. He specializes in cultural studies and cultural history in periods of crisis. He is the author of *Vanguardia y humorismo gráfico en crisis: La Guerra Civil Española (1936–1939) y la Revolución Cubana (1959–1961)* (2015) and script cowriter of the 2015 documentary *José Ricardo Morales: Escrito en el agua*. He is also the principal investigator (with Patricia Oliart) for the international research project "Cultural Narratives of Crisis and Renewal" funded by the European Commission (Marie Curie RISE scheme) for 2015 through 2018.

ISABELLA COSSE is a researcher at CONICET (Consejo Nacional de Investigaciones Científicas y Técnicas National Council of Science and Technology) and teaches at the University of Buenos Aires. Her field of studies is family and childhood history in contemporary Argentina, and she is working on a project on the family and politics during the Cold War. She is author of, among other books, *Estigmas de nacimiento: Peronismo y orden familiar (1946–1955)* (2006), *Pareja, sexualidad y familia en Buenos Aires (1950–1975)* (2010), and *Mafalda: Historia social y política* (2014).

PAULO DRINOT is a senior lecturer in Latin American history at the Institute of the Americas, University College London. He is the author of *The Allure of Labor: Workers, Race, and the Making of the Peruvian State* (2011), editor of *Che's Travels: The Making of a Revolutionary in 1950s Latin America* (2010) and *Peru in Theory* (2014), and coeditor (with Alan Knight) of *The Great Depression in Latin America* (2014).

EDWARD KING is a lecturer in Portuguese and Lusophone studies at the University of Bristol. He is the author of *Science Fiction and Digital Technologies in Argentine and Brazilian Culture* (2013) and *Virtual Orientalism in Brazilian Culture* (2015).

CYNTHIA E. MILTON is the editor of *Art from a Fractured Past: Memory and Truth-Telling in Post–Shining Path Peru* (2014) and a coeditor of *Curating Difficult Knowledge: Violent Pasts in Public Places* (2011) and *The Art of Truth-Telling about Authoritarian Rule* (2005). Major honors include the Bolton-Johnson Prize for *The Many Meanings of Poverty: Colonialism, Social Compacts, and Assistance in Eighteenth-Century Ecuador* (2007) and the Alexander Von Humboldt Experienced Researcher Fellowship. She holds a Canada Research Chair in Latin American history at the Université de Montréal and is a member of the College of New Scholars, Artists, and Scientists of the Royal Society of Canada.

JAMES SCORER is a lecturer in Latin American cultural studies at the University of Manchester. His research areas include the cultures and imaginaries of the Latin American city, especially those of Buenos Aires, and Latin American visual cultures, particularly photography and comics. He has published articles on Tintin's Latin American adventures and on graphic biographies of Ernesto "Che" Guevara. He is the author of *City in Common: Culture and Community in Buenos Aires* (2016).

INDEX